My Second Yea:

Frederick Palmer

Alpha Editions

This edition published in 2024

ISBN : 9789361474279

Design and Setting By
Alpha Editions
www.alphaedis.com
Email - info@alphaedis.com

Contents

I

BACK TO THE FRONT

How America fails to realize the war—Difficulties of realization—Uncle Sam is sound at heart—In London again—A Chief of Staff who has risen from the ranks—Sir William Robertson takes time to think—At the front—Kitchener's mob the new army—A quiet headquarters—Sir Douglas Haig—His office a clearing house of ideas—His business to deal in blows—"The Spirit that quickeneth."

"I've never kept up my interest so long in anything as in this war," said a woman who sat beside me at dinner when I was home from the front in the winter of 1915-16. Since then I have wondered if my reply, "Admirable mental concentration!" was not ironic at the expense of manners and philosophy. In view of the thousands who were dying in battle every day, her remark seemed as heartless as it was superficial and in keeping with the riotous joy of living and prosperity which strikes every returned American with its contrast to Europe's self-denial, emphasized by such details gained by glimpses in the shop windows of Fifth Avenue as the exhibit of a pair of ladies' silk hose inset with lace, price one hundred dollars.

Meanwhile, she was knitting socks or mufflers, I forget which, for the Allies. Her confusion about war news was common to the whole country, which heard the special pleading of both sides without any cross-questioning by an attorney. She remarked how the Allies' bulletins said that the Allies were winning and the German bulletins that the Germans were winning; but so far as she could see on the map the armies remained in much the same positions and the wholesale killing continued. Her interest, I learned on further inquiry, was limited and partisan. When the Germans had won a victory, she refused to read about it and threw down her paper in disgust.

There was something human in her attitude, as human as the war itself. It was a reminder of how far away from the Mississippi is the Somme; how broad is the Atlantic; how impossible it is to project yourself into the distance even in the days of the wireless. She was moving in the orbit of her affairs, with its limitations, just as the soldiers were in theirs. Before the war luxury was as common in Paris as in New York; but with so ghastly a struggle proceeding in Europe it seemed out of keeping that the joy of living should endure anywhere in the world. Yet Europe was tranquilly going its way when the Southern States were suffering pain and hardship worse than any that France and England have known. Paris and London were dining and smiling when Richmond was in flames.

War can be brought home to no community until its own sons are dying and risking death. In nothing are we so much the creatures of our surroundings as in war. For the first few weeks when I was at home, a nation going its way in an era of prosperity had an aspect of vulgarity; peace itself was vulgar by contrast with the atmosphere of heroic sacrifice in which I had lived for over a year. I asked myself if my country could ever rise to the state of exaltation of France and England. Though first thought, judging by superficial appearances alone, might have said "No," I knew that we could if there ever came a call to defend our soil—a call that could be brought home to the valleys of the Hudson and the Mississippi as a call was brought home to the valleys of the Somme, the Meuse and the Marne.

Many Americans had returned from Europe with reports of humiliation endured as a result of their country's attitude. Shopkeepers had made insulting remarks, they said, and in some instances had refused to sell goods. They had been conscious of hostility under the politeness of their French and English friends. A superficial confirmation of their contention might be taken from the poster I noticed on my way from Paddington Station to my hotel upon my arrival in England. It advertised an article in a cheap weekly under the title of "Uncle Sham."

I took this just as seriously as I took a cartoon in a New York evening paper of pro-German tendencies on the day that I had sailed from New York, which showed John Bull standing idly by and urging France on to sacrifices in the defense of Verdun. It was as easy for an American to be indignant at one as for an Englishman at the other, but a little unworthy of the intelligence of either. I was too convinced that Uncle Sam, who does not always follow my advice, is sound at heart and a respectable member of the family of nations to be in the least disturbed in my sense of international good will. If I had been irritated I should have contributed to the petty backbiting by the mischievous uninformed which makes bad blood between peoples.

I knew, too, from experience, as I had kept repeating at home, that when the chosen time arrived for the British to strike, they would prove with deeds the shamelessness of this splash of printer's ink and confound, as they have on the Somme, the witticism of a celebrated Frenchman who has since made his apology for saying that the British would fight on till the last drop of French blood was shed. Besides, on the same day that I saw the poster I saw in a British publication a reproduction of a German cartoon—exemplifying the same kind of vulgar facility—picturing Uncle Sam being led by the nose by John Bull.

Thinking Englishmen and Frenchmen, when they pause in their preoccupation of giving life and fortune for their cause to consider this extraneous subject, realize the widespread sympathy of the United States for the Allied cause and how a large proportion of our people were prepared to go to war after the sinking of the *Lusitania* for an object which could bring them no territorial reward. If we will fight only for money and aggrandizement, as the "Uncle Sham" style of reasoners hold, we should long ago have taken Mexico and Central America. Personally, I have never had anyone say to me that I was "too proud to fight," though if I went about saying that I was ashamed of my country I might; for when I think of my country I think of no group of politicians, financiers, or propagandists, no bureaucracy or particular section of opinion, but of our people as a whole. But unquestionably we were unpopular with the masses of Europeans. A sentence taken out of its context was misconstrued into a catch-phrase indicating the cravenness of a nation wedded to its flesh-pots, which pretended a moral superiority to others whose passionate sacrifice made them supersensitive when they looked across the Atlantic to the United States, which they saw profiting from others' misfortunes.

By living at home I had gained perspective about the war and by living with the war I have gained perspective about my own country. At the front I was concerned day after day with the winning of trenches and the storming of villages whose names meant as little in the Middle West as a bitter fight for good government in a Western city meant to the men at the front. After some months of peace upon my return to England I resented passport regulations which had previously been a commonplace; but soon I was back in the old groove, the groove of war, with war seeming as normal in England as peace seemed in the United States.

In London, recruiting posters with their hectic urgings to the manhood of England to volunteer no longer blanketed the hoardings and the walls of private buildings. Conscription had come. Every able-bodied man must now serve at the command of the government. England seemed to have greater dignity. The war was wholly master of her proud individualism, which had stubbornly held to its faith that the man who fought best was he who chose to fight rather than he who was ordered to fight.

There was a new Chief of Staff at the War Office, Sir William Robertson, who had served for seven years as a private before he received his commission as an officer, singularly expressing in his career the character of the British system, which leaves open to merit the door at the head of a long stairway which calls for hard climbing. England believes in men and he had earned his way to the direction of the most enormous plant with the largest personnel which the British Empire had ever created.

It was somewhat difficult for the caller to comprehend the full extent of the power and responsibility of this self-made leader at his desk in a great room overlooking Whitehall Place, for he had so simplified an organization that had been brought into being in two years that it seemed to run without any apparent effort on his part. The methods of men who have great authority interest us all. I had first seen Sir William at a desk in a little room of a house in a French town when his business was that of transport and supply for the British Expeditionary Force. Then he moved to a larger room in the same town, as Chief of Staff of the army in France. Now he had a still larger one and in London.

I had heard much of his power of application, which had enabled him to master languages while he was gaining promotion step by step; but I found that the new Chief of Staff of the British Army was not "such a fool as ever to overwork," as one of his subordinates said, and no slave to long hours of drudgery at his desk.

"Besides his routine," said another subordinate, speaking of Sir William's method, "he has to do a great deal of thinking." This passing remark was most illuminating. Sir William had to think for the whole. He had trained others to carry out his plans, and as former head of the Staff College who had had experience in every branch, he was supposed to know how each branch should be run.

When I returned to the front, my first motor trip which took me along the lines of communication revealed the transformation, the more appreciable because of my absence, which the winter had wrought. The New Army had come into its own. And I had seen this New Army in the making. I had seen Kitchener's first hundred thousand at work on Salisbury Plain under old, retired drillmasters who, however eager, were hazy about modern tactics. The men under them had the spirit which will endure the drudgery of training. With time they must learn to be soldiers. More raw material, month after month, went into the hopper. The urgent call of the recruiting posters and the press had, in the earlier stages of the war, supplied all the volunteers which could be utilized. It took much longer to prepare equipment and facilities than to get men to enlist. New Army battalions which reached the front in August, 1915, had had their rifles only for a month. Before rifles could be manufactured rifle plants had to be constructed. As late as December, 1915, the United States were shipping only five thousand rifles a week to the British. Soldiers fully drilled in the manual of arms were waiting for the arms with which to fight; but once the supply of munitions from the new plants was started it soon became a flood.

All winter the New Army battalions had been arriving in France. With them had come the complicated machinery which modern war requires. The staggering quantity of it was better proof than figures on the shipping list of the immense tonnage which goes to sea under the British flag. The old life at the front, as we knew it, was no more. When I first saw the British Army in

France it held seventeen miles of line. Only seventeen, but seventeen in the mire of Flanders, including the bulge of the Ypres salient.

By the first of January, 1915, a large proportion of the officers and men of the original Expeditionary Force had perished. Reservists had come to take the vacant places. Officers and non-commissioned officers who survived had to direct a fighting army in the field and to train a new army at home. An offensive was out of the question. All that the force in the trenches could do was to hold. When the world wondered why it could not do more, those who knew the true state of affairs wondered how it could do so much. With flesh and blood infantry held against double its own numbers supported by guns firing five times the number of British shells. The British could not confess their situation without giving encouragement to the Germans to press harder such attacks as those of the first and second battle of Ypres, which came perilously near succeeding.

This little army would not admit the truth even in its own mind. With that casualness by which the Englishman conceals his emotions the surviving officers of battalions which had been battered for months in the trenches would speak of being "top dog, now." While the world was thinking that the New Army would soon arrive to their assistance, they knew as only trained soldiers can know how long it takes to make an army out of raw material. So persistent was their pose of winning that it hypnotized them into conviction. As it had never occurred to them that they could be beaten, so they were not.

If sometimes the logic of fact got the better of simulation, they would speak of the handicap of fighting an enemy who could deliver blows with the long reach of his guns to which they could not respond. But this did not happen often. It was a part of the game for the German to marshal more guns than they if he could. They accepted the situation and fought on. They, too, looked forward to "the day," as the Germans had before the war; and their day was the one when the New Army should be ready to strike its first blow.

There was also a new leader in France, king of the British world there. Sir William sent him the new battalions and the guns and the food for men and guns and his business was to make them into an army. They arrived thinking that they were already one, as they were against any ordinary foe, though not yet in homogeneity of organization against a foe that had prepared for war for forty years and on top of this had had two years' experience in actual battle.

On a quiet byroad near headquarters town, where all the staff business of General Headquarters was conducted, a wisp of a flag hung at the entrance to the grounds of a small modern chateau. There seemed no place in all France more isolated and tranquil, its size forbidding many guests. It was such a house as some quiet, studious man might have chosen to rest in during his summer holiday. The sound of the guns never reached it; the rumble of army transport was unheard.

Should you go there to luncheon you would be received by a young aide who, in army jargon, was known as a "crock"; that is, he had been invalided as the result of wounds or exposure in the trenches and, though unfit for active service, could still serve as aide to the Commander-in-Chief. At the appointed minute of the hour, in keeping with military punctuality, whether of generals or of curtains of fire, a man with iron-gray hair, clear, kindly eyes, and an unmistakably strong chin, came out of his office and welcomed the guests with simple informality. He seemed to have left business entirely behind when he left his desk. You knew him at once for the type of well-preserved British officer who never neglects to keep himself physically fit. It amounts to a talent with British officers to have gone through campaigns in India and South Africa and yet always to appear as fresh as if they had never known anything more strenuous than the leisurely life of an English country gentleman.

I had always heard how hard Sir Douglas Haig worked, just as I had heard how hard Sir William Robertson worked. Sir Douglas, too, showed no signs of pressure, and naturally the masterful control of surroundings without any seeming effort is a part of the equipment of military leaders. The power of the modern general is not evident in any of the old symbols.

It was really the army that chose Sir Douglas to be Commander-in-Chief. Whenever the possibility of the retirement of Sir John French was mentioned and you asked an officer who should take his place, the answer was always either Robertson or Haig. In any profession the members should be the best judges of excellence in that profession, and through eighteen months of organizing and fighting these two men had earned the universal praise of their comrades in arms. Robertson went to London and Haig remained in France. England looked to them for victory.

Birth was kind to Sir Douglas. He came of an old Scotch family with fine traditions. Oxford followed almost as a matter of course for him and afterward he went into the army. From that day there is something in common between his career and Sir William's, simple professional zeal and industry. They set out to master their chosen calling. Long before the public had ever heard of either one their ability was known to their fellow soldiers. No two officers were more averse to any form of public advertisement, which was contrary to their instincts no less than to the ethics of soldiering. In South Africa, which was the practical school where the commanders of the British Army of to-day first learned how to command, their efficient staff work singled them out as coming men. Both had vision. They studied the continental systems of war and when the great war came they had the records which were the undeniable recommendation that singled them out from their fellows. Sir John French and Sir Ian Hamilton belonged to the generation ahead of them, the difference being that between the '50s and the '60s.

It was the test of command of a corps and afterward of an army in Flanders and Northern France which made Sir Douglas Commander-in-Chief, a test of more than the academic ability which directs chessmen on the board: that of the physical capacity to endure the strain of month after month of campaigning, to keep a calm perspective, never to let the mastery of the force under you get out of hand and never to be burdened with any details except those which are vital.

The subordinate who went in an uncertain mood to see either Sir Douglas or Sir William left with a sense of stalwart conviction. Both had the gift of simplifying any situation, however complex. When a certain general became unstrung during the retreat from Mons, Sir Douglas seemed to consider that his first duty was to assist this man to recover composure, and he slipped his arm through the general's and walked him up and down until composure had returned. Again, on the retreat from Mons Sir Douglas said, "We must stay here for the present, if we all die for it," stating this military necessity as coolly as if it merely meant waiting another quarter-hour for the arrival of a guest to dinner.

No less than General Joffre, Sir Douglas lived by rule. He, too, insisted on sleeping well at night and rising fresh for his day's work. During the period of preparation for the offensive his routine began with a stroll in the garden before breakfast. Then the heads of the different branches of his staff in headquarters town came in turn to make their reports and receive instructions. At luncheon very likely he might not talk of war. A man of his education and experience does not lack topics to take his mind off his duties. Every day at half-past two he went for a ride and with him an escort of his own regiment of Lancers. The rest of the afternoon was given over to conferences with subordinates whom he had summoned. On Sunday morning he always went into headquarters town and in a small, temporary wooden chapel listened to a sermon from a Scotch dominie who did not spare its length in awe of the eminent member of his congregation. Otherwise, he left the chateau only when he went to see with his own eyes some section of the front or of the developing organization.

Of course, the room in the chateau which was his office was hung with maps as the offices of all the great leaders are, according to report. It seems the most obvious decoration. Whether it was the latest photograph from an aeroplane or the most recent diagram of plans of attack, it came to him if his subordinates thought it worth while. All rivers of information flowed to the little chateau. He and the Chief of Staff alone might be said to know all that was going on. Talking with him in the office, which had been the study of a French country gentleman, one gained an idea of the things which interested him; of the processes by which he was building up his organization. He was the clearing house of all ideas and through them he was setting the criterion of efficiency. He spoke of the cause for which he was fighting as if this were the great thing of all to him and to every man under him, but without allowing his feelings to interfere with his judgment of the enemy. His opponent was seen without illusion, as soldier sees soldier. To him his problem was not one of sentiment, but of military power. He dealt in blows; and blows alone could win the war.

Simplicity and directness of thought, decision and readiness to accept responsibility, seemed second nature to the man secluded in that little chateau, free from any confusion of detail, who had a task—the greatest ever fallen to the lot of a British commander—of making a raw army into a force which could undertake an offensive against frontal positions considered impregnable by many experts and occupied by the skilful German Army. He had, in common with Sir William Robertson, "a good deal of thinking to do"; and what better place could he have chosen than this retreat out of the sound of the guns, where through his subordinates he felt the pulse of the whole army day by day?

His favorite expression was "the spirit that quickeneth"; the spirit of effort, of discipline, of the fellowship of cohesion of organization—spreading out from the personality at the desk in this room down through all the units to the men themselves. Though officers and soldiers rarely saw him they had felt the impulse of his spirit soon after he had taken command. A new era had come in France. That old organization called the British Empire, loose and decentrated—and holding together because it was so—had taken another step forward in the gathering of its strength into a compact force.

II

VERDUN AND ITS SEQUEL

German grand strategy and Verdun—Why the British did not go to Verdun—What they did to help—Racial characteristics in armies—Father Joffre a miser of divisions—The Somme country—Age-old tactics—If the flank cannot be turned can the front be broken?—Theory of the Somme offensive.

In order properly to set the stage for the battle of the Somme, which was the corollary of that of Verdun, we must, at the risk of appearing to thresh old straw, consider the German plan of campaign in 1916 when the German staff had turned its eyes from the East to the West. During the summer of 1915 it had attempted no offensive on the Western front, but had been content to hold its solid trench lines in the confidence that neither the British nor the French were prepared for an offensive on a large scale.

Blue days they were for us with the British Army in France during July and early August, while the official bulletins revealed on the map how von Hindenburg's and von Mackensen's legions were driving through Poland. More critical still the subsequent period when inside information indicated that German intrigue in Petrograd, behind the Russian lines which the German guns were pounding, might succeed in making a separate peace. Using her interior lines for rapid movement of troops, enclosed by a steel ring and fighting against nations speaking different languages with their capitals widely separated and their armies not in touch, each having its own sentimental and territorial objects in the war, the obvious object of Germany's policy from the outset would be to break this ring, forcing one of the Allies to capitulate under German blows.

In August, 1914, she had hoped to win a decisive battle against France before she turned her legions against Russia for a decision. Now she aimed to accomplish at Verdun what she had failed to accomplish on the Marne, confident in her information that France was exhausted. It was von Hindenburg's turn to hold the thin line while the Germans concentrated on the Western front twenty-six hundred thousand men, with every gun that they could spare and all the munitions that had accumulated after the Russian drive was over. The fall of Paris was unnecessary to their purpose. Capitals, whether Paris, Brussels, or Bucharest, are only the trophies of military victory. Primarily the German object, which naturally included the taking of Verdun, was to hammer at the heart of French defense until France, staggering under the blows, her *morale* broken by the loss of the fortress, her supposedly mercurial nature in the depths of depression, would surrender to impulse and ask for terms.

After the German attacks began at Verdun all the world was asking why the British, who were holding only sixty-odd miles of line at the time and must have large reserves, did not rush to the relief of the French. The French people themselves were a little restive under what was supposed to be British inaction. Army leaders could not reveal their plans by giving reasons—the reasons which are now obvious—for their action or inaction. To some unmilitary minds the situation seemed as simple as if Jones were attacked on the street by Smith and Robinson, while Miller, Jones' friend who was a block away, would not go to his rescue. To others, perhaps a trifle more knowing, it seemed only a matter of marching some British divisions across country or putting them on board a train.

Of course the British were only too ready to assist the French. Any other attitude would have been unintelligent; for, with the French Army broken, the British Army would find itself having to bear unassisted the weight of German blows in the West. There were three courses which the British Army might take.

First. It could send troops to Verdun. But the mixture of units speaking different languages in the intricate web of communications required for directing modern operations, and the mixture of transport in the course of heavy concentrations in the midst of a critical action where absolute cohesion of all units was necessary, must result in confusion which would make any such plan impracticable. Only the desperate situation of the French being without reserve could have compelled its second consideration, as it represented the extreme of that military inefficiency which makes wasteful use of lives and material.

Second. The British could attack along their front as a diversion to relieve pressure on Verdun. For this the Germans were fully prepared. It fell in exactly with their plan. Knowing that the British New Army was as yet undeveloped as an instrument for the offensive and that it was still short of guns and shells, the Germans had struck in the inclement weather of February at Verdun, thinking, and wrongly to my mind, that the handicap to the vitality of their men of sleet, frost and cold, soaking rains would be offset by the time gained. Not only had the Germans sufficient men to carry on the Verdun offensive, but facing the British their numbers were the largest mile for mile since the first battle of Ypres. Familiar with British valor as the result of actual contact in battle from Mons to the Marne and back to Ypres, and particularly in the Loos offensive (which was the New Army's first "eye-opener" to the German staff), the Germans reasoned that, with what one German called "the courage of their stupidity, or the stupidity of their courage," the British, driven by public demand to the assistance of the French, would send their fresh infantry with inadequate artillery support against German machine guns and curtains of fire, and pile up their dead until their losses would reduce the whole army to inertia for the rest of the year.

Of course, the German hypothesis—the one which cost von Falkenhayn his place as Chief of Staff—was based on such a state of exhaustion by the French that a British attack would be mandatory. The initial stage of the German attack was up to expectations in ground gained, but not in prisoners or material taken. The French fell back skilfully before the German onslaught against positions lightly held by the defenders in anticipation of the attack, and turned their curtains of fire upon the enemy in possession of captured trenches. Then France gave to the outside world another surprise. Her spirit, ever brilliant in the offensive, became cold steel in a stubborn and thrifty defensive. She was not "groggy," as the Germans supposed. For every yard of earth gained they had to pay a ghastly price; and their own admiration of French shell and valor is sufficient professional glory for either Pétain, Nivelle, or Mangin, or the private in the ranks.

Third. The British could take over more trench line, thus releasing French forces for Verdun, which was the plan adopted at the conference of the French and British commands. One morning in place of a French army in Artois a British army was in occupation. The round helmets of the British took the place of the oblong helmets of the French along the parapet; British soldiers were in billets in place of the French in the villages at the rear and British guns moved into French gun-emplacements with the orderly precision which army training with its discipline alone secures; while the French Army was on board railway trains moving at given intervals of headway over rails restricted to their use on their way to Verdun where, under that simple French staff system which is the product of inheritance and previous training and this war's experience, they fell into place as a part of the wall of men and cannon.

Outside criticism, which drew from this arrangement the conclusion that it left the British to the methodical occupation of quiet trenches while their allies were sent to the sacrifice, had its effect for a time on the outside public and even on the French, but did not disturb the equanimity of the British staff in the course of its preparations or of the French staff, which knew well enough that when the time came the British Army would not be fastidious about paying the red cost of victory. Four months later when British battalions were throwing themselves against frontal positions with an abandon that their staff had to restrain, the same sources of outside criticism, including superficial gossip in Paris, were complaining that the British were too brave in their waste of life. It has been fashionable with some people to criticize the British, evidently under the impression that the British New Army would be better than a continental army instantly its battalions were landed in France.

Every army's methods, every staff's way of thinking, are characteristic in the long run of the people who supply it with soldiers. The German Army is what it is not through the application of any academic theory of military perfection, but through the application of organization to German character. Naturally phlegmatic, naturally disinclined to initiative, the Germans before the era of modern Germany had far less of the martial instinct than the French. German army makers, including the master one of all, von Moltke, set out to use German docility and obedience in the creation of a machine of singular industry and rigidity and ruthless discipline. Similar methods would mean revolt in democratic France and individualistic England where every man carries Magna Charta, talisman of his own "rights," in his waistcoat pocket.

The French peasant, tilling his fields within range of the guns, the market gardener bringing his products down the Somme in the morning to Amiens, or the Parisian clerk, business man and workman—they are France and the French Army. But the heart-strength and character-strength of France, I think, is her stubborn, conservative, smiling peasant. It is repeating a commonplace to say that he always has a few gold pieces in his stocking. He yields one only on a critical occasion and then a little grumblingly, with the thrift of the bargainer who means that it shall be well spent.

The Anglo-Saxon, whose inheritance is particularly evident in Americans in this respect, when he gives in a crisis turns extravagant whether of money or life, as England has in this war. The sea is his and new lands are his, as they are ours. Australians with their dollar and a half a day, buying out the shops of a village when they were not in the trenches, were astounding to the natives though not in the least to themselves. They were acting like normal Anglo-Saxons bred in a rich island continent. Anglo-Saxons have money to spend and spend it in the confidence that they will make more.

General Joffre, grounded in the France of the people and the soil, was a thrifty general. Indeed, from the lips of Frenchmen in high places the Germans might have learned that the French Army was running short of men. Joffre seemed never to have any more divisions to spare; yet never came a crisis that he did not find another division in the toe of his stocking, which he gave up as grumblingly as the peasant parts with his gold piece.

A miser of divisions, Father Joffre. He had enough for Verdun as we know—and more. While he was holding on the defensive there, he was able to prepare for an offensive elsewhere. He spared the material and the guns to coöperate with the British on the Somme and later he sent to General Foch, commander of the northern group of French Armies, the unsurpassed Iron Corps from Nancy and the famous Colonial Corps.

It was in March, 1916, when suspense about Verdun was at its height, that Sir Douglas Haig, Commander-in-Chief of the group of British Armies, and Sir Henry Rawlinson, who was to be his right-hand man through the offensive as commander of the Fourth Army, went over the ground opposite the British front on the Somme and laid the plans for their attack, and Sir Henry received instructions to begin the elaborate preparations for what was to become the greatest battle of all time. It included, as the first step, the building of many miles of railway and highway for the transport of the enormous requisite quantities of guns and materials.

The Somme winds through rich alluvial lands at this point and around a number of verdant islands in its leisurely course. Southward, along the old front line, the land is more level, where the river makes its bend in front of Péronne. Northward, generically, it rises into a region of rolling country, with an irregularly marked ridge line which the Germans held.

No part of the British front had been so quiet in the summer of 1915 as the region of Picardy. From the hill where later I watched the attack of July 1st, on one day in August of the previous year I had such a broad view that if a shell were to explode anywhere along the front of five miles it would have been visible to me, and I saw not a single burst of smoke from high explosive or shrapnel. Apparently the Germans never expected to undertake any offensive here. All their energy was devoted to defensive preparations, without even an occasional attack over a few hundred yards to keep in their hand. Tranquillity, which amounted to the simulation of a truce, was the result. At different points you might see Germans walking about in the open and the observer could stand exposed within easy range of the guns without being sniped at by artillery, as he would have been in the Ypres salient.

When the British took over this section of line, so short were they of guns that they had to depend partly on French artillery; and their troops were raw New Army battalions or regulars stiffened by a small percentage of veterans of Mons and Ypres. The want of guns and shells required correspondingly more troops to the mile, which left them still relying on flesh and blood rather than on machinery for defense. The British Army was in that middle stage of a few highly trained troops and the first arrival of the immense forces to come; while the Germans occupied on the Eastern front were not of a mind to force the issue. There is a story of how one day a German battery, to vary the monotony, began shelling a British trench somewhat heavily. The British, in reply, put up a sign, "If you don't stop we will fire our only rifle grenade at you!" to which the Germans replied in the same vein, "Sorry! We will stop"—as they did.

The subsoil of the hills is chalk, which yields to the pick rather easily and makes firm walls for trenches. Having chosen their position, which they were able to do in the operations after the Marne as the two armies, swaying back and forth in the battle for positions northward, came to rest, the Germans had set out, as the result of experience, to build impregnable works in the days when forts had become less important and the trench had become supreme. As holding the line required little fighting, the industrious Germans under the stiff bonds of discipline had plenty of time for sinking deep dugouts and connecting galleries under their first line and for elaborating their communication trenches and second line, until what had once been peaceful farming land now consisted of irregular welts of white chalk crossing fields without hedges or fences, whose sweep had been broken only by an occasional group of farm buildings of a large proprietor, a plot of woods, or the village communities where the farmers lived and went to and from their farms which were demarked to the eye only by the crop lines.

One can never make the mistake of too much simplification in the complicated detail of modern tactics where the difficulty is always to see the forest for the trees. Strategy has not changed since prehistoric days. It must always remain the same: feint and surprise. The first primitive man who looked at the breast of his opponent and struck suddenly at his face was a strategist; so, too, the anthropoid at the Zoo who leads another to make a leap for a trapeze and draws it out from under him; so, too, the thug who waits to catch his victim coming unawares out of an alley. Anybody facing more than one opponent will try to protect his back by a wall, which is also strategy—strategy being the veritable instinct of self-preservation which aims at an advantage in the disposition of forces.

Place two lines of fifty men facing each other in the open without officers, and some fellow with initiative on the right or the left end will instinctively give the word and lead a rush for cover somewhere on the flank which will permit an enfilade of the enemy's ranks. Practically all of the great battles of the world have been won by turning an enemy's flank, which compelled him to retreat if it did not result in rout or capture.

The swift march of a division or a brigade from reserve to the flank at the critical moment has often turned the fortune of a day. All manoeuvering has this object in view. Superior numbers facilitate the operation, and victory has most often resolved itself into superior numbers pressing a flank and nothing more; though subsequently his admiring countrymen acclaimed the victor as the inventor of a strategic plan which was old before Alexander took the field, when the victor's genius consisted in the use of opportunities that enabled him to strike at the critical point with more men than his adversary. In flank of the Southern Confederacy Sherman swung through the South; in flank the Confederates aimed to bend back the Federal line at Kulp's Hill and Little Round Top. By the flank Grant pressed Lee back to Appomattox. Yalu,

Liao Yang and Mukden were won in the Russo-Japanese war by flanking movements which forced Kuropatkin to retire, though never disastrously.

Pickett's charge at Gettysburg remains to the American the most futile and glorious illustration of a charge against a frontal position, with its endeavor to break the center. The center may waver, but it is the flanks that go; though, of course, in all consistent operations of big armies a necessary incident of any effort to press back the wings is sufficient pressure on the front, simultaneously delivered, to hold all the troops there in position and keep the enemy command in apprehension of the disaster that must follow if the center were to break badly at the same time that his flanks were being doubled back. The foregoing is only the repetition of principles which cannot be changed by the length of line and masses of troops and incredible volumes of artillery fire; which makes the European war the more confusing to the average reader as he receives his information in technical terms.

The same object that leads one line of men to try to flank another sent the German Army through Belgium in order to strike the French Army in flank. It succeeded in this purpose, but not in turning the French flank; though by this operation, in violation of the territory of a neutral nation, it made enemy territory the scene of future action. One may discuss until he is blue in the face what would have happened if the Germans had thrown their legions directly against the old French frontier. Personally, in keeping with the idea that I expressed in "The Last Shot," I think that they would never have gone through the Trouée de Miracourt or past Verdun.

With a solid line of trenches from Switzerland to the North Sea, any offensive must "break the center," as it were, in order to have room for a flanking operation. It must go against frontal positions, incorporating in its strategy every defensive lesson learned and the defensive tactics and weapons developed in eighteen months of trench warfare. If, as was generally supposed, the precision of modern arms, with rifles and machine guns sending their bullets three thousand yards and curtains of fire delivered from hidden guns anywhere from two to fifteen miles away, was all in favor of the defensive, then how, when in the days of muzzle-loading rifles and smooth-bore guns frontal attacks had failed, could one possibly succeed in 1916?

Again and again in our mess and in all of the messes at the front, and wherever men gathered the world over, the question, Can the line be broken? has been discussed. As discussed it is an academic question. The practical answer depends upon the strength of the attacking force compared to that of the defending force. If the Germans could keep only five hundred thousand men on the Western front they would have to withdraw from a part of the line, concentrate on chosen positions and depend on tactics to defend their exposed flanks in pitched battle. Three million men, with ten thousand guns, could not break the line against an equally skilful army of three millions with ten thousand guns; but five millions with fifteen thousand guns might break the line held by an equally skilful army of a million with five thousand guns. Thus, you are brought to a question of numbers, of skill and of material. If the object be attrition, then the offensive, if it can carry on its attacks with less loss of men than the defensive, must win. With the losses about equal, the offensive must also eventually win if it has sufficient reserves.

There could be no restraining the public, with the wish father to the thought, from believing that the attack of July 1st on the Somme was an effort at immediate decision, though the responsible staff officer was very careful to state that there was no expectation of breaking the line and that the object was to gain a victory in *morale*, train the army in actual conditions for future offensives, and, when the ledger was balanced, to prove that, with superior gunfire, the offensive could be conducted with less loss than the defensive under modern conditions. This, I think, may best be stated now. The results we shall consider later.

One thing was certain, with the accruing strength of the British and the French Armies, they could not rest idle. They must attack. They must take the initiative away from the Germans. The greater the masses of Germans which were held on the Western front under the Allied pounding, the better the situation for the Russians and the Italians; and, accordingly, the plan for the summer of 1916 for the first time permitted all the Allies, thanks to increased though not adequate munitions—there never can be that—to conduct something like a common offensive. That of the Russians, starting earlier than the others, was the first to pause, which meant that the Anglo-French and the Italian offensives were in full blast, while the Russians, for the time being, had settled into new positions.

Preparation for this attack on the Somme, an operation without parallel in character and magnitude unless it be the German offensive at Verdun which had failed, could not be too complete. There must be a continuous flow of munitions which would allow the continuation of the battle with blow upon blow once it had begun. Adequate realization of his task would not hasten a general to undertake it until he was fully ready, and military preference, if other considerations had permitted, would have postponed the offensive till the spring of 1917.

III

A CANADIAN INNOVATION

Gathering of the clans from Australia, New Zealand and Canada—England sends Sir Douglas Haig men but not an army—Methods of converting men into an army—The trench raid a Canadian invention—Development of trench raiding—The correspondents' quarters—Getting ready for the "big push"—A well-kept secret.

"Some tough!" remarked a Canadian when he saw the Australians for the first time marching along a French road. They and the New Zealanders were conspicuous in France, owing to their felt hats with the brim looped up on the side, their stalwart physique and their smooth-shaven, clean-cut faces. Those who had been in Gallipoli formed the stiffening of veteran experience and comradeship for those fresh from home or from camps in Egypt.

Canadian battalions, which had been training in Canada and then in England, increased the Canadian numbers until they had an army equal in size to that of Meade or Lee at Gettysburg. English, Scotch, Welsh, Irish, South Africans and Newfoundlanders foregathering in Picardy, Artois and Flanders left one wondering about English as "she is spoke." On the British front I have heard every variety, including that of different parts of the United States. One day I received a letter from a fellow countryman which read like this:

"I'm out here in the R.F.A. with 'krumps' bursting on my cocoanut and am going to see it through. If you've got any American newspapers or magazines lying loose please send them to me, as I am far from California."

The clans kept arriving. Every day saw new battalions and new guns disembark. England was sending to Sir Douglas Haig men and material, but not an army in the modern sense. He had to weld the consignments into a whole there in the field in face of the enemy. Munitions were a matter of resource and manufacturing, but the great factory of all was the factory of men. It was not enough that the gunners should know how to shoot fairly accurately back in England, or Canada, or Australia. They must learn to coöperate with scores of batteries of different calibers in curtains of fire and, in turn, with the infantry, whose attacks they must support with the finesse of scientific calculation plus the instinctive *liaison* which comes only with experience under trained officers, against the German Army which had no lack of material in its conscript ranks for promotion to fill vacancies in the officers' lists.

From seventeen miles of front to twenty-seven, and then to sixty and finally to nearly one hundred, the British had broadened their responsibility, which meant only practice in the defensive, while the Germans had had two years' practice in the offensive. The two British offensives at Neuve Chapelle had included a small proportion of the battalions which were to fight on the Somme; and the third, incomparably more ambitious, faced heavier concentration of troops and guns than its predecessors.

What had not been gained in battle practice must be approximated in drill. Every battalion commander, every staff officer and every general who had had any experience, must be instructor as well as director. They must assemble their machine and tune it up before they put it on a stiffer road than had been tried before.

The British Army zone in France became a school ground for the Grand Offensive; and while the people at home were thinking, "We've sent you the men and the guns—now for action!" the time of preparation was altogether too short for the industrious learners. Every possible kind of curriculum which would simulate actual conditions of attack had been devised. In moving about the rear the rattle of a machine gun ten miles back of the line told of the machine gun school; a series of explosions drew attention to bombers working their way through practice trenches in a field; a heavier explosion was from the academy for trench mortars; a mighty cloud of smoke and earth rising two or three hundred feet was a new experiment in mining. Sir Douglas went on the theory that no soldier can know his work too well. He meant to allow no man in his command to grow dull from idleness.

Trench warfare had become systematized, and inevitably the holding of the same line for month after month was not favorable to the development of initiative. A man used to a sedentary life is not given to physical action. One who is always digging dugouts is loath to leave the habitation which has cost him much labor in order to live in the open.

Battalions were in position for a given number of days, varying with the character of the position held, when they were relieved for a rest in billets. While in occupation they endured an amount of shell fire varying immensely between different sectors. A few men were on the watch with rifles and machine guns for any demonstration by the enemy, while the rest were idle when not digging. They sent out patrols at night into No Man's Land for information; exchanged rifle grenades, mortars and bombs with the enemy. Each week brought its toll of casualties, light in the tranquil places, heavy in the wickedly hot corner of the Ypres salient, where attacks and counter-attacks never ceased and the apprehension of having your parapet smashed in by an artillery "preparation," which might be the forerunner of an attack, was unremittingly on the nerves.

It was a commonplace that any time you desired you could take a front of a thousand or two yards simply by concentrating your gunfire, cutting the enemy's barbed wire and tearing the sandbags of his parapet into ribbons, with resulting fearful casualties to him; and then a swift charge under cover of the artillery hurricane would gain possession of the débris, the enemy's wounded and those still alive in his dugouts. Losses in operations of this kind usually were much lighter in taking the enemy's position than in the attempt to hold it, as he, in answer to your offensive, turned the full force of his guns upon his former trench which your men were trying to organize into one of their own. Later, under cover of his own guns, his charge recovered the ruins, forcing the party of the first part who had started the "show" back to his own former first line trench, which left the situation as it was before with both sides a loser of lives without gaining any ground and with the prospect of drudgery in building anew their traverses and burrows and filling new sandbags.

It was the repetition of this sort of "incident," as reported in the daily *communiqués*, which led the outside world to wonder at the fatuousness and the satire of the thing, without understanding that its object was entirely for the purpose of *morale*. An attack was made to keep the men up to the mark; a counter-attack in order not to allow the enemy ever to develop a sense of superiority. Every soldier who participated in a charge learned something in method and gained something in the quality considered requisite by his commanders. He had met face to face in mortal hand-to-hand combat in the trench traverses the enemy who had been some invisible force behind a gray line of parapet sniping at him every time he showed his head.

Attack and counter-attack without adding another square yard to the territory in your possession—these had cost hundreds of thousands of casualties on the Western front. The next step was to obtain the *morale* of attack without wasting lives in trying to hold new ground.

Credit for the trench raid, which was developed through the winter of 1915, belongs to the Canadian. His plan was as simple as that of the American Indian who rushed a white settlement and fled after he was through scalping; or the cowboys who shot up a town; or the Mexican insurgents who descend upon a village for a brief visit of killing and looting. The Canadian proposed to enter the German trenches by surprise, remain long enough to make the most of the resulting confusion, and then to return to his own trenches without trying to hold and organize the enemy's position and thus draw upon his head while busy with the spade a murderous volume of shell fire.

The first raids were in small parties over a narrow front and the tactics those of the frontiersman, who never wants in individual initiative and groundcraft. Behind their lines the Canadians rehearsed in careful detail again and again till each man was letter perfect in the part that he was to play in the "little surprise being planned in Canada for Brother Boche." The time chosen for the exploit was a dark, stormy night, when the drumbeat of rain and the wind blowing in their direction would muffle the movements of the men as they cut paths through the barbed wires for their panther-like rush. It was the kind of experiment whose success depends upon every single participant keeping silence and performing the task set for him with fastidious exactitude.

The Germans, confident in the integrity of their barbed wire, with all except the sentries whose ears and eyes failed to detect danger asleep in their dugouts, found that the men of the Maple Leaf had sprung over the parapet and were at the door demanding surrender. It was an affair to rejoice the heart of Israel Putnam or Colonel Mosby, and its success was a new contribution in tactics to stalemate warfare which seemed to have exhausted every possible invention and novelty. Trench raids were made over broader and broader fronts until they became considerable operations, where the wire was cut by artillery which gave the same kind of support to the men that it was to give later on in the Grand Offensive.

There was a new terror to trench holding and dwelling. Now the man who lay down in a dugout for the night was not only in danger of being blown heavenward by a mine, or buried by the explosion of a heavy shell, or compelled to spring up in answer to the ring of the gong which announced a gas attack, but he might be awakened at two a.m. (a favorite hour for raids) by the outcry of sentries who had been overpowered by the stealthy rush of shadowy figures in the night, and while he got to his feet be killed by the burst of a bomb thrown by men whom he supposed were also fast asleep in their own quarters two or three hundred yards away.

Trench-raid rivalry between battalions, which commanders liked to instil, inevitably developed. Battalions grew as proud of their trench raids as battleships of their target practice. A battalion which had not had a successful trench raid had something to explain. What pride for the Bantams—the little fellows below regulation height who had enlisted in a division of their own on Lord Kitchener's suggestion—when in one of their trench raids they brought back some hulking, big Germans and a man's size German machine gun across No Man's Land!

Raiders never attempted to remain long in the enemy's trenches. They killed the obdurate Germans, took others prisoners and, aside from the damage that they did, always returned with identifications of the battalions which occupied the position, while the prisoners brought in yielded valuable information.

The German, more adaptive than creative, more organizing than pioneering, was not above learning from the British, and soon they, too, were undertaking surprise parties in the night. Although they tightened the discipline for the defensive of both sides, trench raids were of far more service to the British than to the Germans; for the British staff found in them an invaluable method of preparation for the offensive. Not only had the artillery practice in supporting actual rather than theoretical attacks, but when the men went over the parapet it was in face of the enemy, who might turn on his machine guns if not silenced by accurate gunfire. They learned how to coördinate their efforts, whether individually or as units, both in the charge and in cleaning out the German dugouts. Their sense of observation, adaptability and team play was quickened in the life-and-death contact with the foe.

Through the spring months the trench raids continued in their process of "blooding" the new army for the "big push." Meanwhile, the correspondents, who were there to report the operations of the army, were having as quiet a time as a country gentleman on his estate without any of the cares of his superintendent.

Our homing place from our peregrinations about the army was not too far away from headquarters town to be in touch with it or too near to feel the awe of proximity to the directing authority of hundreds of thousands of men. Trench raids had lost their novelty for the public which the correspondents served. A description of a visit to a trench was as commonplace to readers as the experience itself to one of our seasoned group of six men. We had seen all the schools of war and the Conscientious Objectors' battalion, too— those extreme pacifists who refuse to kill their fellow man. Their opinions being respected by English freedom and individualism, they were set to repairing roads and like tasks.

The war had become completely static. Unless some new way of killing developed, even the English public did not care to read about its own army. When my English comrades saw that a petty scandal received more space in the London papers than their accounts of a gallant air raid, they had moments of cynical depression.

Between journeys we took long walks, went birds'-nesting and chatted with the peasants. What had we to do with war? Yet we never went afield to trench or headquarters, to hospital or gun position, without finding something new and wonderful to us if not to the public in that vast hive of military industry.

"But if we ever start the push they'll read every detail," said our wisest man. "It's the push that is in everybody's mind. The man in the street is tired of hearing about rehearsals. He wants the curtain to go up."

Each of us knew that the offensive was coming and where, without ever speaking of it in our mess or being supposed to know. Nobody was supposed to know, except a few "brass hats" in headquarters town. One of the prime requisites of the gold braid which denotes a general or of the red band around the cap and the red tab on the coat lapel which denote staff is ability to keep a secret; but long association with an army makes it a sort of second nature, even with a group of civilians. When you met a Brass Hat you pretended to believe that the monotony of those official army reports about shelling a new German redoubt or a violent artillery duel, or four enemy planes brought down, which read the same on Friday as on Thursday, was to continue forever. The Brass Hats pretended to believe the same among themselves. For all time the British and the French Armies were to keep on hurling explosives at the German Army from the same positions.

Occasionally a Brass Hat did intimate that the offensive would probably come in the spring of 1917, if not later, and you accepted the information as strictly confidential and indefinite, as you should accept any received from a Brass Hat. It never occurred to anybody to inquire if "1917" meant June or July of 1916. This would be as bad form as to ask a man whose head was gray last year and is black this year if he dyed his hair.

Those heavy howitzers, fresh from the foundry, drawn by big caterpillar tractors, were all proceeding in one direction—toward the Somme. Villages along their route were filling with troops. The nearer the front you went, the greater the concentration of men and material. Shells, the size of the milk cans at suburban stations, stood in close order on the platforms beside the sidings of new light railways; shells of all calibers were piled at new ammunition dumps; fields were cut by the tracks of guns moving into position; steam rollers were road-making in the midst of the long processions of motor trucks, heavy laden when bound toward the trenches and empty when returning; barbed-wire enclosures were ready as collecting stations for prisoners; clusters of hospital tents at other points seemed out of proportion to the trickle of wounded from customary trench warfare.

All this preparation, stretching over weeks and months, unemotional and methodical, infinite in detail, prodigious in effort, suggested the work of engineers and contractors and subcontractors in the building of some great bridge or canal, with the workmen all in the same kind of uniform and with managers, superintendents and foremen each having some insignia of rank and the Brass Hats and Red Tabs the inspectors and auditors.

The officer installing a new casualty clearing station, or emplacing a gun, or starting another ammunition dump, had not heard of any offensive. He was only doing what he was told. It was not his business to ask why of any Red Tab, any more than it was the business of a Red Tab to ask why of a Brass Hat, or his business to know that the same sort of thing was going on over a front of sixteen miles. Each one saw only his little section of the hive. Orders strictly limited workers to their sections at the same time that their lips were sealed. Contractors were in no danger of strikes; employees received no extra pay for overtime. It was as evident that the offensive was to be on the Somme as that the circus has come to town, when you see tents rising at dawn in a vacant lot while the elephants are standing in line.

Toward the end of June I asked the Red Tab who sat at the head of our table if I might go to London on leave. He was surprised, I think, but did not appear surprised. It is one of the requisites of a Red Tab that he should not. He said that he was uncertain if leave were being granted at present. This was unusual, as an intimation of refusal had never been made on any previous occasion. When I said that it would be for only two or three days, he thought that it could be arranged all right. What this considerate Red Tab meant was that I should return "in time." Yet he had not mentioned that there was to be any offensive and I had not. We had kept the faith of military secrecy. Besides, I really did not know, unless I opened a pigeonhole in my brain. It was also my business not to know—the only business I had with the "big push" except to look on.

Over in London my friends surprised me by exclaiming, "What are you doing here?" and, "Won't you miss the offensive which is about to begin?" Now, what would a Brass Hat say in such an awkward emergency? Would he look wise or unwise when he said it? Trying to look unwise, I replied: "They have the men now and can strike any time that they please. It's not my place to know where or when. I asked for leave and they gave it." I was quite relieved and felt that I was almost worthy of a secretive Brass Hat myself, when one man remarked: "They don't let you know much, do they?"

To keep such immense preparations wholly a secret among any English-speaking people would be out of the question. Only the Japanese are mentally equipped for security of information. With other races it is a struggling effort. Can you imagine Washington keeping a military secret? You could hear the confidential whispers all the way from the War Department to the Capitol. In such a great movement as that of the Somme one weak link in a chain of tens of thousands of officers is enough to break it, not to mention a million or so of privates.

IV

READY FOR THE BLOW

French national spirit—Our gardeners—Tuning up for the attack—Policing the sky—Sausage balloons—Matter-of-fact, systematic war—A fury of trench raids—Reserves marching forward—Organized human will—Sons of the old country ready to strike—The greatest struggle of the war about to begin.

Our headquarters during my first summer at the front had been in the flat border region of the Pas de Calais, which seemed neither Flanders nor France. Our second summer required that we should be nearer the middle of the British line, as it extended southward, in order to keep in touch with the whole. In the hilly country of Artois a less comfortable chateau was compensated for by the smiling companionship of neighbors in the fields and villages of the real France.

The quality of this sympathetic appeal was that of the thoroughbred racial and national spirit of a great people, in the politeness which gave to a thickset peasant woman a certain grace, in the smiles of the land and its inhabitants, in that inbred patriotism which through the centuries has created a distinctive civilization called French by the same ready sacrifices for its continuity as those which were made on the Marne and at Verdun. Flanders is not France, and France is increasingly French as you proceed from Ypres to Amiens, the capital of Picardy. I was glad that Picardy had been chosen as the scene of the offensive. It made the blow seem more truly a blow for France. I was to learn to love Picardy and its people under the test of battle.

In order that we might be near the field of the Somme we were again to move our quarters, and we had the pang of saying good-by to another garden and another gardener. All the gardeners of our different chateaux had been philosophers. It was Louis who said that he would like to make all the politicians who caused wars into a salad, accompanying his threat with appropriate gestures; Charles who thought that once the "Boches" were properly pruned they might be acceptable second-rate members of international society; and Leon who wanted the Kaiser put to the plow in a coat of corduroy as the best cure for his conceit. That afternoon, when *au revoirs* were spoken and our cars wound in and out over the byroads of the remote countryside, not a soldier was visible until we came to the great main road, where we had the signal that peaceful surroundings were finally left behind in the distant, ceaseless roar of the guns, like some gigantic drumbeat calling the armies to combat.

A giant with nerves of telephone wires and muscles of steel and a human heart seemed to be snarling his defiance before he sprang into action. We knew the meaning of the set thunders of the preliminary bombardment. That night to the eastward the sky was an aurora borealis of flashes; and the next day we sought the source of the lightnings.

Seamed and tracked and gashed were the slopes behind the British line and densely peopled with busy men in khaki. Every separate scene was familiar to us out of our experience, but every one had taken on a new meaning. The whole exerted a majestic spell. Graded like the British social scale were the different calibers of guns. Those with the largest reach were set farthest back. Fifteen-inch howitzer dukes or nine-inch howitzer earls, with their big, ugly mouths and their deliberate and powerful fire, fought alone, each in his own lair, whether under a tree or in the midst of the ruins of a village. The long naval guns, though of smaller caliber, had a still greater reach and were sending their shells five to ten miles beyond the German trenches.

The eight-inch and six-inch howitzers were more gregarious. They worked in groups of four and sometimes a number of batteries were in line. Beyond them were those alert commoners, the field guns, rapid of fire with their eighteen-pound shells. These seemed more tractable and companionable, better suited for human association, less mechanically brutal. They were not monstrous enough to require motor tractors to draw them at a stately gait, but behind their teams could be up and away across the fields on short notice, their caissons of ammunitions creaking behind them. Along the communication trenches perspiring soldiers carried "plum puddings" or the trench-mortar shells which were to be fired from the front line and boxes of egg-shaped bombs which fitted nicely in the palm of the hand for throwing.

It seemed that all the guns in the world must be firing as you listened from a distance, although when you came into the area where the guns were in tiers behind the cover of a favorable slope you found that many were silent. The men of one battery might be asleep while its neighbor was sending shells with a one-two-three deliberation. Any sleep or rest that the men got must be there in the midst of this crashing babel from steel throats. Again, the covers were being put over the muzzles for the night, or, out of what had seemed blank hillside, a concealed battery which had not been firing before sent out its vicious puffs of smoke before its reports reached your ears. Every battery was doing as it was told from some nerve-center; every one had its registered target on the map—a trench, or a road, or a German battery, or where it was thought that a German battery ought to be.

The flow of ammunition for all came up steadily, its expenditure regulated on charts by officers who kept watch for extravagance and aimed to make every shell count. A fortune was being fired away every hour; a sum which would send a youth for a year to college or bring up a child went into a single large shell which might not have the luck to kill one human being as excuse for its existence; an endowment for a maternity hospital was represented in a day's belch of destruction from a single acre of trodden wheat land. One trench mortar would consume in an hour plum puddings for an orphan school. For you might pause to think of it in this way if you chose. Thousands do at the front.

Down on the banks of the Somme the blue uniforms of the French in place of the British khaki hovered around the gun-emplacements; the *soixante-quinze* with its virtuoso artistic precision was neighbor to the British eighteen-pounder. Guns, guns, guns—French and English! The same nests of them opposite Gommecourt and at Estrées thundered across at one another from either bank of the Somme through summer haze over the green spaces of the islands edged with the silver of its tranquil flow in the moonlight or its glare in the sunlight.

Not the least of the calculations in this activity was to screen every detail from aerial observation. New hangars had risen at the edge of level fields, whence the swift fighting machines of an aircraft concentration in keeping with the concentration of guns and all other material rose to reconnaissance, or to lie in wait as a falcon to pounce upon an invading German plane. Thus the sky was policed by flight against prying aerial eyes. If one German plane could descend to an altitude of a thousand feet, its photographs would reveal the location of a hundred batteries to German gunners and show the plan of concentration clearly enough to leave no doubt of the line of attack; but the anti-aircraft guns, plentiful now as other British material, would have caught it going, if not coming, provided it escaped being jockeyed to death by half a dozen British planes with their machine guns rattling.

To "camouflet" became a new English verb British planes tested out a battery's visibility from the air. Landscape painters were called in to assist in the deceit. One was set to "camouflet" the automobile van for the pigeons which, carried in baskets on the men's backs in charges, were released as another means of sending word of the progress of an attack obscured in the shell-smoke. This conscientious artist "camoufleted" the pigeon-van so successfully that the pigeons could not find their way home.

Night was the hour of movement. At night the planes, if they went forth, saw only a vague and shadowy earth. The sausage balloons, German and Allied, those monitors of the sky, a line of opaque, weird question marks against the blue, stared across at each other out of range of the enemy's guns, "spotting" the fall of shells for their own side from their suspended basket observation posts from early morning until they were drawn in by their gasoline engines with the coming of dusk. Clumsy and helpless they seemed;

but in common with the rest of the army they had learned to reach their dugouts swiftly at the first sign of shell fire, and descended then with a ridiculous alacrity which suggested the possession of the animal intelligence of self-preservation. Occasionally one broke loose and, buffeted like an umbrella down the street by the wind, started for the Rhine. And the day before the great attack the British aviation corps sprang a surprise on the German sausages, six of which disappeared in balls of flame.

A one-armed man of middle age from India, who offered to do his "bit," refused a post at home in keeping with his physical limitations. His eyes were all right, he said, when he nominated himself as a balloon observer, and he never suffered from sea-sickness which sausage balloons most wickedly induce. Many a man who has ascended in one not only could see nothing, but wanted to see nothing, and turning spinach lopping over the basket rail prayed only that the engine would begin drawing in immediately.

One day the one-armed pilot was up with a "joy-rider"; that is, an officer who was not a regular aerial observer but was sight-seeing. The balloon suddenly broke loose with the wind blowing strong toward Berlin, which was a bit awkward, as he remarked, considering that he had an inexperienced passenger.

"We mustn't let the Boches get us!" he said. "Look sharp and do as I say."

First, he got the joy-rider into the parachute harness for such emergencies and over the side, then himself, both descending safely on the right side of the British trenches—which was rather "smart work," as the British would say, but all to the taste of the one-armed pilot who was looking for adventures. I have counted thirty-three British sausage balloons within my range of vision from a hill. The previous year the British had not a baker's dozen.

What is lacking? Have we enough of everything? These questions were haunting to organizers in those last days of preparation.

After dark the scene from a hill, as you rode toward the horizon of flashes, was one of incredible grandeur. Behind you, as you looked toward the German lines, was the blanket of night pierced and slashed by the flashes of gun blasts; overhead the bloodcurdling, hoarse sweep of their projectiles; and beyond the darkness had been turned into a chaotic, uncanny day by the jumping, leaping, spreading blaze of explosives which made all objects on the landscape stand out in flickering silhouette. Spurts of flame from the great shells rose out of the bowels of the earth, softening with their glow the sharp, concentrated, vicious snaps of light from shrapnel. Little flashes played among big flashes and flashes laid over flashes shingle fashion in a riot of lurid competition, while along the line of the German trenches at some places lay a haze of shimmering flame from the rapid fire of the trench mortars.

The most resourceful of descriptive writers is warranted in saying that the scene was indescribable. Correspondents did their best, and after they had squeezed the rhetorical sponge of its last drop of ink distilled to frenzy of adjectives in inadequate effort, they gaspingly laid their copy on the table of the censor, who minded not "word pictures" which contained no military secrets.

Vision exalted and numbed by the display, one's mind sought the meaning and the purpose of this unprecedented bombardment, with its precision of the devil's own particular brand of "kultur," which was to cut the Germans' barbed wire, smash in their trenches, penetrate their dugouts, close up their communication trenches, do unto their second line the same as to their first line, bury their machine guns in débris, crush each rallying strong point in that maze of warrens, burst in the roofs of village billets over their heads, lay a barrier of death across all roads and, in the midst of the process of killing and wounding, imprison the men of the front line beyond relief by fresh troops and shut them off from food and munitions. Theatric, horrible and more than that—matter-of-fact, systematic war! There was relatively little response from the German batteries, whose silence had a sinister suggestion. They waited on the attack as the target of their revenge for the losses which they were suffering.

By now they knew from the bombardment, if not from other sources, that a British attack was coming at some point of the line. Their flares were playing steadily over No Man's Land to reveal any movement by the British or the French. From their trenches rose signal rockets—the only real fireworks, leisurely and innocent, without any sting of death in their sparks—which seemed to be saying "No movement yet" to commanders who could not be reached by any other means through the curtains of fire and to artillerists who wanted to turn on their own curtains of fire instantly the charge started. Then there were other little flashes and darts of light and flame which insisted on adding their moiety to the garish whole. And under the German trenches at several points were vast charges of explosives which had been patiently borne under ground through arduously made tunnels.

So much for the machinery of material. Thus far we have mentioned only guns and explosions, things built of steel to fire missiles of steel and things on wheels, and little about the machine of human beings now to come abreast of the tape for the charge, the men who had been "blooded," the "cannon fodder." Every shell was meant for killing men; every German battery and machine gun was a monster frothing red at the lips in anticipation of slaughter.

A fury of trench raids broke out from the Somme to Ypres further to confuse the enemy as to the real front of attack. Men rushed the trenches which they were to take and hold later, and by their brief visit learned whether or not the barbed wire had been properly cut to give the great charge a clear pathway and whether or not the German trenches were properly mashed. They brought in prisoners whose identification and questioning were invaluable to the intelligence branch, where the big map on the wall was filled in with the location of German divisions, thus building up the order of battle, so vital to all plans, with its revelation of the disposition and strength of the enemy's forces. It was known that the Germans were rapidly bringing up new batteries north of the Ancre while low visibility postponed the day of the attack.

The men that worked on the new roads keeping them in condition for the passage of the heavy transport, whether columns of motor trucks, or caissons, or the great tractors drawing guns, were no less a part of the scheme than the daring raiders. Every soldier who was going over the parapet in the attack must have his food and drink and bombs to throw and cartridges to fire after he had reached his objective.

Most telling of all the innumerably suggestive features to me were the streets of empty white tents at the casualty clearing stations, and the empty hospital cars on the railway sidings, and the new enclosures for prisoners—for these spoke the human note. These told that man was to be the target.

The staff might plan, gunners might direct their fire accurately against unseen targets by the magic of their calculations, generals might prepare their orders, the intricate web of telephone and telegraph wires might hum with directions, but the final test lay with him who, rifle and bomb ready in hand, was going to cross No Man's Land and take possession of the German trenches. A thousand pictures cloud the memory and make a whole intense in one's mind, which holds all proudly in admiration of human stoicism, discipline and spirit and sadly, too, with a conscious awe in the possession as of some treasure intrusted to him which he cheapens by his clumsy effort at expression.

Stage by stage the human part had moved forward. Khaki figures were swarming the village streets while the people watched them with a sort of worshipful admiration of their stalwart, trained bodies and a sympathetic appreciation of what was coming. These men with their fair complexion and strange tongue were to strike against the Germans. Two things the French had learned about the English: they were generous and they were just, though phlegmatic. Now they were to prove that with their methodical deliberation they were brave. Some would soon die in battle—and for France.

By day they loitered in the villages waiting on the coming of darkness, their training over—nothing to do now but wait. If they went forward it was by platoons or companies, lest they make a visible line on the chalky background of the road to the aviator's eye. A battalion drawn up in a field around a battalion commander, sitting his horse sturdily as he gave them final advice, struck home the military affection of loyalty of officer to man and man to officer. A soldier parting at a doorway from a French girl in whose eyes he had found favor during a brief residence in her village struck another chord. That elderly woman with her good-by to a youth was speaking as she would to her own son who was at the front and unconsciously in behalf of some English mother. Up near the trenches at dusk, in the last billet before the assembly for attack, company officers were recalling the essentials of instructions to a line standing at ease at one side of the street while caissons of shells had the right of way.

With the coming of night battalions of reserves formed and set forth on the march, going toward the flashes in the heavens which illumined the men in their steady tramp, the warmth of their bodies and their breaths pressing close to your ear as you turned aside to let them pass. "East Surreys," or "West Ridings," or "Manchesters" might come the answer to inquiries. All had the emblems of their units in squares of cloth on their shoulders, and on the backs of some of the divisions were bright yellow or white patches to distinguish them from Germans to the gunners in the shell-smoke.

Nothing in their action at first glance indicated the stress of their thoughts. Officers and men, their physical movements set by the mold of discipline, were in gesture, in voice, in manner the same as when they were on an English road in training. This was a part of the drill, a part of man's mastery of his emotions. None were under any illusions as soldiers of other days had been. Few nursed the old idea of being the lucky man who would escape. They knew the chances they were taking, the meaning of frontal attacks and of the murderous and wholesale quickness of machine gun methods.

Will, organized human will, was in their steps and shining out of their eyes. It occurred to me that they might have escaped this if England had kept out of the war at the price of something with which Englishmen refused to part. "The day" was coming, "the day" they had foreseen, "the day" for which their people waited.

When they were closing in with death, the clans which make up the British Empire kept faith with their character as do all men. These battalions sang the songs and whistled the tunes of drill grounds at home, though in low notes lest the enemy should hear, and lapsed into silence when they drew near the front and filed through the communication trenches.

Quiet the English, that great body of the army which sees itself as the skirt for the Celtic fringe, ploddingly undemonstrative with memories of the phlegm of their history holding emotions unexpressed; the Scotch in their kilts, deep-chested, with their trunk-like legs and broad hips, braw of face under their mushroom helmets, seemed like mediæval men of arms ready in spirit as well as looks for fierce hand-to-hand encounters; the Welsh, more emotional than the English, had songs which were pleasant to the ear if the words were unrecognizable; and the ruddy-faced Irish, with their soft voices, had a beam in their eyes of inward anticipation of the sort of thing to come which no Irishman ever meets in a hesitating mood. No overseas troops were there except the Newfoundland battalion; for only sons of the old country were to strike on July 1st.

Returning from a tour at night I had absorbed what seemed at one moment the unrealness and at another the stern, unyielding reality of the scenes. The old French territorial, with wrinkled face and an effort at a military mustache, who came out of his sentry box at a control post squinting by the light of a lantern held close to his nose at the bit of paper which gave the bearer freedom of the army and nodding with his polite word of concurrence, was a type who might have stopped a traveler in Louis XIV.'s time. All the farmers sleeping in the villages who would be up at dawn at their work, all the people in Amiens, knew that the hour was near. The fact was in the air no less than in men's minds. Nobody mentioned that the greatest struggle of the war was about to begin. We all knew that it was in hearts, souls, fiber.

There were moments when imagination gave to that army in its integrity of organization only one heart in one body. Again, it was a million hearts in a million bodies, deaf except to the voice of command. Most amazing was the absence of fuss whether with the French or the British. Everybody seemed to be doing what he was told to do and to know how to do it. With much to be left to improvisation after the attack began, nothing might be neglected in the course of preparation.

In other days where infantry on the march deployed and brought up suddenly against the enemy in open conflict the anticipatory suspense was not long and was forgotten in the brief space of conflict. Here this suspense really had been cumulative for months. It built itself up, little by little, as the material and preparations increased, as the battalions assembled, until sometimes, despite the roar of the artillery, there seemed a great silence while you waited for a string, drawn taut, to crack.

On the night of June 30th the word was passed behind a closed door in the hotel that seven-thirty the next morning was the hour and the spectators should be called at five—which seemed the final word in staff prevision.

V

THE BLOW

Plans at headquarters—A battle by inches—In the observation post—The débris of a ruined village—"Softening" by shell fire—A slice out of the front—The task of the infantryman—The dawn before the attack—Five minutes more—A wave of men twenty-five miles long—Mist and shell-smoke—Duty of the war-correspondent.

I was glad to have had glimpses of every aspect of the preparation from battalion headquarters in the front line trenches to General Headquarters, which had now been moved to a smaller town near the battlefield where the intelligence branch occupied part of a schoolhouse. In place of exercises in geography and lithographs of natural history objects, on the schoolroom walls hung charts of the German Order of Battle, as built up through many sources of information, which the British had to face. There was no British Order of Battle in sight. This, as the Germans knew it, you might find in a German intelligence office; but the British were not going to aid the Germans in ascertaining it by giving it any publicity.

By means of a map spread out on a table an officer explained the plan of attack with reference to broad colored lines which denoted the objectives. The whole was as explicit as if Bonaparte had said:

"We shall engage heavily on our left, pound the center with our artillery, and flank on our right."

The higher you go in the command the simpler seem the plans which by direct and comprehensive strokes conceal the detail which is delegated down through the different units. At Gommecourt there was a salient, an angle of the German trench line into the British which seemed to invite "pinching," and this was to be the pivot of the British movement. The French who were on both sides of the Somme were to swing in from their southern flank of attack near Soyecourt in the same fashion as the British from the northern, thus bringing the deepest objective along the river in the direction of Péronne, which would fall when eventually the tactical positions commanding it were gained.

Not with the first rush, for the lines of the objective were drawn well short of it, but with later rushes the British meant to gain the irregular ridge formation from Thiepval to Longueval, which would start them on the way to the consummation of their siege hammering. It was to be a battle by inches; the beginning of a long task. German *morale* was still high on the Western front; their numbers immense. *Morale* could be broken, numbers worn down, only by pounding.

Granted that the attack of July 1st should succeed all along the line, it would gain little ground; but it would everywhere break through the first line fortifications over a front of more than twenty-five miles, the British for about fifteen and the French for about ten. The soldierly informant at "Intelligence" reminded the listener, too, that battalions which might be squeezed or might run into unexpected obstacles would suffer fearfully as in all great battles and one must be careful not to be over-depressed by the accounts of the survivors or over-elated by the roseate narratives of battalions which had swept all before them with slight loss.

The day before I saw the map of the whole I had seen the map of a part at an Observation Post at Auchonvillers. The two were alike in a standardized system, only one dealt with corps and the other with battalions. A trip to Auchonvillers at any time during the previous year or up to the end of June, 1916, had not been fraught with any particular risk. It was on the "joy-riders'" route, as they say.

When I said that the German batteries were making relatively little reply to the preliminary British bombardment I did not mean to imply that they were missing any opportunities. At the dead line for automobiles on the road the burst of a shrapnel overhead had a suggestiveness that it would not have had at other times. Perhaps the Germans were about to put a barrage on the road. Perhaps they were going to start their guns in earnest. Happily, they have always been most considerate where I was concerned and they were only throwing in a few shells in the course of artillery routine, which happened also on our return from the Observation Post. But they were steadily attentive with "krumps" to a grove where some British howitzers sought the screen of summer foliage. If they could put any batteries out of action while they waited for the attack this was good business, as it meant fewer guns at work in support of the British charge.

An artilleryman, perspiring and mud-spattered from shell-bursts, who came across the fields, said: "They knocked off the corner of our gun-pit and got two men. That's all." His eyes were shining; he was in the elation of battle. Casualties were an incident in the preoccupation of his work and of the thought: "At last we have the shells! At last it is our turn!"

On our way forward we passed more batteries and wisely kept to the open away from them, as they are dangerous companions in an artillery duel. Then we stepped into the winding communication trench with its system of wires fast to the walls, and kept on till we passed under a lifted curtain into a familiar chamber roofed with heavy cement blocks and earth.

"Safe from a direct hit by five-point-nines," said the observation officer, a regular promoted from the ranks who had been "spotting" shells since the war began. "A nine-inch would break the blocks, but I don't think that it would do us in."

Even if it did "do us in," why, we were only two or three men. All this protection was less perhaps to insure safety than to insure security of observation for these eyes of the guns. The officer was as proud of his O.P. as any battalion commander of his trench or a battery commander of his gun-position, which is the same kind of human pride that a man has in the improvements on his new country estate.

There was a bench to sit on facing the narrow observation slit, similar to that of a battleship's conning tower, which gave a wide sweep of vision. A commonplace enough *mise-en-scène* on average days, now significant because of the stretch of dead world of the trench systems and No Man's Land which was soon to be seething with the tumult of death.

Directly in front of us was Beaumont-Hamel. Before the war it had been like hundreds of other villages. Since the war its ruins were like scores of others in the front line. Parts of a few walls were standing. It was difficult to tell where the débris of Beaumont-Hamel began and that of the German trench ended. Dust was mixed with the black bursts of smoke rising from the conglomerate mass of buildings and streets thrown together by previous explosions. The effect suggested the regular spout of geysers from a desert rock crushed by charges of dynamite.

Could anybody be alive in Beaumont-Hamel? Wasn't this bombardment threshing straw which had long since yielded its last kernel of grain? Wasn't it merely pounding the graves of a garrison? Other villages, equally passive and derelict, were being submitted to the same systematic pounding, which was like timed hammer-beats.

"We keep on softening them," said the observer.

Soldiers have a gift for apt words to describe their work, as have all professional experts. Softening! It personified the enemy as something hard and tough which would grow pulpy under enough well-mapped blows striking at every vital part from dugouts to billets.

All the barbed-wire entanglements in front of the first-line trenches appeared to be cut, mangled, twisted into balls, beaten back into the earth and exhumed again, leaving only a welt of crater-spotted ground in front of the chalky contour of the first-line trenches which had been mashed and crushed out of shape.

"Yes, the Boche's first line looks rather messy," said the officer. "We've been giving him an awful doing these last few days. Turning our attention mostly to the second line, now. That's our lot, there," he added, indicating a cluster of bursts over a nest of burrows farther up on the hillside.

"Any attempts to repair their wire at night?" I asked.

"No. They have to do it under our machine gun fire. Any Boches who have survived are lying doggo."

How many dugouts were still intact and secure refuges for the waiting Germans? Only trench raids could ascertain. As well might the observer with his glasses or an aeroplane looking down try to take a census of the number of inhabitants of a prairie dog village who were all in their holes.

The officer spread out his map marked "Secret and confidential," delimiting the boundaries of a narrow sector. He had nothing to do with what lay to the right and left—other sectors, other men's business—of the area inclosed in the clear, heavy lines crosswise of British and German trenches—a slice out of the front, as it were. Speaking over the telephone to the blind guns, he was interested only in the control of gunfire in this sector. The charge to him was lines on the map parallel with the trenches which would be at given points at given moments—lines which he must support when their soldier counterparts were invisible through the shell-smoke in the nice calculation of time and range which should put the shells into the enemy and never into the charging man.

To infantry commanders with similar maps those lines were breathing human lines of men whom they had trained, and the gunfire a kind of spray which the gunners were to adjust for the protection of the battalions when they should cross that dead space. Once the British were in the German front trenches, details which had been told off for the purpose were to take possession of the dugouts and "breach" them of prisoners and disarm all other Germans, lest they fire into the backs of those who carried the charge farther on to the final stage of the objective. What awaited them they would know only when they climbed over the parapet and became silhouettes of vulnerable flesh in the open. Yes, one had the system in the large and the small, by the army, the corps, the division, the brigade, the battalion, and the man, the individual infantryman who was to suffer that hazard of marching in the open toward the trenches which not guns, or motor trucks, or trench-mortar shells could take, but only he could take and hold.

The advantage of watching the attack from this O.P. in comparison with that of other points was mooted; for the spectator had to choose his seat for the panorama. This time we sought a place where we hoped to see something of the battle as a whole.

"*C'est arrivé!*" said the old porter to me at the door when I left the hotel before dawn. The great day had arrived!

Amiens was in darkness, with the lightnings of the guns which had never ceased their labors through the night flashing in the heavens their magnetic summons to battle. When a dip into a valley shut out their roar a divine hush lay over the world. On either side of the main road was the peace of the hour before the dawn which would send the peasants from their beds to the fields. There were no lights yet in the villages. It had not occurred to the inhabitants to try to see the battle. They knew that they would be in the way; sentries or gunners would halt them.

The traffic was light and all vehicles, except a flying staff officer's car, were going their methodical way. Vaguely, as an aviation station was passed, planes were visible being pushed out of their sheds; the hum of propellers being tried out was faintly heard. The birds of battle were testing their wings before flight and every one out of the hundreds which would take part that day had his task set, no less than had a corps, a regiment of artillery, or the bombers in a charge.

"This is the place," was the word to the chauffeur as we swept up a grade in the misty darkness.

Stretched from trunk to trunk of the trees beside the road were canvas screens to hide the transport from enemy observation. Passing between them had the effect of going through the curtains into a parterre box. Light was just breaking and we were in a field of young beets on the crest of a rise, with no higher ground beyond us all the way to Thiepval, which was in the day's objective, and to Pozières, which was beyond it. Ordinarily, on a clear day we should have had from here a view over five or six miles of front and through our glasses the action should have been visible in detail.

This morning the sun was not showing his head and the early mist lay opaque over all the positions, holding in place the mighty volume of smoke from bursting shells. As it was not seven o'clock the sun might yet realize its duty in July and dissipate this shroud, which was so thick that it partially obscured the flashes of the guns and the shell-bursts.

Seven-ten came and seven-twenty and still no more light. It was too late now to seek another hill and, if we had sought one, we should have had no better view. At least, we were seeing as much as the Commander of the Fourth Army in his dugout near by. The artillery fire increased. Every gun was now firing, all stretching their powers to the maximum. The mist and smoke over the positions seemed to tremble with the blasts. Near-by shells, especially German, broke brilliantly against a background so thick that it swallowed up the flashes of more distant shells in its garishly illumined density. Thousands of officers were studying their wrist watches for the tick of "zero" as the minute-hands moved on with merciless fatalism; and hundreds of thousands of men who had come into position overnight were in line in the trenches looking to their officers for the word.

Our little group in the beet field was restless and silent; or if we spoke it was not of what was oppressing our minds and stilling our heartbeats. Our glasses gave no aid; they only made the fog thicker. Had we been in the first-line British trenches we could hardly have seen the men who left them through this wall of smoke and mist as they entered the German first line and the answering German "krumps" would have driven us to the dugouts and German curtains of fire held us prisoner.

One of us called attention to a lark that had risen and was singing with all the power in his little throat. Another mentioned a squadron of aeroplanes against the background of a soft and domeless sky, flying with the precision of wild geese. We knew that the German guns were responding now, for the final blasts of British concentration had been a sufficient signal of attack if some British prisoner taken in a trench raid had not revealed the hour.

Seven-twenty-five! someone said, but not one of us needed any reminder. Five minutes more and the great experiment would begin. Had Sir Douglas Haig made an army equal to the task? What would be the answer to skeptics who said that the London cockneys and the Manchester factory hands and all the others without military training could not be made into a force skilful enough to take those trenches? Was the feat of conquering those fortifications within the bounds of human courage, skill and resource?

Not what one saw but what one felt and knew counted. A crowd is spellbound in watching a steeplejack at work, or an aviator doing a "loop-the-loop," or an acrobat swinging from one bar to another above the sawdust ring, or the "leap of death" of the movies; and here we were in the presence of a multitude who were running a far greater risk in an untried effort, with their inspiration not a breathless audience but duty. For none wanted to die. All were human in this. None had any sense of the glorious sport of war, only that of grim routine.

Our group was not particularly religious, but I think that we were all uttering a prayer for England and France. At seven-thirty something seemed to crack in our brains. There was no visible sign that a wave of men twenty-five miles long, reaching from Gommecourt to Soyecourt, wherever the trenches ran across fields, through villages and along slopes to the banks of the Somme and beyond, had left their parapets. I knew the men who were going into that charge too well to have any apprehension that any battalion would falter. The thing was to be done and they were to do it. Now they were out in No Man's Land; now they were facing the reception prepared for them. Thousands might already be down. We could discern that the German guns, long waiting for their prey, were seeking it in eager ferocity as they laid their curtains of fire on the appointed places which they had registered. The hell of the poets and the priests must have some emotion, some temperamental variation. This was sheer mechanical hell, its pulse that of the dynamo and the engine.

Seven-forty-five! Helplessly we stared at the blanket. If the charge had gone home it was already in the German trenches. For all we knew it might have been repulsed and its remnants be struggling back through the curtains of artillery fire and the sweep of machine gun fire. As the sun came out without clearing away the mist and shell-smoke over the field we had glimpses of some reserves who had looked like a yellow patch behind a hill deploying to go forward, suggestive of yellow-backed beetles who were the organized servitors of a higher mind on some other planet.

This was all we saw; and to make more of it would not be fair to other occasions when views of attacks were more intimate. Yet I would not change the impression now. It has its place in the spectator's history of the battle.

VI

FIRST RESULTS OF THE SOMME

At the little schoolhouse—Twenty miles of German fortifications taken—Doubtful situation north of Thiepval—Prisoners and wounded—Defeat and victory—The topography of Thiepval—Sprays of bullets and blasts of artillery fire—"The day" of the New Army—The courage of civilized man—Fighting with a kind of divine stubbornness—Braver than the "Light Brigade"—Died fighting as final proof of the New Army's spirit—Crawling back through No Man's Land—Not beaten but roughly handled.

In the room at the head of the narrow stairs in the schoolhouse of the quiet headquarters town we should have the answer to the question, Has the British attack succeeded? which was throbbing in our pulsebeats. By the same map on the table in the center of the room showing the plan of attack with its lines indicating the objectives we should learn how many of them had been gained. The officer who had outlined the plan of battle with fine candor was equally candid about its results, so far as they were known. Not only did he avoid mincing words, but he avoided wasting them.

From Thiepval northward the situation was obscure. The German artillery response had been heavy and the action almost completely blanketed from observation. Some detachments must have reached their objective, as their signals had been seen. From La Boisselle southward the British had taken every objective. They were in Mametz and Montauban and around Fricourt. For the French it had been a clean sweep, without a single repulse. Twenty miles of those formidable German fortifications were in the possession of the Allies.

On the ledge of the schoolroom window, with the shrill voices of the children at recess playing in the yard below rising to my ears, I wrote my dispatch for the press at home, less conscious then than now of the wonder of the situation. Downstairs the curé of the church next door was standing on the steps, an expectant look in his eyes. When I told him the news his smile and the flash of his eye, which lacked the meekness usually associated with the Church, were good to see.

"And the French?" he asked.

"All of their objectives!"

"Ah!" He drew a deep breath and rubbed his hands together softly. "And prisoners?"

"A great many."

"Ah! And guns?"

"Yes."

Thus he ran up the scale of happiness. I left him on the steps of the church with a proud, glad, abstracted look.

Beyond the town peaceful fields stretched away to the battle area, where figures packed together inside the new prisoners' inclosures made a green blot. Litters were thick in the streets of the casualty clearing stations which had been empty yesterday. There were no idle ambulances now. They had passengers in green as well as in khaki. The first hospital trains were pulling out from the rail-head across from a clearing station. Thus promptly, as foreseen, the processes of battle had worked themselves out.

From "light" cases and from "bad" cases, from officers and men, you had the account of an individual's supreme experience, infinitesimal compared to the whole but when taken together making up the whole. The wounded in the Thiepval-Gommecourt sector spoke of having "crawled" back across No Man's Land. South of Thiepval they had "walked" back. This, too, told the story of the difference between repulse and victory.

As the fight went for each man in the fray, so the battle went to his conception. The spectator going here and there could hear accounts at one headquarters of battalions that were beyond the first-line trenches and at another of battalions whose survivors were back in their own trenches. He could hear one wounded man say: "It was too stiff, sir. There was no getting through their curtains of fire against their machine guns, sir;" and another: "We went into their first line without a break and right on, gathering in Boches on the way."

Victory is sweet. It writes itself. Perhaps because failure is harder to write, though in this case it is equally glorious, we shall have this first. To make the picture of that day clearer, imagine a movement of the whole arm, with the shoulder at Gommecourt and the fist swinging in at Montauban, crushing its way against those fortifications. It broke through for a distance of more than from the elbow to the fingers' ends twenty miles southward from Thiepval— a name to bear in mind. Men crossing the open under protecting waves of shell fire had proved that men in dugouts with machine guns were not invincible.

From a certain artillery observation post in a tree you had a good view of Thiepval, already a blackened spot with the ruins of the chateau showing white in its midst and pricked by the toothpick-like trunks of trees denuded of their limbs, which were to become such a familiar sight on the battlefield. It was uphill all the way to Thiepval for the British. A river so-called, really a brook, the Ancre, runs at the foot of the slope and turns eastward beyond Thiepval, where a ridge called Crucifix Ridge north-east of the village takes its name from a Christ with outstretched arms visible for many miles around. Then on past the bend of the Ancre the British and the German positions continued to the Gommecourt salient.

Along these five miles the odds of terrain were all against the British. The high ground which they sought to gain was of supreme tactical value. Nature was an ally of soldierly industry in constructing defenses. The German staff expected the brunt of the offensive in this sector and every hour's delay in the attack was invaluable for their final preparations. Thiepval, Beaumont-Hamel and Gommecourt would not be yielded if there were any power of men or material at German command to keep them. Indeed, the Germans said that Thiepval was impregnable. Their boast was good on July 1st but not in the end, as we shall see, for, before the summer was over, Thiepval was to be taken with less loss to the British than to the defenders.

At Beaumont-Hamel and Thiepval, particularly, and in all villages house cellars had been enlarged and connected by new galleries, the débris from the buildings forming a thicker roof against penetration by shells. Where there had seemed no life in Beaumont-Hamel battalions were snug in their refuges as the earth around trembled from the explosions. Those shell-threshed parapets of the first-line German trenches which appeared to represent complete destruction had not filled in all the doorways of dugouts which big shells had failed to reach. The cut and twisted fragments of barbed wire which were the remains of the maze of entanglements fringing the parapets no longer protected them from a charge; but the garrisons depended upon another kind of defense which sent its deadly storms against the advancing infantry.

The British battalions that went over the parapet from Thiepval northward were of the same mettle as those that took Montauban and Mametz; their training and preparation the same. Where battalions to the southward swept forward according to plan and the guns' pioneering was successful, those on this front in many cases started from trenches already battered in by German shell fire. A few steps across that dead space and officers knew that the supporting artillery, working no less thoroughly in its preliminary bombardment here than elsewhere, had not the situation in hand.

All the guns which the Germans had brought up during the time that weather delayed the British attack added their weight to the artillery concentration. Down the valley of the Ancre at its bend they had more or less of an enfilade. Machine guns had survived in their positions in the débris of the trenches or had been mounted overnight and others appeared from manholes in front of the trenches. Sprays of bullets cut crosswise of the blasts of the German curtains of artillery fire. How any men could go the breadth of No Man's Land and survive would have been called miraculous in other days; in these days we know that it was due to the law of chance which will wound one man a dozen times and never bark the skin of another.

Any troops might have been warranted in giving up the task before they reached the first German trench. Veterans could have retired without criticism. This is the privilege of tried soldiers who have won victories and are secured by such an expression as, "If the Old Guard saw that it could not be done, why, then, it could not." But these were New Army men in their first offensive. Their victories were yet to be won. This was "the day."

Each officer and each man had given himself up as a hostage to death for his cause, his pride of battalion and his manhood when he went over the parapet. The business of the officers was to lead their men to certain goals; that of the men was to go with the officers. All very simple reasoning, this, yet hardly reason: the second nature of training and spirit. How officers had studied the details of their objectives on the map in order to recognize them when they were reached! How like drill it was the way that those human waves moved forward! But they were not waves for long in some instances, only survivors still advancing as if they were parts of a wave, unseen by their commanders in the shell-smoke, buffeted by bursts of high explosives, with every man simply keeping on toward the goal till he arrived or fell. Foolhardy, you say. Perhaps. It is an easy word to utter over a map after the event. You would think of finer words if you had been at the front.

Would England have wanted her New Army to act otherwise?—the first great army that she had put into the field on trial on the continent of Europe against an army which had, by virtue of its own experience, the right to consider the newcomers as amateurs? They became more skilful later; but in war all skill is based on such courage as these men showed that day. Those who sit in offices in times of peace and think otherwise had better be relieved. It is the precept that the German Army itself taught and practiced at Ypres and Verdun. On July 1st a question was answered for anyone who had been in the Manchurian war. He learned that those bred in sight of cathedrals in the civilization of the epic poem can surpass without any inspiration of oriental fatalism or religious fanaticism the courage of the land of Shintoism and Bushido.

In most places the charge reached the German trenches. There, frequently outnumbered by the garrison, the men stabbed and bombed, fought to put out machine guns that were turned on them and so stay the tide coming out of the mouths of dugouts—simply fought and kept on fighting with a kind of divine stubbornness.

Tennyson's "Light Brigade" seems bombast and gallery play after July 1st. In that case some men on horses who had received an order rode out and rode back, and verse made ever memorable this wild gallop of exhilaration with horses bearing the men. The battalions of July 1st went on their own feet driven by their own will toward their goals, without turning back. Surviving officers with objectives burned in their brains led the surviving men past the first-line trenches if the directions required this. "Theirs not to reason why— theirs but to do and die—cannon to right of them volleyed and thundered,"—old-fashioned, smoke-powder cannon firing round shot for the Light Brigade; for these later-day battalions every kind of modern shell and machine guns, showers of death and sheets of death!

The goal—the goal! Ten men out of a hundred reached it in a few cases and when they arrived they sent up rocket signals to say that they were there! there! there! Two or three battalions literally disappeared into the blue. I thought that the Germans might have taken a considerable number of prisoners, but not so. Those isolated lots who went on to their objectives regardless of every other thought died fighting, as final proof of the New Army's spirit, against the Germans enraged by their heavy losses from the preliminary British bombardment.

It was where gaps existed and gallantry went blindly forward, unable in the fog of shell-smoke to see whether the units on the right or the left were up, that these sacrifices of heroism were made; but where command was held over the line and the opposition was not of a variable kind counsel was taken of the impossible and retreat was ordered. That is, the units turned back toward their own trenches under direction. They had to pass through the same curtain of shell fire in returning as in charging, and ahead of them through the blasts they drove their prisoners.

"Never mind. It's from your own side!" said one Briton to a German who had been knocked over by a German "krump" when he picked himself up; and the German answered that this did not make him like it any better.

Scattered with British wounded taking cover in new and old shell-craters was No Man's Land as the living passed. A Briton and his prisoner would take cover together. An explosion and the prisoner might be blown to bits, or if the captor were, another Briton took charge of the prisoner. Persistently stubborn were the captors in holding on to prisoners who were trophies out of that inferno, and when a Briton was back in the first-line trench with his German his delight was greater in delivering his man alive than in his own safety. Out in No Man's Land the wounded hugged their shell-craters until the fire slackened or night fell, when they crawled back.

Where early in the morning it had appeared as if the attack were succeeding reserve battalions were sent in to the support of those in front, and as unhesitatingly and steadily as at drill they entered the blanket of shell-smoke with its vivid flashes and hissing of shrapnel bullets and shell-fragments. Commanders, I found, stood in awe of the steadfast courage of their troops.

Whether officers or men, those who came out of hell were still true to their heritage of English phlegm.

Covered with chalk dust from crawling, their bandages blood-soaked, bespattered with the blood of comrades as they lay on litters or hobbled down a communication trench, they looked blank when they mentioned the scenes that they had witnessed; but they gave no impression of despair. It did not occur to them that they had been beaten; they had been roughly handled in one round of a many-round fight. Had a German counter-attack developed they would have settled down, rifle in hand, to stall through the next round. And that young officer barely twenty, smiling though weak from loss of blood from two wounds, refusing assistance as he pulled himself along among the "walking wounded," showed a bravery in his stoicism equal to any on the field when he said, "It did not go well this time," in a way that indicated that, of course, it would in the end.

It was over one of those large scale, raised maps showing in facsimile all the elevations that a certain corps commander told the story of the whole attack with a simplicity and frankness which was a victory of character even if he had not won a victory in battle. He rehearsed the details of preparation, which were the same in their elaborate care as those of corps which had succeeded; and he did not say that luck had been against him—indeed, he never once used the word—but merely that the German fortifications had been too strong and the gunfire too heavy. He bore himself in the same manner that he would in his house in England; but his eyes told of suffering and when he spoke of his men his voice quavered.

Where the young officer had said that it had not gone well this time and a private had said, "We must try again, sir!" the general had said that repulse was an incident of a prolonged operation in the initial stage, which sounded more professional but was no more illuminating. All spoke of lessons learned for the future. Thus they had stood the supreme test which repulse alone can give.

What could an observer say or do that was not banal in the eyes of men who had been through such experiences? Only listen and look on with the awe of one who feels that he is in the presence of immortal heroism. And an hour's motor ride away were troops in the glow of that success which is without comparison in its physical elation—the success of arms.

VII

OUT OF THE HOPPER OF BATTLE

An army of movement—Taking over the captured space—At Minden Post, a crossroads of battle—German prisoners—Their desire to live—Their variety—The ambulance line—The refuse from the hopper of battle—Resting in the battle line—Reminiscences of the fighters—A mighty crater—The dugouts around Fricourt—Method of taking a dugout—The litter over the field.

When I went southward through that world of triumph back of Mametz and Montauban I kept thinking of a strong man who had broken free of his bonds and was taking a deep breath before another effort. Where from Thiepval to Gommecourt the men who had expected to be organizing new trenches were back in their old ones and the gunners who had hoped to move their guns forward were in the same positions and all the plans for supplying an army in advance were still on paper, to the southward anticipation had become realization and the system devised to carry on after success was being applied.

A mighty, eager industry pervaded the rear. Here, at last, was an army of movement. New roads must be made in order that the transport could move farther forward; medical corps men were establishing more advanced clearing stations; new ammunition dumps were being located; military police were adapting traffic regulations to the new situation. Old trenches had been filled up to give trucks and guns passageway. In every face was the shining desire which overcomes fatigue. An army long trench-tied was stretching its limbs as it found itself in the open. At corps headquarters lines were drawn on the maps of positions gained and beyond them the lines of new objectives.

Could it be possible that our car was running along that road back of the first-line trenches where it would have been death to show your head two days ago? And could battalions in reserve be lying in the open on fields where forty-eight hours previously a company would have drawn the fire of half a dozen German batteries? Was it dream or reality that you were walking about in the first-line German trenches? So long had you been used to stationary warfare, with your side and the other side always in the same places hedged in by walls of shell fire, that the transformation seemed as amazing as if by some magic overnight lower Broadway with all its high buildings had been moved across the North River.

Among certain scenes which memory still holds dissociated from others by their outstanding characterization, that of Minden Post remains vivid as illustrating the crossroads man-traffic of battle. A series of big dugouts, of houses and caves with walls of sandbags, back of the first British line near Carnoy was a focus of communication trenches and the magnet to the men hastening from bullet-swept, shell-swept spaces to security. The hot breath of the firing-line had scorched them and cast them out and they came together in congestion at this clearing station like a crowd at a gate. Eyes were bloodshot and set in deep hollows from fatigue, those of the British having the gleam of triumph and those of the Germans a dazed inquiry as they awaited directions.

Only a half-hour before, perhaps, the Germans had been fighting with the ferocity of racial hate and the method of iron discipline. Now they were simply helpless, disheveled human beings, their short boots and green uniforms whitened by chalk dust. Hunger had weakened the stamina of many of them in the days when the preliminary British bombardment had shut them off from supplies; but none looked as if he were really underfed. I never saw a German prisoner who was except for the intervals when battle kept the food waiting at the rear away from his mouth, though some who were under-sized and ill-proportioned looked incapable of absorbing nutrition.

In order to make them fight better they had been told that the British gave no quarter. Out of hell, with shells no longer bursting overhead or bullets whimpering and hissing past, they were conscious only that they were alive, and being alive, though they had risked life as if death were an incident, now freed of discipline and of the exhilaration of battle, their desire to live was very human in the way that hands shot up if a sharp word were spoken to them by an officer. They were wholly lacking in military dignity as they filed by; but it returned as by a magic touch when a non-commissioned officer was bidden to take charge of a batch and march them to an inclosure. Then, in answer to the command shoulders squared, heels rapped together, and the instinct of long training put a ramrod to their backbones which stiffened mere tired human beings into soldiers. Distinct gratitude was evident when their papers were taken for examination over the return of their identification books, which left them still docketed and numbered members of "system" and not mere lost souls as they would otherwise have considered themselves.

"All kinds of Boches in our exhibit!" said a British soldier.

As there were, in truth: big, hulking, awkward fellows, beardless youths, men of forty with stoops formed in civil life, professional men with spectacles fastened to their ears by cords and fat men with the cranial formation and physiognomy in keeping with French comic pictures of the "type Boche."

Mixed with the British wounded they came, tall and short, thin and portly, the whole a motley procession of friend and foe in a strange companionship which was singularly without rancor. I saw only one incident of any harshness of captor to prisoner. A big German ran against the wounded arm of a

Briton, who winced with pain and turned and gave the German a punch in very human fashion with his free arm. Another German with his slit trousers' leg flapping around a bandage was leaning on the arm of a Briton whose other arm was in a sling. A giant Prussian bore a spectacled comrade pickaback. Germans impressed as litter-bearers brought in still forms in khaki. Water and tobacco, these are the bounties which no man refuses to another at such a time as this. The gurgle of a canteen at a parched mouth on that warm July day was the first gift to wounded Briton or German and the next a cigarette.

Every returning Briton was wounded, of course, but many of the Germans were unwounded. Long rows of litters awaited the busy doctors' visit for further examination. First dressings put on by the man himself or by a comrade in the firing-line were removed and fresh dressings substituted. Ambulance after ambulance ran up, the litters of those who were "next" were slipped in behind the green curtains, and on soft springs over spinning rubber tires the burdens were sped on their way to England.

Officers were bringing order out of the tide which flowed in across the fields and the communication trenches as if they were used to such situations, with the firing-line only two thousand yards away. The seriously wounded were separated from the lightly wounded, who must not expect to ride but must go farther on foot. The shell-mauled German borne pickaback by a comrade found himself in an ambulance across from a Briton and his bearer was to know sleep after a square meal in the prisoners' inclosure.

And all this was the refuse from the hopper of battle, which has no service for prisoners unless to carry litters and no use at all for wounded; and it was only a by-product of the proof of success compared to a trip over the field itself—a field still fresh.

Artillery caissons and ambulances and signal wire carts and other specially favored transport—favored by risk of being in range of hundreds of guns— now ran along the road in the former No Man's Land which for nearly two years had had no life except the patrols at night. The bodies of those who fell on such nocturnal scouting expeditions could not be recovered and their bones lay there in the midst of rotting green and khaki in the company of the fresh dead of the charge who were yet to be buried.

There was the battalion which took the trenches resting yonder on a hillside, while another battalion took its place in the firing-line. The men had stripped off their coats; they were washing and making tea and sprawling in the sunshine, these victors, looking across at curtains of fire where the battle was raging. Thus reserves might have waited at Gettysburg or at Waterloo.

"They may put some shells into you," I suggested to their colonel.

"Perhaps," he said. The prospect did not seem to disturb him or the men. It was a possibility hazy to minds which asked only sleep or relaxation after two sleepless nights under fire. "The Germans haven't any aeroplanes up to enable them to see us and no sausage balloons, either. Since our planes brought down those six in flames the day before the attack the others have been very coy."

His young officers were all New Army products; he, the commander, being the only regular. There were still enough regulars left to provide one for each of the New Army battalions, in some cases even two.

"The men were splendid," he said, "just as good as regulars. They went in without any faltering and we had a stiffish bit of trench in front of us, you know. It's jolly out here, isn't it?"

He was tired and perhaps he would be killed to-morrow, but nothing could prevent him from going some distance to show us the way to the trenches that his men had taken. They were heroes to him and he was one to them; and they had won. That was the thing, victory, though they regarded it as a matter of course, which gave them a glow warmer than the sunlight as they lay at ease on the grass. They had "been in;" they had seen the day for which they had long waited. A quality of mastery was in their bearing, but their elation was tempered by the thought of the missing comrades, the dead.

"I wish as long as Bill had to go that he hadn't fallen before we got to the trench," said one soldier. "He had set his heart on seeing what a Boche dugout was like."

"George was beside me when a Boche got him with a bomb. I did for the Boche with a bayonet," said another.

"When the machine gun began I thought that it would get us all, but we had to go on."

They were matter-of-fact, dwelling on the simple essentials. Men had died; men had been wounded; men had survived. This was all according to expectation. Mostly, they did not rehearse their experiences. Their brains had had emotion enough; their bodies asked for rest. They lay silently enjoying the fact of life and sunlight. Details which were lost in the haze of action would develop in the memory in later years like the fine points of a photographic plate.

The former German trench on a commanding knoll had little resemblance to a trench. Here artillerists had fulfilled infantry requirements to the letter. Areas of shell-craters lay on either side of the tumbled walls and dugout entrances were nearly all closed. The infantry which took the position met no fire in front, but had an enfilade at one point from a machine gun. Where the dead lay told exactly the breadth of its sweep through which the charge had unfalteringly passed; and this was only a first objective. As you could see, the charge had gone on to its second with slight loss. A young officer after being wounded had crawled into a shell-crater, drawn his rubber sheet over him and so had died peacefully, the clot of his life's blood on the earth beside him.

In the field of ruins around Fricourt a mighty crater of one of the mines exploded on July 1st at the hour of attack was large enough to hold a battalion. Germans had gone aloft in a spatter with its vast plume of smoke and dust scooped from the bowels of the earth. Famous since to sightseers of war were the dugouts around Fricourt which were the last word in German provision against attack. The making of dugouts is standardized like everything else in this war. There is the same angle of entrance, the same flight of steps to that underground refuge, in keeping with the established pattern. Depth, capacity and comfort are the result of local initiative and industry. There may be beds and tables and tiers of bunks. Many such chambers were as undisturbed as if never a shell had burst in the neighborhood. The Germans in occupation had been told to hold on; a counter-attack would relieve them. The faith of some of them endured so well that they had to be blasted out by explosives before they would surrender.

There was reassurance in the proximity of such good dugouts when habitable to a correspondent if shells began to fall, as well as protection for the British in reserve. Some whence came foul odors were closed by the British as the simplest form of burial for the dead within who had waited for bombs to be thrown before surrendering. For the method of taking a dugout had long since become as standardized as its construction. The men inside could have their choice from the Briton at the entrance.

"Either file out or take what we send," as a soldier put it. "We can't leave you there to come out and fire into our backs, as the Kaiser told you to do, when we've started on ahead."

You could follow for miles the ruins of the first line, picking your way among German dead in all attitudes, while a hand or a head or a foot stuck out of the shell-hammered chalk mixed with flesh and fragments of clothing, the thing growing nauseatingly horrible and your wonder increasing as to how gunfire had accomplished the destruction and how men had been able to conquer the remains that the shells had left. It was a prodigious feat, emphasizing again the importance of the months of preparation.

And the litter over the whole field! This, in turn, expressed how varied and immense is the material required for such operations. One had in mind the cleaning up after some ghastly debauch. Shell-fragments were mixed with the earth; piles of cartridge cases lay beside pools of blood. Trench mortars poked their half-filled muzzles out of the toppled trench walls. Bundles of rocket flares, empty ammunition boxes, steel helmets crushed in by shell-fragments, gasbags, eye-protectors against lachrymatory shells, spades, water bottles, unused rifle grenades, egg bombs, long stick-handled German bombs, map cases, bits of German "K.K." bread, rifles, the steel jackets of shells and unexploded shells of all calibers were scattered about the field between the irregular welts of chalky soil where shell fire had threshed them to bits.

The rifles and accoutrements of the fallen were being gathered in piles, this being, too, a part of a prearranged system, as was the gathering of the wounded and later of the dead who had worn them. Big, barelegged forms of the sturdy Highland regiment which would not halt for a machine gun were being brought in and laid in a German communication trench which had only to be closed to make a common grave, each identification disk being kept as a record of where the body lay. Another communication trench near by was reserved for German dead who were being gathered at the same time as the British. In life the foes had faced each other across No Man's Land. In death they were also separated.

Up to the first-line German trenches, of course, there were only British dead, those who had fallen in the charge. It was this that made it seem as if the losses had been all on one side. In the German trenches the entries on the other side of the ledger appeared; and on the fields and in the communication trenches lay green figures. Over that open space they were scattered green dots; again, where they had run for cover to a wood's edge, they lay thick as they had dropped under the fire of a machine gun which the British had brought into action. A fierce game of hare and hounds had been played. Both German and British dead lay facing in the same direction when they were in the open, the Germans in retreat, the British in pursuit. An officer called attention to this grim proof that the initiative was with the British.

By the number of British dead lying in No Man's Land or by the blood clots when the bodies had been removed, it was possible to tell what price battalions had paid for success. Nothing could bring back the lives of comrades who had fallen in front of Thiepval to the survivors of that action; but could they have seen the broad belts of No Man's Land with only an occasional prostrate figure it would have had the reassurance that another time they might have easier going. Wherever the Germans had brought a machine gun into action the results of its work lay a stark warning of the necessity of silencing these automatic killers before a charge. Yet from Mametz to Montauban the losses had been light, leaving no doubt that the Germans, convinced that the weight of the attack would be to the north, had been caught napping.

The Allies could not conceal the fact and general location of their offensive, but they did conceal its plan as a whole. The small number of shell-craters attested that no such artillery curtains of fire had been concentrated here as from Thiepval to Gommecourt. Probably the Germans had not the artillery to spare or had drawn it off to the north.

All branches of the winning army making themselves at home in the conquered area among the dead and the litter behind the old German first line—this was the fringe of the action. Beyond was the battle itself, with the firing-line still advancing under curtains of shell-bursts.

VIII

FORWARD THE GUNS!

An audacious battery—"An unusual occasion"—Guns to the front at night—Close to the firing-line—Not so dangerous for observers—The German lines near by—Advantages of even a gentle slope—Skilfully chosen German positions—A game of hide and seek with death—Business-like progress—Haze, shell-smoke and moving figures—Each figure part of the "system."

Hadn't that battery commander mistaken his directions when he emplaced his howitzers behind a bluff in the old No Man's Land? Didn't he know that the German infantry was only the other side of the knoll and that two or three score German batteries were in range? I looked for a tornado to descend forthwith upon the gunners' heads. I liked their audacity, but did not court their company when I could not break a habit of mind bred in the rules of trench-tied warfare where the other fellow was on the lookout for just such fair targets as they.

For the moment these "hows" were not firing and the gunners were in a little circumscribed world of their own, dissociated from the movement around them as they busily dug pits for their ammunition. In due course someone might tell them to begin registering on a certain point or to turn loose on one which they had already registered. Meanwhile, very workmanlike in their shirt-sleeves, they had no concern with the traffic in the rear, except as it related to their own supply of shells, or with the litter of the field, or the dead, or the burial parties and the scattered wounded passing back from the firing-line. Their business relations were exclusively with the battle area hidden by the bluff. I thought that they were "rather fond of themselves" (as the British say) that morning, though not so much so, perhaps, as the crew of the eighteen pounders still farther forward within about a thousand yards of the Germans whom they were pelting with shrapnel.

Ordinarily, the eighteen pounders were expected to keep a distance of four or five thousand yards; but this was "rather an unusual occasion" as an officer explained. It would never do for the eighteen pounders to be wall-flowers; they must be on the ballroom floor. Had these men who were mechanically slipping shells into the gun-breeches slept last night or the previous night? Oh, yes, for two or three hours when they were not firing.

What did fatigue matter to an eighteen-pounder spirit released from the eternal grind of trench warfare and pushing across the open in the way that eighteen pounders were meant to do? Weren't they horse artillery? What use had they had for their horses in the immovable Ypres salient except when they drew back their guns to the billets after their tour of duty?—they who had drilled and drilled in evolutions in England under the impression that field guns were a mobile arm!

When orders came on the afternoon of July 1st to go ahead "right into it" it was like a summons to a holiday for a desk-ridden man brought up in the Rockies. Out into the night with creaking wheels and caissons following with sharp words of urging from the sergeant, "Now, wheelers, as I taught you at Aldershot," as they went across old trenches or up a stiff slope and into the darkness, with transport giving them the right of way, and on to a front that was in motion, with officers studying their maps and directions by the pocket flashlight—this was something like. And a young lieutenant hurried forward to where the rifles were talking to signal back the results of the guns firing from the midst of the battle. Something like, indeed! The fellows training their pieces in keeping with his instructions might be in for a sudden concentration of blasts from the enemy, of course. Wasn't that part of the experience? Wasn't it their place to take their share of the pounding, and didn't they belong to the guns?

These were examples close at hand, but sprinkled about the well-won area I saw the puffs from other British batteries which, after a nocturnal journey, morning found close to the firing-line. While I was moving about in the neighborhood I cast glances in the direction of that particular battery of eighteen pounders which was still serenely firing without being disturbed by the German guns. There was something unreal about it after nearly two years of the Ypres salient.

But the worst shock to a trench-tied habit of mind was when I stood upon the parapet of a German trench and saw ahead the British firing-line and the German, too. I ducked as instinctively, according to past training, as if I had seen a large, black, murderous thing coming straight for my head. In the stalemate days a dozen sharpshooters waiting for such opportunities would have had a try at you; a machine gun might have loosened up, and even batteries of artillery in their search for game to show itself from cover did not hesitate to snipe with shells at an individual.

I must be dead; at least, I ought to be according to previous formulæ; but realizing that I was still alive and that nothing had cracked or whistled overhead, I took another look and then remained standing. I had been considering myself altogether too important a mortal. German guns and snipers were not going to waste ammunition on a non-combatant on the skyline when they had an overwhelming number of belligerent targets. A few shrapnel breaking remotely were all that we had to bother us, and these were sparingly sent with the palpable message, "We'll let you fellows in the rear know what we would do to you if we were not so preoccupied with other business."

I was near enough to see the operations; to have gone nearer would have been to face in the open the sweep of bullets over the heads of the British front line hugging the earth, which is not wise in these days of the machine gun. A correspondent likes to see without being shot at and his lot is sometimes to be shot at without being able to see anything except the entrance of a dugout, which on some occasions is more inviting than the portals of a palace.

In the distance was the main German second trench line on the crest of Longueval and High Wood Ridge, which the British were later to win after a struggle which left nothing of woods or villages or ridges except shell-craters. Naturally, the Germans had not restricted their original defenses to the ridge itself, any more than the French had theirs to the hills immediately in front of Verdun. They had placed their original first-line trenches along the series of advantageous positions on the slope and turned every bit of woods and every eminence into a strong point on the way back to the second line, whose barbed-wire entanglements rusted by long exposure were distinct under the glasses. A German officer stood on the parapet looking out in our direction, probably trying to locate the British infantry advance which was hugging a fold in the ground and resting there for the time being. I imagined how beaver-like were the Germans in the second line strengthening their defenses. I scanned all the slopes facing us in the hope of seeing a German battery. There must be one under those balls of black smoke from high explosives from British guns and another a half mile away under the same kind of shower.

"They withdrew most of their guns behind the ridge overnight," said an officer, "in order to avoid capture in case we made another rush."

On the other side of this natural wall they would be safe from any except aerial observation, and the advanced British batteries, though all in the open, were in folds in the ground, or behind bluffs, or just below the skyline of a rise where they had found their assigned position by the map. How much a few feet of depression in a field, a slightly sunken road, the grade of a gentle slope, which hid man or gun from view counted for I did not realize that day as I was to realize in the fierce fight for position which was to come in succeeding weeks.

It was easy to understand why the Germans had made a strong point in the first line where I was standing, for it was a position which, in relation to both the British and the German trenches, would instantly appeal to the tactical eye. Here they had emplaced machine guns manned by chosen desperate men which had given the British charge its worst experience over a mile front. I could see all the movement over a broad area to the rear which, however, the rise under my feet hid from the ridge where the German officer stood. The advantage which the Germans had after their retreat from the Marne was brought home afresh once you were on conquered ground. A mile more or less of depth had no sentimental interest to them, for they were on foreign soil. They had chosen their positions by armies, by corps, by battalions, by hundreds of miles and tens of miles and tens of yards with the view to a command of observation and ground. This was a simple application of the formula as old as man; but it was their numbers and preparedness that permitted its application and wherever the Allies were to undertake the offensive they must face this military fact, which made the test of their skill against frontal positions all the stiffer and added tribute to success.

The scene in front reminded one of a great carpet which did not lie flat on the floor but was in undulations, with the whole on an incline toward Longueval and High Wood Ridge. The Ridge I shall call it after this, for so it was in capital letters to millions of French, British and German soldiers in the summer of 1916. And this carpet was peopled with men in a game of hide and seek with death among its folds.

No vehicle, no horse was anywhere visible. Yet it was a poignantly live world where the old trench lines had been a dead world—a world alive in the dots of men strung along the crest, in others digging new trenches, in messengers and officers on the move, in clumps of reserves behind a hillock or in a valley. Though bursting shrapnel jackets whipped out the same kind of puffs as always from a flashing center which spread into nimbus radiant in the sunlight and the high explosives sent up the same spouts of black smoke as if a stick of dynamite had burst in a coal box, the shell fire seemed different; it had a quality of action and adventure in comparison with the monotonous exhibition which we had watched in stalemate warfare. Death now had some element of glory and sport. It was less like set fate in a stationary shambles.

Directly ahead was a bare sweep of field of waste wild grass between the German communication trenches where wheat had grown before the war, and the British firing-line seemed like heads fastened to a greenish blanket. Holding the ground that they had gained, they were waiting on something to happen elsewhere. Others must advance before they could go farther.

The battle was not general; it raged at certain points where the Germans had anchored themselves after some recovery from the staggering blow of the first day. Beyond Fricourt the British artillery was making a crushing concentration on a clump of woods. This seemed to be the hottest place of all. I would watch it. Nothing except the blanket of shell-smoke hanging over the trees was visible for a time, unless you counted figures some distance away moving about in a sort of detached pantomime.

Then a line of British infantry seemed to rise out of the pile of the carpet and I could see them moving with a drill-ground steadiness toward the edge of the woods, only to be lost to the eye in a fold of the carpet or in a changed background. There had been something workmanlike and bold about their rigid, matter-of-fact progress, reflective of man-power in battle as seen very distinctly for a space in that field of baffling and shimmering haze. I thought that I had glimpses of some of them just before they entered the woods and that they were mixing with figures coming out of the woods. At any rate, what was undoubtedly a half company of German prisoners were soon coming down the slope in a body, only to disappear as if they, too, were playing their part in the hide and seek of that irregular landscape with its variation from white chalk to dark green foliage.

Khaki figures stood out against the chalk and melted into the fields or the undergrowth, or came up to the skyline only to be swallowed into the earth probably by the German trench which they were entering. I wondered if one group had been killed, or knocked over, or had merely taken cover in a shell-crater when a German "krump" seemed to burst right among them, though at a distance of even a few hundred yards nothing is so deceiving as the location of a shell-burst in relation to objects in line with it. The black cloud drew a curtain over them. When it lifted they were not on the stage. This was all that one could tell.

What seemed only a platoon became a company for an instant under favorable light refraction. The object of British khaki, French blue and German green is invisibility, but nothing can be designed that will not be visible under certain conditions. A motley such as the "tanks" were painted would be best, but the most utilitarian of generals has not yet dared to suggest motley as a uniform for an army. It occurred to me how distinct the action would have been if the participants had worn the blue coats and red trousers in which the French fought their early battles of the war.

All was confused in that mixture of haze and shell-smoke and maze of trenches, with the appearing and disappearing soldiers living patterns of the carpet which at times itself seemed to move to one's tiring, intensified gaze. Each one was working out his part of a plan; each was a responsive unit of the system of training for such affairs.

The whole would have seemed fantastic if it had not been for the sound of the machine guns and the rifles and the deeper-throated chorus of the heavy guns, which proved that this was no mesmeric, fantastic spectacle but a game with death, precise and ordered, with nothing that could be rehearsed left to chance any more than there was in the regulation of the traffic which was pressing forward, column after column, to supply the food which fed the artillery-power and man-power that should crush through frontal positions.

IX

WHEN THE FRENCH WON

A big man's small quarters—General Foch—French capacity for enjoying a victory—Winning quality of French as victors—When the heart of France stood still—The bravery of the race—Germany's mistaken estimate of France—Why the French will fight this war to a finish—French and Germans as different breeds as ever lived neighbor—The democracy of the French—*Élan*—"War of movement."

The farther south the better the news. There was another world of victory on the other side of a certain dividing road where French and British transport mingled. That world I was to see next on a day of days—a holiday of elation.

A brief note, with its permission to "circulate within the lines," written in a bold hand in the chateau where General Foch directed the Northern Group of French Armies, placed no limitation on freedom of movement for my French friend and myself.

Of course, General Foch's chateau was small. All chateaux occupied by big commanders are small, and as a matter of method I am inclined to think. If they have limited quarters there is no room for the intrusion of anyone except their personal staff and they can live with the simplicity which is a soldier's barrack training.

Joffre, Castelnau and Foch were the three great names in the French Army which the public knew after the Marne, and of the three Foch has, perhaps, more of the dash which the world associates with the French military type. He simplified victory, which was the result of the same arduous preparation as on the British side, with a single gesture as he swept his pencil across the map from Dompierre to Flaucourt. Thus his army had gone forward and that was all there was to it, which was enough for the French and also for the Germans on this particular front.

"It went well! It goes well!" he said, with dramatic brevity. He had made the plans which were so definite in the bold outline to which he held all subordinates in a coördinated execution; and I should meet the men who had carried out his plans, from artillerists who had blazed the way to infantry who had stormed the enemy trenches. There was no mistaking his happiness. It was not that of a general, but the common happiness of all France.

Victory in France for France could never mean to an Englishman what it meant to a Frenchman. The Englishman would have to be on his own soil before he could understand what was in the heart of the French after their drive on the Somme. I imagined that day that I was a Frenchman. By proxy

I shared their joy of winning, which in a way seemed to be taking an unfair advantage of my position, considering that I had not been fighting.

There is no race, it seems to me, who know quite so well how to enjoy victory as the French. They make it glow with a rare quality which absorbs you into their own exhilaration. I had the feeling that the pulse of every citizen in France had quickened a few beats. All the peasant women as they walked along the road stood a little straighter and the old men and old women were renewing their youth in quiet triumph; for now they had learned the first result of the offensive and might permit themselves to exult.

Once before in this war at the Marne I had followed the French legions in an advance. Then victory meant that France was safe. The people had found salvation through their sacrifice, and their relief was so profound that to the outsider they seemed hardly like the French in their stoic gratitude. This time they were articulate, more like the French of our conception. They could fondle victory and take it apart and play with it and make the most of it.

If I had no more interest in the success of one European people than another, then as a spectator I should choose that it should be to the French, provided that I was permitted to be present. They make victory no raucous-voiced, fleshy woman, shrilly gloating, no superwoman, cold and efficient, who considers it her right as a superior being, but a gracious person, smiling, laughing, singing in a human fashion, whether she is greeting winning generals or privates or is looking in at the door of a chateau or a peasant's cottage.

An old race, the French, tried out through many victories and defeats until a vital, indescribable quality which may be called the art of living governs all emotions. Victory to the Germans could not mean half what it would to the French. The Germans had expected victory and had organized for it for years as a definite goal in their ambitions. To the French it was a visitation, a reward of courage and kindly fortune and the right to be the French in their own world and in their own way, which to man or to State is the most justifiable of all rights.

Twice the heart of France had stood still in suspense, first on the Marne and then at the opening onslaught on Verdun; and between the Marne and Verdun had been sixteen months when, on the soil of their France and looking out on the ruins of their villages, they had striven to hold what remained to them. They had been the great martial people of Europe and because Napoleon III. tripped them by the fetish of the Bonaparte name in '70, people thought that they were no longer martial. This puts the world in the wrong, as it implies that success in war is the test of greatness. When the world expressed its surprise and admiration at French courage France smiled politely, which is the way of France, and in the midst of the shambles, as she strained every nerve, was a little amused, not to say irritated, to think that Frenchmen had to prove again to the world that they were brave.

Whether the son came from the little shops of Paris, from stubborn Brittany, the valley of the Meuse, or the vineyards, war made him the same kind of Frenchman that he was in the time of Louis XIV. and Napoleon, fighting now for France rather than for glory as he did in Napoleon's time; a man cured of the idea of conquest, advanced a step farther than the stage of the conqueror, and his courage, though slower to respond to wrath, the finer. He had proven that the more highly civilized a people, the more content and the more they had to lose by war, the less likely they were to be drawn into war, the more resourceful and the more stubborn in defense they might become—especially that younger generation of Frenchmen with their exemplary habits and their fondness for the open air.

If France had been beaten at the Marne, notice would have been served on humanity that thrift and refinement mean enervation. We should have believed in the alarmists who talk of oriental hordes and of the vigor of primitive manhood overcoming art and education.

The Germans could not give up their idea that both the French and the English must be dying races. The German staff had been well enough informed to realize that they must first destroy the French Army as the continental army most worthy of their steel and, at the same time, they could not convince themselves that France was other than weak. She loved her flesh-pots too well; her families would yield and pay rather than sacrifice only sons.

At any time since October, 1914, the French could have had a separate peace; but the answer of the Frenchman, aside from his bounden faith to the other Allies, was that he would have no peace that was given—only a peace that was yielded. France would win by the strength of her manhood or she would die. When the war was over a Frenchman could look a German in the face and say, "I have won this peace by the force of my blows;" or else the war would go on to extermination.

At intervals in the long, long months of sacrifice France was very depressed; for the French are more inclined than the English to be up and down in their emotions. They have their bad and their good days. Yet, when they were bluest over reports of the retreat from the Marne or losses at Verdun they had no thought of making terms. Depression merely meant that they would all have to succumb without winning. Thus, after the weary stalling and resistance of the blows at Verdun, never making any real progress in driving the enemy out of France, ever dreaming of the day when they should see the Germans' backs, France had waited for the movement that came on the Somme.

The people were always talking of this offensive. They had heard that it was under way. Yet, how were they to know the truth? The newspapers gave vague hints; gossip carried others, more concrete, sometimes correct but usually incorrect; and all that the women and the old men and the children at home could do was to keep on with the work. And this they did; it is instinct. Then one morning news was flashed over France that the British and the French had taken over twenty thousand prisoners. The tables were turned at last! France was on the march!

"Do you see why we love France?" said my friend T——, who was with me that day, as with a turn of the road we had a glimpse of the valley of the Somme. He swung his hand toward the waving fields of grain, the villages and plots of woods, as the train flew along the metals between rows of stately shade trees. "It is France. It is bred in our bones. We are fighting for that— just what you see!"

"But wouldn't you take some of Germany if you could?" I asked.

"No. We want none of Germany and we want no Germans. Let them do as they please with what is their own. They are brave; they fight well; but we will not let them stay in France."

Look into the faces of the French soldiers and look into the faces of Germans and you have two breeds as different as ever lived neighbor in the world. It would seem impossible that there could be anything but a truce between them and either preserve its own characteristics of civilization. The privilege of each to survive through all the centuries has been by force of arms and, after the Marne and Verdun, the Somme put the seal on the French privilege to survive. If there be any hope of true internationalism among the continental peoples I think that it can rely on the Frenchman, who only wants to make the most of his own without encroaching on anybody's else property and is disinterested in human incubation for the purpose of overwhelming his neighbors. True internationalism will spring from the provincialism that holds fast to its own home and does not interfere with the worship by other countries of their gods.

All this may seem rambling, but to a spectator of war indulging in a little philosophy it goes to the kernel of the meaning of victory to the French and to my own happiness in seeing the French win. Sometimes the Frenchman seems the most soldierly of men; again, a superficial observer might wonder if the French Army had any real discipline. And there, again, you have French temperament; the old civilization that has defined itself in democracy. For the French are the most democratic of all peoples, not excluding ourselves. That is not saying that they are the freest of all peoples, because no people on earth are freer than the English or the American.

An Englishman is always on the lookout lest someone should interfere with his individual rights as he conceives them. He is the least gregarious of all Europeans in one sense and the French the most gregarious, which is a factor contributing to French democracy. It is his gregariousness that makes the Frenchman polite and his politeness which permits of democracy. An officer may talk with a private soldier and the private may talk back because of French politeness and equality, which yield fellowship at one moment and the next slip back into the bonds of discipline which, by consent of public opinion, have tightened until they are as strict as in Napoleon's day. Gregariousness was supreme on this day of victory; democracy triumphant. Democracy had proved itself again as had English freedom against Prussian system. Vitality is another French possession and this means industry. The German also is industrious, but more from discipline and training than from a philosophy of life. French vitality is inborn, electrically installed by the sunshine of France.

When a battery of French artillery moves along the road it is democratic, but when it swings its guns into action it is military. Then its vitality is something that is not the product of training, something that training cannot produce. A French battalion moving up to the trenches seems not to have any particular order, but when it goes over the parapet in an attack it has the essence of military spirit which is coördination of action. No two French soldiers seem quite alike on the march or when moving about a village on leave. Each seems three beings: one a Frenchman, one a soldier, a third himself. German psychology left out the result of the combination, just as it never considered that the British could in two years submerge their individualism sufficiently to become a military nation.

There is a French word, *élan*, which has been much overworked in describing French character. Other nations have no equivalent word; other races lack the quality which it expresses, a quality which you get in the wave of a hand from a peasant girl to a passing car, in the woman who keeps a shop, in French art, habits, literature. To-day old Monsieur Élan was director-general of the pageant.

This people of apt phrases have one for the operations before the trench system was established; it is the "war of movement." That was the word, movement, for the blue river of men and transport along the roads to the front. We were back to the "war of movement" for the time being, at any rate; for the French had broken through the German fortifications for a depth of four to five miles in a single day.

X

ALONG THE ROAD TO VICTORY

A thrifty victory—Seventeen-inch guns asleep—A procession of guns that gorged the roads—French rules of the road—Absence of system conceals an excellent system—Spoils of war—The Colonial Corps—The "chocolates"—"Boches"—Dramatic victors—The German line in front of the French attack—Galloping *soixante-quinzes*.

Anyone with experience of armies cannot be deceived about losses when he is close to the front. Even if he does not go over the field while the dead of both sides are still lying there, infallible signs without a word being spoken reflect the truth. It was shining in panoplies of smiles with the French after the attack of July 1st. Victory was sweet because it came at slight cost. Staff officers could congratulate themselves on having driven a thrifty bargain. Casualty clearing stations were doing a small business; prisoners' inclosures a driving one.

"We've nothing to fire at," said an officer of heavy artillery. "Our targets are out of reach. The Germans went too fast for us; they left us without occupation."

Where with the British I had watched the preparations for the offensive develop, the curtain was now raised on the French preparations, which were equally elaborate, after the offensive had gone home. General Joffre had spared more guns from Verdun for the Somme than optimism had supposed possible. Those immense fellows of caliber from twelve to seventeen-inch, mounted on railway trucks, were lions asleep under their covers on the sidings which had been built for them. Their tracks would have to be carried farther forward before they roared at the Germans again.

Five miles are not far for a battalion to march, though an immense distance to a modern army with its extensive and complicated plant. Even the aviators wanted to be nearer the enemy and were looking for a new park. Sheds where artillery horses had been sheltered for more than a year were empty; camps were being vacated; vast piles of shells must follow the guns which the tractors were taking forward. The nests of spacious dugouts in a hillside nicely walled in by sandbags had served their purpose. They were beyond the range of any German guns.

For the first time you realized what the procession which gorged the roads would be like if the Western front were actually broken. Guns of every caliber from the 75's to the 120's and 240's, ammunition pack trains, ambulances horse-drawn and motor-drawn, big and little motor trucks, staff officers' cars, cycle riders and motor cycle riders, small two-wheeled carts, all were mixed with the flow of infantry going and coming and crowding the road-menders off the road.

There was none of the stateliness of the columns of British motor trucks and none of the rigidity of British marching. It all seemed a great family affair. When one wondered what part any item of the variegated transport played it was always promptly explained.

Officers and men exchanged calls of greeting as they passed. Eyes were flashing to the accompaniment of gestures. There were arguments about right of way in which the fellow with the two-wheeled cart held his own with the chauffeur of the three-ton motor truck. But the argument was accompanied by action. In some cases it was over, a decision made and the block of traffic broken before a phlegmatic man could have had discussion fairly under way. For Frenchmen are nothing if not quick of mind and body and whether a Frenchman is pulling or pushing or driving he likes to express the emotions of the moment. If a piece of transport were stalled there would be a chorus of exclamations and running disputes as to the method of getting it out of the rut, with the result that at the juncture when an outsider might think that utter confusion was to ensue, every Frenchman in sight had swarmed to the task under the direction of somebody who seemed to have made the suggestion which won the favor of the majority.

Much has been written about the grimness of the French in this war. Naturally they were grim in the early days; but what impresses me most about the French Army whenever I see it is that it is entirely French. Some people had the idea that when the French went to war they would lose their heads, run to and fro and dance about and shout. They have not acted so in this war and they never have acted so in any other war. They still talk with eyes, hands and shoulders and fight with them, too.

The tide never halted for long. It flowed on with marvelous alacrity and a seeming absence of system which soon convinced you as concealing a very excellent system. Every man really knew where he was going; he could think for himself, French fashion. Near the front I witnessed a typical scene when an officer ran out and halted a soldier who was walking across the fields by himself and demanded to know who he was and what he was doing there.

"I am wounded, sir," was the reply, as he opened his coat and showed a bandage. "I am going to the casualty clearing station and this is the shortest way"—not to mention that it was a much easier way than to hug the edge of the road in the midst of the traffic.

The battalions and transport which made up this tide of an army's rear trying to catch up with its extreme front had a view, as the road dipped into a valley, of the trophies which are the proof of victory. Here were both guns and prisoners. Among the guns nicely parked you might have your choice between the latest 77's out of Krupps' and pieces of the vintage of the '80's. One 77 had not a blemish; another had its muzzle broken off by the burst of a shell, its spokes slashed by shell-fragments, and its armored shield, opened by a jagged hole, was as crumpled as if made of tin.

Four of the old fortress type had a history. They bore the mark of their French maker. They had fired at the Germans from Maubeuge and after having been taken by the Germans were set to fire at the French. One could imagine how the German staff had scattered such pieces along the line when in stalemate warfare any kind of gun that had a barrel and could discharge a shell would add to the volume of gunfire.

Such a ponderous piece with its heavy, old-fashioned trail and no recoil cylinder was never meant to play any part in an army of movement. You could picture how it had been dragged up into position back of the German trenches and how a crew of old Landsturm gunners had been allowed a certain number of shells a day and told off to fire them at certain villages and crossroads, with that systematic regularity of the German artillery system which often defeats its own purpose, as we on the Allies' side well know.

Very likely, as often happened, the crew fired six rounds before breakfast and eight at four o'clock in the afternoon, and the rest of the time they might sit about playing cards. Of course, retreat was out of the question with a gun of this sort. Yet through the twenty months that the opposing armies had sniped at each other from the same positions the relic had done faithful auxiliary service. The French could move it on to some other part of the line now where no offensive was expected and some old territorials could use it as the old Landsturmers had used it.

All the guns in this park had been taken by the Colonial Corps, which thinks itself a little better than the Nancy (or Iron) Corps, a view with which the Iron Corps entirely disagreed. Scattered among the Colonial Corps, whether on the march or in billets, were the black men. There is no prejudice against the "chocolates," as they are called, who provide variation and amusement, not to mention color. Most adaptable of human beings is the negro, whom you find in all lands and engaged in all kinds of pursuits, reflecting always the character of his surroundings. If his French comrades charged he would charge and just as far; if they fell back he would fall back and just as far. No Frenchman could approach the pride of the blacks over those captured guns, which brought grins that left only half of their ebony countenances as a background for the whites of their eyes and teeth.

The tide of infantry, vehicles and horses flowing past must have been a strange world to the German prisoners brought past it to the inclosures, when they had not yet recovered from their astonishment at the suddenness of the French whirlwind attack. The day was warm and the ground dry, and those prisoners who were not munching French bread were lying sardine fashion pillowing their heads on one another, a confused mass of arms and legs, dead to the world in sleep—a green patch of humanity with all the fight out of them, without weapons or power of resistance, guarded by a single French soldier, while the belligerent energy of war was on that road a hundred yards away.

"They are good Boches, now," said the French sentry; "we sha'n't have to take that lot again."

Boches! They are rarely called anything else at the front. With both French and English this has become the universal word for the Germans which will last as long as the men who fought in this war survive. Though the Germans dislike it that makes no difference. They will have to accept it even when peace comes, for it is established. One day they may come to take a certain pride in it as a distinction which stands for German military efficiency and racial isolation. The professional soldier expressing his admiration of the way the German charges, handles his artillery, or the desperate courage of his machine gun crews may speak of him as "Brother Boche" or the "old Boche" in a sort of amiable recognition of the fact of how worthy he is of an enemy's steel if only he would refrain from certain unsportsmanlike habits.

At length the blue river on the way to the front divided at a crossroad and we were out on the plain which swept away to the bend of the Somme in front of Péronne. Officers returning from the front when asked how the battle was going were never too preoccupied to reply. It was anybody's privilege to ask a question and everybody seemed to delight to answer it. I talked with a group of men who were washing down their bread with draughts of red wine, their first meal after they had been through two lines of trenches. Their brigade had taken more prisoners than it had had casualties. Their dead were few and less mourned because they had fallen in such a glorious victory. Rattling talk gave gusto to every mouthful.

Unlike the English, these victors were articulate; they rejoiced in their experiences and were glad to tell about them. If one had fought it out at close quarters with a German and got his man, he made the incident into a dramatic episode for your edification. It was war; he had been in a charge; he had escaped alive; he had won. He liked the thrill of his exploit and enjoyed the telling, not allowing it to drag, perhaps, for want of a leg. Every Frenchman is more or less of a general, as Napoleon said, and every one knew the meaning of this victory. He liked to make the most of it and relive it.

After having seen the trenches that the British had taken on the high ground around Fricourt, I was the more interested to see those that the French had taken on July 1st. The British had charged uphill against the strongest fortifications that the Germans could devise in that chalky subsoil so admirably suited for the purpose. Those before the French were not so strong and were in alluvial soil on the plain. Many of the German dugouts in front of Dompierre were in relatively as good condition as those at Fricourt, though not so numerous or so strong; which meant that the artillery of neither army had been able completely to destroy them. The ground on the plain permitted of no such advantageous tactical points for machine guns as those which had confronted the British, in front of whom the Germans had massed immense reserves of artillery, particularly in the Thiepval-Gommecourt sector where the British attack had failed, besides having the valuable ridge of Bapaume at their backs. In front of the French the Germans had smaller forces of artillery on the plain where the bend of the Somme was at their backs.

This is not detracting from the French success, which was complete and masterful. The coördination of artillery and infantry must have been perfect, as you could see when you went over the field where there were surprisingly few French dead and the German dead, though more plentiful than the French, were not very numerous. It seemed that the French artillery had absolutely pinioned the Germans to their trenches and communication trenches in the Dompierre sector and the French appearing close under their own shells in a swift and eager wave gathered in all the German garrison as prisoners. The ruins of the villages might have been made either by French, British or German artillery. There is true internationalism in artillery destruction.

It was something to see the way that French transport and reserves were going right across the plain in splendid disregard of any German artillery concentration. But, as usual, they knew what they were doing. No shells fell among them while I was at the front, and out on the plain where the battle still raged the *soixante-quinze* batteries were as busy as knitting-machines working some kind of magic which protected that column from tornadoes of the same kind that they themselves were sending. The German artillery, indeed, seemed a little demoralized. Krump-krump-krump, they put a number of shells into a group of trees beside the road where they mistakenly thought that there was a battery. Swish-swish-swish came another salvo which I thought was meant for us, but it passed by and struck where there was no target.

I have had glimpses of nearly every feature of war, but there was one in this advance which was not included in my experiences. The French infantry was hardly in the first-line German trench when the ditch had been filled in and the way was open for the *soixante-quinze* to go forward. For the guns galloped into action just as they might have done at manoeuvers. Some dead artillery horses near the old trench line told the story of how a German shell must have stopped one of the guns, which was small price to pay for so great a privilege as—let us repeat—galloping the guns into action across the trenches in broad daylight and keeping close to the infantry as it advanced from position to position on the plain.

Here was a surviving bit of the glory and the sport of war, whose passing may be one of the great influences in preventing future wars; but there being war and the French having to win that war, why, the spectacle of this marvelous field gun, so beloved of its alert and skilful gunners, playing the part that was intended for it on the heels of the enemy made a thrilling incident in the history of modern France. The French had shown on that day that they had lost none of their initiative of Napoleon's time, just as the British had shown that they could be as stubborn and determined as in Wellington's.

XI

THE BRIGADE THAT WENT THROUGH

A young brigadier—A regular soldier—No heroics—How his brigade charged—Systematically cleaning up the dugouts—"It was orders. We did it."—The second advance—Holding on for two sleepless days and nights—Soda water and cigars—Yorkshiremen, and a stubborn lot—British phlegm—Five officers out of twenty who had "gone through"—Stereotyped phrases and inexpressible emotions.

No sound of the guns was audible in this quiet French village where a brigade out of the battle line was in rest. The few soldiers moving about were looking in the shop windows, trying their French with the inhabitants, or standing in small groups. Their faces were tired and drawn as the only visible sign of the torment of fire that they had undergone. They had met everything the German had to offer in the way of projectiles and explosives; but before we have their story we shall have that of the young brigadier-general who had his headquarters in one of the houses. His was the brigade that went "through," and he was the kind of brigadier who would send a brigade "through."

With its position in the attack of July 1st in the joint, as it were, between the northern sector where the German line was not broken and the southern where it was, this brigade had suffered what the charges which failed had suffered and it had known the triumph of those which had succeeded, at a cost in keeping with the experience.

The brigadier was a regular soldier and nothing but a soldier from head to foot, in thought, in manner and in his decisive phrases. Nowadays, when we seem to be drawing further and further away from versatility, perhaps more than ever we like the soldier to be a soldier, the poet to be a poet, the surgeon to be a surgeon; and I can even imagine this brigadier preferring that if another man was to be a pacifist he should be a real out and out pacifist. You knew at a glance without asking that he had been in India and South Africa, that he was fond of sport and probably fond of fighting. He had rubbed up against all kinds of men, as the British officer who has the inclination may do in the course of his career, and his straight eye—an eye which you would say had never been accustomed to indefiniteness about anything—must have impressed the men under his command with the confidence that he knew his business and that they must follow him. Yet it could twinkle on occasion with a pungent humor as he told his story, which did not take him long but left you long a-thinking. A writer who was as good a writer as he was a soldier if he had had the same experience could have made a book out of it; but then he could not have been a man of action at the same time.

He made it clear at once that he had not led his brigade in person over the parapet, or helped in person to bomb the enemy's dugouts, or indulged in any other kind of gallery play. I do not think that all the drawing-rooms in London or all the reception committees which receive gallant sons in their home towns could betray him into the faintest simulation of the pose of a hero. He was not a hero and he did not believe in heroics. His occupation was commanding men and taking trenches.

Not once did he utter anything approaching a boast over a feat which his friends and superiors had expected of him. This would be "swank," as they call it, only he would characterize it by even a stronger word. He is the kind of officer, the working, clear-thinking type, who would earn promotion by success at arms in a long war, while the gallery-play crowd whose promotion and favors come by political gift and academic reports in time of peace would be swept into the dustbin. He was simply a capable fighter; and war is fighting.

His men had gone over the "lid" in excellent fashion, quite on time. He had seen at once what they were in for, but he had no doubt that they would keep on, for he had warned them to expect machine gun fire and told them what to do in case it came. They applied the system in which he had trained them with a coolness that won his approbation as a directing expert—his matter-of-fact approbation in the searching analysis of every detail, with no ecstasies about their unparalleled gallantry. He expected them to be gallant. However, I could imagine that if you said a word against them his eyes would flash indignation. They were his men and he might criticize them, but no one else might except a superior officer. The first wave reached the first-line German trench on time, that is, half of them did; the rest, including more than half of the officers, were down, dead or wounded, in No Man's Land in the swift crossing of two hundred yards of open space.

He had watched their advance from the first-line British trench. Later, when the situation demanded it, I learned that he went up to the captured German line and on to the final objective, but this fact was drawn out of him. It might lead to a misunderstanding; you might think that he had been taking as much risk as his officers and men, and risk of any kind for him was an incident of the business of managing a brigade.

"How about the dugouts?" I asked.

This was an obvious question. The trouble on July 1st had been, as we know, that the Germans hiding in their dugouts had rushed forth as soon as the British curtain of fire lifted and sometimes fought the British in the trench traverses with numbers superior. Again, they had surrendered, only to overpower their guards, pick up rifles and man their machine guns after the first wave had passed on, instead of filing back across No Man's Land in the regular fashion of prisoners.

"I was looking out for that," said the brigadier, like a lawyer who has stated his opponent's case; but other commanders had taken the same precautions with less fortunate results. When he said that he was "looking out for that" it meant, in his case, that he had so thoroughly organized his men—and he was not the only brigadier who had, he was a type—in view of every emergency in "cleaning up" that the Germans did not outwit them. The half which reached the German trench had the situation fully in hand and details for the dugouts assigned before they went on. And they did go on. This was the wonderful thing.

"With your numbers so depleted, wasn't it a question whether or not it was wise for you to attempt to carry out the full plan?"

He gave me a short look of surprise. I realized that if I had been one of the colonels and made such a suggestion I should have drawn a curtain of fire upon myself.

"It was orders," he said, and added: "We did it."

Yes, they did it—when commanding officers, majors and senior captains were down, when companies without any officers were led by sergeants and even by corporals who knew what to do, thanks to their training.

In order to reach the final objective the survivors of the first charge which had gone two hundred yards to the first line must cover another thousand, which must have seemed a thousand miles; but that was not for them to consider. The spirit of the resolute man who had drilled them, if not his presence, was urging them forward. They reached the point where the landmarks compared with their map indicated their stopping place—about one-quarter of the number that had left the British trench.

They had enough military sense to realize that if they tried to go back over the same ground which they had crossed there might be less than one-quarter of the fourth remaining. They preferred to die with their faces rather than their backs to the enemy. No, they did not mean to die. They meant to hold on and "beat the Boche," according to their teaching.

As things had been going none too well with the brigade on their left their flank was exposed. They met this condition by fortifying themselves against enfilade in an old German communication trench and rushing other points of advantage to secure their position. When a German machine gun was able to sweep them, a corporal slipped up another communication trench and bombed it out of business. Running out of bombs of their own, they began gathering German bombs which were lying about plentifully and threw these at the Germans. Short of rifle ammunition they found that there was ammunition for the German rifles which had been captured. They were not choice about their methods and neither were the Germans in that cheek-by-jowl affair with both sides so exhausted that a little more grit on one side struck the balance in its favor.

This medley of British and Germans in a world of personal combat shared shell fire, heat and misery. The British sent their rocket signals up to say that they had arrived. In two or three other instances the signals had meant that a dozen men only had reached their objective, a force unable to hold until reinforcements could come. Not so this time. The little group held; they held even when the Germans got some fresh men and attempted a counter-attack; they held until assistance came. For two sleepless days and nights under continual fire they remained in their dearly won position until, under cover of darkness, they were relieved.

In the most tranquil of villages the survivors looking in shop windows and trying out their French might wonder how it was that they were alive, though they were certain that their brigadier thought well of them. Ask them or their officers what they thought of their brigadier and they were equally certain of that, too. Theirs was the best brigadier in the army. Think what this kind of confidence means to men in such an action when their lives are the pawns of his direction!

I felt a kind of awe in the presence of one of the battalions in billet in a warehouse, more than in the presence of prime ministers or potentates. Most of them were blinking and mind-stiff after having slept the clock around. They were Yorkshiremen, chiefly workers in worsted mills and a stubborn lot.

"What did you most want to do when you got out of the fight?" I asked.

They spoke with one voice which left no question of their desires in a one-two-three order. They wanted a wash, a shave, a good meal, and then sleep. And personal experiences? Tom called on Jim and Jim had bayoneted two Germans, he said; then Jim called on Bill, who had had a wonderful experience according to Jim, though all that Bill made of it was that he got there first with his bombs. Told among themselves the stories might have been thrilling. Before a stranger they were mere official reports. It had been quick work, too quick for anything but to dodge for cover and act promptly in your effort to get the other fellow before he got you.

Generically, they had a job to do and they did it just as they would have done one in the factories at home. They were not so interested in any exhibition of courage as in an encounter which had the element of sport. Each narrator invariably returned to the subject of soda water. The outstanding novelty of the charge to these men was the quantity of soda water in bottles which they had found in the German dugouts. They went on to their second objective with bottles of soda water in their pockets and German light cigars in the corners of their mouths and stopped to drink soda water between bombing rushes after they had arrived. It was a hot, thirsty day.

Through the curtains of artillery fire which were continually maintained back of their new positions supplies could not be brought up, but Boche provisions saved the day. In fact, I think this was one of the reasons why they felt almost kindly toward the Germans. They found the canned meat excellent, but did not care for the "K.K." bread.

Thus in the dim light of the warehouse they talked on, making their task appear as a half-holiday of sport. It seemed to me that this was in keeping with their training; the fashionable attitude of the British soldier toward a horrible business. If this helps him to endure what these men had endured without flinching, with comrades being blown to bits around them by shell-bursts, why, then, it is the attitude best suited to develop the fighting quality of the British. They had it from their officers who, in turn, perhaps, had it in part from such British regulars as the brigadier, though mostly I think that it was inborn racial phlegm.

I met the five officers who were the survivors of the twenty in one battalion, the five who had "carried through." One was a barrister, another just out of Oxford, a third, as I remember, a real estate broker in a small town. They told their stories without a gesture, quite as if they were giving an account of a game of golf. It might have seemed callous, but you knew better.

You knew when they said that it was "a bit stiff," or "a bit thick," or "it looked as if they had us," what inexpressible emotion lay behind the accepted army phrases. The truth was they would not permit themselves to think of the void in their lines made by the death of their comrades. They had drawn the curtain on all incidents which had not the appeal of action and finality as a part of the business of "going through." One officer with a twitch of the lips remarked almost casually that new officers and drafts were arriving and that it would seem strange to see so many new faces in the mess.

Those of their old comrades who were not dead were already in hospital in England. When an officer who had been absent joined the group he brought the news that one of their number who had been badly hit would live. The others' quiet ejaculation of "Good!" had a thrill back of it which communicated its joy to me. Eight of the wounded had not been seriously hit, which meant that these would return and that, after all, only four were dead. This was the first intimate indication I had of how the offensive exposing the whole bodies of men in a charge against the low-velocity shrapnel bullets and high-velocity bullets from rifles and machine guns must result in the old ratio of only one mortal wound for every five men hit.

There was consolation in that fact. It was another advantage of the war of movement as compared with the war of shambles in trenches. And none, from the general down to the privates, had really any idea of how glorious a part they had played. They had merely "done their bit" and taken what came their way—and they had "gone through."

XII

THE STORMING OF CONTALMAISON

The mighty animal of war makes ready for another effort—New charts at headquarters—The battle of the Somme the battle of woods and villages—A terrible school of war in session—Mametz—A wood not "thinned"—The Quadrangle—Marooned Scots—"Softening" a village—Light German cigars—Going after Contalmaison—Aeroplanes in the blue sky—Midsummer fruitfulness and war's destruction—Making chaos of a village—Attack under cover of a wall of smoke—A melodrama under the passing shells.

If the British and the French could have gone on day after day as they had on July 1st they would have put the Germans out of France and Belgium by autumn. Arrival at the banks of the Rhine and even the taking of Essen would have been only a matter of calculation by a schedule of time and distance. After the shock of the first great drive in which the mighty animal of war lunged forward, it had to stretch out its steel claws to gain further foothold and draw its bulky body into position for another huge effort. Wherever the claws moved there were Germans, who were too wise soldiers to fall back supinely on new lines of fortifications and await the next general attack. They would parry every attempt at footholds of approach for launching it; pound the claws as if they were the hands of an invader grasping at a window ledge.

At headquarters there was a new chart with different colored patches numbered by the days of the month beginning July 1st, each patch indicating the ground that had been won on that day. Compare their order with a relief map and in one-two-three fashion you were able to grasp the natural tactical sequence; how one position was taken in order to command another. Sometimes, though, they represented the lines of least resistance. Often the real generals were the battalions on the battle front who found the weak points and asked permission to press on. The principle was the same as water finding its level as it spreads from a reservoir.

I have often thought that a better name for the battle of the Somme would be the battle of woods and villages. Their importance never really dawned on the observer until after July 1st. Or, it might be called the battle of the spade. Give a man an hour with a spade in that chalky subsoil and a few sandbags and he will make a fortress for himself which only a direct hit by a shell can destroy. He ducks under the sweep of bullets when he is not firing and with his steel helmet is fairly safe from shrapnel while he waits in his lair until the other fellow comes.

Thus the German depended on the machine gun and the rifle to stop any charge which was not supported by artillery fire sufficient to crush in the trenches and silence his armament. When it was, he had his own artillery to turn a curtain of fire onto the charge in progress and to hammer the enemy if he got possession. This was obviously the right system—in theory. But the theory did not always work out, as we shall see. Its development through the four months that I watched the Somme battle was only less interesting than the development of offensive tactics by the British and the French. Every day this terrible school of war was in session, with a British battalion more skilful and cunning every time that it went into the firing-line.

Rising out of the slopes toward the Ridge in green patches were three large woods, not to mention small ones, under a canopy of shell-smoke, Mametz, Bernafay and Trônes, with their orgies of combat hidden under their screens of foliage. They recall the Wilderness—a Wilderness lasting for days, with only one feature of the Wilderness lacking which was a conflagration, but with lachrymatory and gas shells and a few other features that were lacking in Virginia. In the next war we may have still more innovations. Ours is the ingenious human race.

It is Mametz with an area of something over two hundred acres that concerns us now. The Germans thought highly of Mametz. They were willing to lose thousands of lives in order to keep it in their possession. For two years it had not been thinned according to French custom; now shells and bullets were to undertake the task which had been neglected. So thick was the undergrowth that a man had to squeeze his way through and an enemy was as well ambushed as a field mouse in high grass.

The Germans had run barriers of barbed wire through the undergrowth. They had their artillery registered to fringe the woods with curtains of fire and machine guns nestling in unseen barricades and trenches. Through the heart of it they had a light railway for bringing up supplies. All these details had been arranged in odd hours when they were not working on the main first- and second-line fortifications during their twenty months of preparation. I think they must have become weary at times of so much "choring," judging by a German general's order after his inspection of the second line, in which he said that the battalions in occupation were a lazy lot who were a disgrace to the Fatherland. After the battle began they could add to the defenses improvements adapted to the needs of the moment. Of course, large numbers of Germans were killed and wounded by British shell fire in the process of "thinning" out the woods; but that was to be expected, as the Germans learned during the battle of the Somme.

How the British ever took Mametz Wood I do not understand; or how they took Trônes Wood later, for that matter. A visit to the woods only heightened perplexity. I have seen men walk over broken bottles with bare feet, swallow swords and eat fire and knew that there was some trick about it, as there was about the taking of Mametz.

The German had not enough barbed wire to go all the way around the woods, or, at least, British artillery would not let him string any more and he thought that the British would attack where they ought to according to rule; that is, by the south. Instead, they went in by the west, where the machine guns were not waiting and the heavy guns were not registered, as I understand it. A piece of strategy of that kind might have won a decisive battle in an old-time war, but I confess that it did not occur to me to ask who planned it when I heard the story. Strategists became so common on the Somme that everybody took them as much for granted as that every battalion had a commander.

Mametz was not taken with the first attack. The British were in the woods once and had to come out; but they had learned that before they could get a proper *point d'appui* they must methodically "clean up" a small grove, a neighboring cemetery, an intricate maze of trenches called the Quadrangle, and a few other outlying obstacles. In the first rush a lot of Tyneside Scots were marooned from joining in the retreat. They fortified themselves in German dugouts and waited in siege, these dour men of the North. When the British returned eighty of the Scots were still full of fight if short of food and "verra well" otherwise, thank you. At times they had been under blasts of shells from both sides, and again they had been in an oasis of peace, with neither British nor German gunners certain whether they would kill friend or foe.

Going in from the west while the Germans had their curtains of fire registered elsewhere, the British grubbed their way in one charge through most of Mametz and when night fell in the midst of the undergrowth, with a Briton not knowing whether it was Briton or German lying on the other side of a tree-trunk, they had the satisfaction of possessing four big guns which the Germans had been unable to withdraw, and had ascertained also that the Germans had a strong position protected by barbed wire at the northern end of the woods.

"This will require a little thinking," as one English officer said, "but of course we shall take it."

The purchase on Mametz and the occupation of Bailiff's Wood, the Quadrangle, La Boisselle and Ovillers-la-Boiselle brought the circle of advancing British nearer to Contalmaison, which sat up on the hills in a sea of chalk seams. Contalmaison was being gradually "softened" by the artillery. The chateau was not yet all down, but after each bite by a big shell less of the white walls was visible when the clouds of smoke from the explosion lifted.

Bit by bit the guns would get the chateau, just as bit by bit a stonemason chips a block down to the proper dimensions to fit it into place in a foundation.

A visit to La Boisselle on the way to Contalmaison justified the expectation as to what was in store for Contalmaison. I saw the blackened and shell-whittled trunks of two trees standing in La Boisselle. Once with many others they had given shade in the gardens of houses; but there were no traces of houses now except as they were mixed with the earth. The village had been hammered into dust. Yet some dugouts still survived. Keeping at it, the British working around these had eventually forced the surrender of the garrison, who could not raise their heads to fire without being met by a bullet or a bomb-burst from the watchful besiegers.

"Slow work, but they had to come out," was the graphic phrase of one of the captors, "and they looked fed up, too. They had even run out of cigars"— which settled it.

Oh, those light German cigars! Sometimes I believe that they were the real mainstay of the German organization. Cigars gone, spirit gone! I have seen an utterly weary German prisoner as he delivered his papers to his captor bring out his last cigar and thrust it into his mouth to forestall its being taken as tribute, with his captor saying with characteristic British cheerfulness, "Keep it, Bochy! It smells too much like a disinfectant for me, but let's have your steel helmet"—the invariable prize demanded by the victor.

The British had already been in Contalmaison, but did not stay. "Too many German machine guns and too much artillery fire and not enough men," to put it with colloquial army brevity. It often happened that a village was entered and parts of it held during a day, then evacuated at night, leaving the British guns full play for the final "softening." These initial efforts had the result of reconnaissances in force. They permitted a thorough look around the enemy's machine gun positions so as to know how to avoid their fire and "do them in," revealed the cover that would be available for the next advance, and brought invaluable information to the gunners for the accurate distribution of their fire. Always some points important for future operations were held.

"We are going after Contalmaison this afternoon," said a staff officer at headquarters, "and if you hurry you may see it."

As a result, I witnessed the most brilliant scene of battle of any on the Somme, unless it was the taking of Combles. There was bright sunshine, with the air luminously clear and no heat waves. From my vantage point I could see clear to the neighborhood of Péronne. The French also were attacking; the drumhead fire of their *soixante-quinze* made a continuous roll, and the puffs of shrapnel smoke hung in a long, gossamery cloud fringing the horizon and the canopy of the green ridges.

Every aeroplane of the Allies seemed to be aloft, each one distinct against the blue with shimmering wings and the soft, burnished aureole of the propellers. They were flying at all heights. Some seemed almost motionless two or three miles above the earth, while others shot up from their aerodromes.

Planes circling, planes climbing, planes slipping down aerial toboggan slides with propellers still, planes going as straight as crows toward the German line to be lost to sight in space while others developed out of space as swift messengers bound for home with news of observations, planes touring a sector of the front, swooping low over a corps headquarters to drop a message and returning to their duty; planes of all types, from the monsters with vast stretch of wing and crews of three or more men, stately as swans, to those gulls, the saucy little Nieuports, shooting up and down and turning with incredible swiftness, their tails in the air; planes and planes in a fantastic aerial minuet, flitting around the great sausage balloons stationary in the still air.

With ripening grain and sweet-smelling harvests of clover and hay in the background and weeds and wild grass in the foreground, the area of vegetation in the opulence of midsummer was demarked from the area of shell-craters, trenches and explosions. You had the majesty of battle and the desolation of war; nature's eternal seeding and fruiting alongside the most ruthless forms of destruction. In the clear air the black bursts of the German high explosives hammering Mametz Wood, as if in revenge for its loss, seemed uglier and more murderous than usual; the light smoke of shrapnel had a softer, more lingering quality; soldiers were visible distinctly at a great distance in their comings and goings; the water carts carrying water up to the first line were a kind of pilgrim circuit riders of that thirsty world of deadly strife; a file of infantry winding up the slope at regular intervals were silhouettes as like as beads on a string. The whole suggested a hill of ants which had turned their habits of industry against an invader of their homes in the earth, and the columns of motor trucks and caissons ever flowing from all directions were as a tide, which halted at the foot of the slope and then flowed back.

There were shell-bursts wherever you looked, with your attention drawn to Contalmaison as it would be to a gathering crowd in the thick of city traffic. All the steel throats in clumps of woods, under cover of road embankments, in gullies and on the reverse side of slopes, were speaking. The guns were giving to Contalmaison all they had to give and the remaining walls of the chateau disappeared in a fog like a fishing smack off the Grand Banks. Super-refined, man-directed hell was making sportive chaos in the village which it hid with its steaming breath cut by columns of black smoke from the H.E.'s and crowned with flashes of shrapnel; and under the sun's rays the gases from the powder made prismatic splendor in flurries and billows shot with the tints of the rainbow.

Submerging a simple farming hamlet in this kind of a tempest was only part of the plan of the gunners, who cut a pattern of fire elsewhere in keeping with the patterns of the German trenches, placing a curtain of fire behind the town and another on the edge, and at other points not a curtain but steady hose-streams of fire. Answering German shells revealed which of the chalky scars on the slope was the British first-line trench, and from this, as steam from a locomotive runs in a flying plume along the crest of a railway cutting, rose a billowing wall of smoke which was harmless, not even asphyxiating, its only purpose being to screen the infantry attack, with a gentle breeze sweeping it on into the mantle over Contalmaison as the wind carries the smoke of a prairie fire. Lookout Mountain was known as the battle in the clouds, where generals could not see what their troops were doing. Now all battles are in a cloud.

From the first-line British trench the first wave of the British attack moved under cover of the smoke-screen and directly you saw that the shells had ceased to fall in Contalmaison. Its smoke mantle slowly lifting revealed fragmentary walls of that sturdy, defiant chateau still standing. Another wave of British infantry was on its way. Four waves in all were to go in, each succeeding one with its set part in supporting the one in front and in mastering the dugouts and machine gun positions that might have survived.

With no shells falling in Contalmaison, the bomb and the bayonet had the stage to themselves, a stage more or less hemmed in by explosions and with a sweep of projectiles from both sides passing over the heads of the cast in a melodrama which had "blessed little comedy relief," as one soldier put it. The Germans were already shelling the former British first line and their supports, while the British maintained a curtain of fire on the far side of the village to protect their infantry as it worked its way through the débris, and any fire which they had to spare after lifting it from Contalmaison they were distributing on different strong points, not in curtains but in a repetition of punches. It was the best artillery work that I had seen and its purpose seemed that of a man with a stick knocking in any head that appeared from any hole.

Act III. now. The British curtain of fire was lifted from the far edge of the village, which meant that the infantry according to schedule should be in possession of all of the village. But they might not stay. They might be forced out soon after they sent up their signals. When the Germans turned on a curtain of fire succeeding the British fire this was further evidence of British success sufficient to convince any skeptic. The British curtain was placed beyond it to hold off any counter-attack and prevent sniping till the new occupants of the premises had "dug themselves in."

The Germans had not forgotten that it was their turn now to hammer Contalmaison, through which they thought that British reserves and fresh supplies of bombs must come; and I saw one of the first "krumps" of this concentration take another bite out of the walls of the chateau.

By watching the switching of the curtains of fire I had learned that this time Contalmaison was definitely held; and though they say that I don't know anything about news, I beat the *communiqué* on the fact as the result of my observation, which ought at least to classify me as a "cub" reporter.

XIII

A GREAT NIGHT ATTACK

Following hard blows with blows—Trônes Woods—Attack and counter-attack—A heavy price to pay—"The spirit that quickeneth" knew no faltering—Second-line German fortifications—A daringly planned attack—"Up and at them!"—An attack not according to the scientific factory system—The splendid and terrible hazard—Gun flashes in the dark numerous as fireflies—Majestic, diabolical, beautiful—A planet bombarding with aerolites—Signal flares in the distance—How far had the British gone?—Sunrise on the attack—Good news that day.

Of all the wonderful nights at the front that of July 13th-14th was distinctive for its incomparable suspense. A great experiment was to be tried; at least, so it seemed to the observer, though the staff did not take that attitude. It never does once it has decided upon any daring enterprise. When you send fifty thousand men into a charge that may fail with a loss of half of their number or may brilliantly succeed with a loss of only five per cent., none from the corps commanders and division commanders, who await results after the plans are made, down to the privates must have any thought except that the plan is right and that it will go through.

There is no older military maxim than to follow up any hard blow with other blows, in order that the enemy may have no time to recuperate; but in moving against a frontal line under modern conditions the congestion of transport and ammunition which must wait on new roads and the filling in of captured trenches makes a difficult problem in organization. Never had there been and never were there necessary such numbers of men and such quantities of material as on the Somme front.

The twelve days succeeding July 1st had seen the taking of minor position after position by local concentrations of troops and artillery fire, while the army as a whole had been preparing for another big attack at the propitious moment when these preliminary gains should justify it.

Half a tactical eye could see that the woods of Mametz, Bernafay and Trônes must be held in order to allow of elbow room for a mass movement over a broad front. The German realized this and after he had lost Mametz and Bernafay he held all the more desperately to Trônes, which, for the time being, was the superlative horror in woods fighting, though we were yet to know that it could be surpassed by Delville and High Woods.

In Trônes the Germans met attack with counter-attack again and again. The British got through to the east side of the woods, and in reply the Germans sent in a wave forcing the British back to the west, but no farther. Then the

British, reinforced again, reached the east side. Showers of leaves and splinters descended from shell-bursts and machine guns were always rattling. The artillery of both sides hammered the approaches of the woods to prevent reinforcements from coming up.

In the cellars of Guillemont village beyond Trônes the Germans had refuges for concentrating their reserves to feed in more troops, whose orders, as all the prisoners taken said, were to hold to the last man. Trônes Wood was never to be yielded to the British. Its importance was too vital. Grim national and racial pride and battalion pride and soldierly pride grappled in unyielding effort and enmity. The middle of the woods became a neutral ground where the wounded of the different sallies lay groaning from pain and thirst. Small groups of British had dug themselves in among the Germans and, waterless, foodless, held out, conserving their ammunition or, when it was gone, waiting for the last effort with the bayonet.

For several days the spare British artillery had been cutting the barbed wire of the second line and smashing in the trenches; and the big guns which had been advanced since July 1st were sending their shells far beyond the Ridge into villages and crossroads and other vital points, in order to interfere with German communications.

The Thiepval-Gommecourt line where the British had been repulsed on July 1st had reverted to something approaching stalemate conditions, with the usual exchange of artillery fire, and it was along the broader front where the old German first line had been broken through that the main concentrations of men and guns were being made in order to continue the advance for the present through the opening won on July 1st. The price paid for the taking of the woods and for repeated attacks where initial attacks had failed might seem to the observer—unless he knew that the German losses had been equally heavy if not heavier since July 1st—disproportionate not only to the ground gained but also to general results up to this time which, and this was most important, had demonstrated, as a promise for the future, that the British New Army could attack unremittingly and successfully against seasoned German troops in positions which the Germans had considered impregnable.

"The spirit that quickeneth" knew no faltering. Battle police were without occupation. There were no stragglers. With methodical, phlegmatic steadiness the infantry moved up to the firing-line when its turn came.

The second-line German fortifications, if not as elaborate, were even better situated than the first; not on the crest of the Ridge, of course, where they would be easily swept by artillery blasts, but where the latest experience demonstrated that they could make the most of the commanding high ground with the least exposure. Looking through my glasses I could see the portion of the open knoll stretching from Longueval to High Wood which was to be the object of the most extensive effort since July 1st.

As yet, except in trench raids over narrow fronts, there had been no attempt to rush a long line under cover of darkness because of the difficulty of the different groups keeping touch and identifying their objectives.

The charge of July 1st had been at seven-thirty in the morning. Contalmaison had been stormed in the afternoon. Fricourt was taken at midday. When the bold suggestion was made that over a three-mile front the infantry should rush the second-line trenches in the darkness, hoping to take the enemy by surprise, it was as daring a conception considering the ground and the circumstances as ever came to the mind of a British commander and might be said to be characteristic of the dash and so-called "foolhardiness" of the British soldier, accustomed to "looking smart" and rushing his enemy from colonial experiences. Nelson had the "spirit that quickeneth" when he turned his blind eye to the enemy. The French, too, are for the attack. It won Marengo and Austerlitz. No general ever dared more than Frederick the Great, not even Cæsar. Thus the great races of history have won military dominion.

"Up and at them!" is still the shibboleth in which the British believe, no less than our pioneers and Grant and Stonewall Jackson believed in it, and nothing throughout the Somme battle was so characteristically British as not only the stubbornness of their defense when small parties were surrounded, but the way in which they would keep on attacking and the difficulty which generals had not in encouraging initiative but in keeping battalions and brigades from putting into practice their conviction that they could take a position on their own account if they could have a chance instead of waiting on a systematic advance.

Thus, an attack on that second line on the Ridge after the Germans had had two weeks of further preparation was an adventure of an order, in the days of mechanical transport, aeroplanes and indirect artillery fire when all military science is supposed to be reduced to a factory system, worthy of the days of the sea-rovers and of Clive, of Washington's crossing of the Delaware or of the storming of Quebec, when a bold confidence made gamble for a mighty stake.

So, at least, it seemed to the observer, though, as I said, the staff insisted that it was a perfectly normal operation. The Japanese had made many successful night attacks early in the Russo-Japanese war, but these had been against positions undefended by machine gun fire and curtains of artillery fire. When the Japanese reached their objective they were not in danger of being blasted out by high explosives and incidentally they were not fighting what has been called the most highly trained army on earth on the most concentrated front that has ever been known in military history.

But "Up and at them!" Sir Douglas Haig, who had "all his nerve with him," said to go ahead. At three-thirty a.m., a good hour before dawn, that wave of men three miles long was to rush into the night toward an invisible objective, with the darkness so thick that they could hardly recognize a figure ten yards away. Yet as one English soldier said, "You could see the German as soon as he saw you and you ought to be able to throw a bomb as quickly as he and a bayonet would have just as much penetration at three-thirty in the morning as at midday."

When I saw the battalions who were to take part in the attack marching up I realized, as they did not, the splendid and terrible hazard of success or failure, of life or death, which was to be theirs. Along the new roads they passed and then across the conquered ground, its uneven slopes made more uneven by continued digging and shell fire, and disappeared, and Night dropped her curtain on the field with no one knowing what morning would reveal.

The troops were in position; all was ready; all the lessons learned from the attack of July 1st were to be applied. At midnight there was no movement except of artillery caissons; gunners whose pieces two hours later were to speak with a fury of blasts were sound asleep beside their ammunition. The absolute order in this amazing network of all kinds of supplies and transport contributed to the suspense. Night bombardments we had already seen, and I would not dwell on this except that it had the same splendor by night that the storming of Contalmaison had by day.

The artillery observer for a fifteen-inch gun was a good-humored host. He was putting his "bit," as the British say, into Bazentin-le-Petit village and the only way we knew where Bazentin was in the darkness was through great flashes of light which announced the bursting of a fifteen-hundred-pound shell that had gone hurtling through the air with its hoarse, ponderous scream. All the slope up to the Ridge was merged in the blanket of night. Out of it came the regular flashes of guns for a while as the prelude to the unloosing of the tornado before the attack.

Now that we saw them all firing, for the first time we had some idea of the number that had been advanced into the conquered territory since July 1st. The ruins and the sticks of trees of Fricourt and Mametz with their few remaining walls stood out spectral in the flashes of batteries that had found nesting places among the débris. The whole slope had become a volcanic uproar. One might as well have tried to count the number of fireflies over a swamp as the flashes. The limitation of reckoning had been reached. Guns ahead of us and around us and behind us as usual, in a battle of competitive crashes among themselves, and near by we saw the figures of the gunners outlined in instants of weird lightning glow, which might include the horses of a caisson in a flicker of distinct silhouette flashed out of the night and then lost in the night, with the riders sitting as straight as if at drill. Every voice had one message, "This for the Ridge!" which was crowned by hell's tempest of shell-bursts to prepare the way for the rush by the infantry at "zero."

The thing was majestic, diabolical, beautiful, absurd—anything you wished to call it. Look away from the near-by guns where the faces of the gunners were illumined and you could not conceive of the scene as being of human origin; but mixing awed humility with colossal egoism in varying compounds of imagination and fact, you might think of your little group of observers as occupying a point of view in space where one planet hidden in darkness was throwing aerolites at another hidden in darkness striking it with mighty explosions, and the crashes and screams were the sound of the missiles on their unlighted way.

It was still dark when three-thirty came and pyrotechnics were added to the display, which I could not think of as being in any sense pyrotechnical, when out of the blanket as signals from the planet's surface in the direction of some new manoeuver appeared showers of glowing red sparks, which rose to a height of a hundred feet with a breadth of thirty or forty feet, it seemed at that distance. One shower was in the neighborhood of Ovillers, one at La Boisselle and one this side of Longueval. Then in the distance beyond Longueval the sky was illumined by a great conflagration not on the fireworks program, which must have been a German ammunition dump exploded by British shells.

It was our planet, now, and a particular portion of it in Picardy. No imaginative translation to space could hold any longer. With the charge going in, the intimate human element was supreme. The thought of those advancing waves of men in the darkness made the fiery display a dissociated objective spectacle. On the Ridge more signal flares rose and those illumining the dark masses of foliage must be Bazentin Wood gained, and those beyond must be in the Bazentin villages, Little Bazentin and Big Bazentin, though neither of them, like most of the villages, numbering a dozen to fifty houses could be much smaller and be called villages.

This was all the objective. Yes, but though the British had arrived, as the signals showed, could they remain? It seemed almost too good to be true. And that hateful Trônes Wood? Had we taken that, too, as a part of the tidal wave of a broad attack instead of trying to take it piecemeal?

Our suspense was intensified by the thought that this action might be the turning-point in the first stage of the great Somme battle. We strained our eyes into the darkness studying, as a mariner studies the sky, the signs with which we had grown familiar as indicative of results. There was a good augury in the comparatively slight German shell fire in response, though we were reminded that it might at any minute develop with sudden ferocity.

Now the flashes of the guns grew dim. A transformation more wonderful than artillery could produce, that of night into day, was in process. Not a curtain but the sun's ball of fire, undisturbed by any efforts of the human beings on a few square miles of earth, was holding to his schedule in as kindly a fashion as ever toward planets which kept at a respectful distance from his molten artillery concentration.

Out of the blanket which hid the field appeared the great welts of chalk of the main line trenches, then the lesser connecting ones; the woods became black patches and the remaining tree-trunks gaunt, still and dismal sentinels of the gray ruins of the villages, until finally all the conformations of the scarred and tortured slope were distinct in the first fresh light of a brilliant summer's day. Where the blazes had been was the burst of black smoke from shells and we saw that it was still German fire along the visible line of the British objective, assuring us that the British had won the ground which they had set out to take and were holding it.

"Up and at them!" had done the trick this time, and trick it was; a trick or stratagem, to use the higher sounding word; a trick in not waiting on the general attack for the taking of Trônes according to obvious tactics, but including Trônes in the sweep; a trick in the daring way that the infantry was sent in ahead of the answering German curtain of fire.

All the news was good that day. The British had swept through Bazentin Wood and taken the Bazentin villages. They held Trônes Wood and were in Delville and High Woods. A footing was established on the Ridge where the British could fight for final mastery on even terms with the enemy. "Slight losses" came the reports from corps and divisions and confirmation of official reports was seen in the paucity of the wounded arriving at the casualty clearing stations and in the faces of officers and men everywhere. Even British phlegm yielded to exhilaration.

XIV

THE CAVALRY GOES IN

The "dodo" band—Cavalry a luxury—Cavalry, however, may not be discarded—What ten thousand horse might do—A taste of action for the cavalry—An "incident"—Horses that had the luck to "go in"—Cavalrymen who showed signs of action—The novelty of a cavalry action—A camp group—Germans caught unawares—Horsemen and an aeroplane—Retiring in good order—Just enough casualties to give the fillip of danger to recollection.

Sometimes a squadron of cavalry, British or Indian, survivors of the ardent past, intruded in a mechanical world of motor trucks and tractors drawing guns. With outward pride these lean riders of burnished, sleek horses, whose broad backs bore gallantly the heavy equipment, concealed their irritation at idleness while others fought. They brought picturesqueness and warm-blooded life to the scene. Such a merciless war of steel contrivances needed some ornament. An old sergeant one day, when the cavalry halted beside his battalion which was resting, in an exhibit of affectionate recollection exclaimed:

"It's good to stroke a horse's muzzle again! I was in the Dragoon Guards once, myself."

Sometimes the cavalry facetiously referred to itself as the "Dodo" band, with a galling sense of helplessness under its humor; and others had thought of it as being like the bison preserved in the Yellowstone Park lest the species die out.

A cynical general said that a small force of cavalry was a luxury which such a vast army of infantry and guns might afford. In his opinion, even if we went to the Rhine, the cavalry would melt in its first charge under the curtains of fire and machine gun sprays of the rearguard actions of the retreating enemy. He had never been in the cavalry, and any squadron knew well what he and all of those who shared his views were thinking whenever it passed over the brow of a hill that afforded a view of the welter of shell fire over a field cut with shell-craters and trenches which are pitfalls for horses. Yet it returned gamely and with fastidious application to its practice in crossing such obstacles in case the command to "go in" should ever come. Such preparations were suggestive to extreme skeptics of the purchase of robes and the selection of a suitable hilltop of a religious cult which has appointed the day for ascension.

Excepting a dash in Champagne, not since trench warfare began had the cavalry had any chance. The thought of action was an hypothesis developed from memory of charges in the past. Aeroplanes took the cavalry's place as scouts, machine guns and rifles emplaced behind a first-line trench which had succumbed to an attack took its place as rearguard, and aeroplane patrols its place as screen.

Yet any army, be it British, French, or German, which expected to carry through an offensive would not turn all its cavalry into infantry. This was parting with one of the old three branches of horse, foot and gun and closing the door to a possible opportunity. If the Japanese had had cavalry ready at the critical moment after Mukden, its mobility would have hampered the Russian retreat, if not turned it into a rout. When you need cavalry you need it "badly," as the cowboy said about his six-shooter.

Should the German line ever be broken and all that earth-tied, enormous, complicated organization, with guns emplaced and its array of congested ammunition dumps and supply depots, try to move on sudden demand, what added confusion ten thousand cavalry would bring! What rich prizes would await it as it galloped through the breach and in units, separating each to its objective according to evolutions suited to the new conditions, dismounted machine guns to cover roads and from chosen points sweep their bullets into wholesale targets! The prospect of those few wild hours, when any price in casualties might be paid for results, was the inspiration of dreams when hoofs stamped in camps at night or bits champed as lances glistened in line above khaki-colored steel helmets on morning parade.

A taste, just a taste, of action the cavalry was to have, owing to the success of the attack of July 14th, which manifestly took the Germans by surprise between High and Delville Woods and left them staggering with second-line trenches lost and confusion ensuing, while guns and scattered battalions were being hurried up by train in an indiscriminate haste wholly out of keeping with German methods of prevision and precision. The breach was narrow, the field of action for horses limited; but word came back that over the plateau which looked away to Bapaume between Delville and High Woods there were few shell-craters and no German trenches or many Germans in sight as day dawned.

Gunners rubbed their eyes at the vision as they saw the horsemen pass and infantry stood amazed to see them crossing trenches, Briton and Indian on their way up the slope to the Ridge. How they passed the crest without being decimated by a curtain of fire would be a mystery if there were any mysteries in this war, where everything seems to be worked out like geometry or chemical formulæ. The German artillery being busy withdrawing heavy guns and the other guns preoccupied after the startling results of an attack not down on the calendar for that day did not have time to "get on" the cavalry when they were registered on different targets—which is suggestive of what might come if the line were cleft over a broad front. A steel band is strong until it breaks, which may be in many pieces.

"Did you see the charge?" you ask. No, nor even the ride up the slope, being busy elsewhere and not knowing that the charge was going to take place. I could only seek out the two squadrons who participated in the "incident," as the staff called it, after it was over. Incident is the right word for a military sense of proportion. When the public in England and abroad heard that the cavalry were "in" they might expect to hear next day that the Anglo-French Armies were in full pursuit of the broken German Armies to the Rhine, when no such outcome could be in the immediate program unless German numbers were cut in two or the Prussian turned Quaker.

An incident! Yes, but something to give a gallop to the pen of the writer after the monotony of gunfire and bombing. I was never more eager to hear an account of any action than of this charge—a cavalry charge, a charge of cavalry, if you please, on the Western front in July, 1916.

In one of the valleys back of the front out of sight of the battle there were tired, tethered horses with a knowing look in their eyes, it seemed to me, and a kind of superior manner toward the sleek, fresh horses which had not had the luck to "go in"; and cavalrymen were lying under their shelters fast asleep, their clothing and accoutrements showing the unmistakable signs of action. We heard from their officers the story of both the Dragoon Guards and the Deccan Horse (Indian) who had known what it was to ride down a German in the open.

The shade of Phil Sheridan might ponder on what the world was coming to that we make much of such a small affair; but he would have felt all the glowing satisfaction of these men if he had waited as long as they for any kind of a cavalry action. The accounts of the two squadrons may go together. Officers were shaving and aiming for enough water to serve as a substitute for a bath. The commander with his map could give you every detail with a fond, lingering emphasis on each one, as a battalion commander might of a first experience in a trench raid when later the same battalion would make an account of a charge in battle which was rich with incidents of hand-to-hand encounters and prisoners breached from dugouts into an "I-came-I-saw" narrative, and not understand why further interest should be shown by the inquirer in what was the everyday routine of the business of war. For the trite saying that everything is relative does not forfeit any truth by repetition.

The cavalry had done everything quite according to tactics, which would only confuse the layman. The wonder was that any of it had come back alive. On that narrow front it had ridden out toward the Germany Army with nothing between the cavalry and the artillery and machine guns which had men on horses for targets. In respect to days when to show a head above a trench meant death the thing was stupefying, incredible. These narrators forming a camp group, with lean, black-bearded, olive-skinned Indians in attendance bringing water in horse-buckets for the baths, and the sight of kindly horses' faces smiling at you, and the officers themselves horsewise and with the talk and manner of horsemen—only they made it credible. How real it was to them! How real it became to me!

There had been some Germans in hiding in the grass who were taken unawares by this rush of gallopers with lances. Every participant agreed as to the complete astonishment of the enemy. It was equivalent to a football player coming into the field in ancient armor and the more of a surprise considering that those Germans had been sent out after a morning full of surprises to make contact with the British and reëstablish the broken line.

Not dummies of straw this time for the lance's sharp point, but startled men in green uniform—the vision which had been in mind when every thrust was made at the dummies! This was what cavalry was for, the object of all the training. It rode through quite as it would have ridden fifty or a hundred years ago. A man on the ground, a man on a horse! This feature had not changed.

"You actually got some?"

"Oh, yes!"

"On the lances?"

"Yes."

From the distance came the infernal sound of guns in their threshing contest of explosions which made this incident more impressive than any account of a man buried by shells, of isolated groups holding out in dugouts, or of venturesome soldiers catching and tossing back German bombs at the man who threw them, because it was unique on the Somme. Both British and Indians had had the same kind of an opportunity. After riding through they wheeled and rode back in the accepted fashion of cavalry.

By this time some of the systematic Germans had recollected that a part of their drill was how to receive a cavalry charge, and when those who had not run or been impaled began firing and others stood ready with their bayonets but with something of the manner of men who were not certain whether they were in a trance or not, according to the account, a German machine gun began its wicked staccato as another feature of German awakening to the situation.

This brings us to the most picturesque incident of the "incident." Most envied of all observers of the tournament was an aviator who looked down on a show bizarre even in the annals of aviation. The German planes had been driven to cover, which gave the Briton a fair field. A knightly admiration, perhaps a sense of fellowship not to say sympathy with the old arm of scouting from the new, possessed him; or let it be that he could not resist a part in such a rare spectacle which was so tempting to sporting instinct. He swooped toward that miserable, earth-tied turtle of a machine gun and emptied his drum into it. He was not over three hundred feet, all agree, above the earth, when not less than ten thousand feet was the rule.

"It was jolly fine of him!" as the cavalry put it. To have a charge and then to have that happen—well, it was not so bad to be in the cavalry. The plane drew fire by setting all the Germans to firing at it without hitting it, and the machine gun, whether silenced or not, ceased to bother the cavalry, which brought back prisoners to complete a well-rounded adventure before withdrawing lest the German guns, also entering into the spirit of the situation, should blow men and horses off the Ridge instead of leaving them to retire in good order.

Casualties: about the same number of horses as men. Riders who had lost their horses mounted riderless horses. A percentage of one in six or seven had been hit, which was the most amazing part of it; indeed, the most joyful part, completing the likeness to the days when war still had the element of sport. There had been killed and wounded or it would not have been a battle, but not enough to cast a spell of gloom; just enough to be a part of the gambling hazard of war and give the fillip of danger to recollection.

XV

ENTER THE ANZACS

Newfoundland sets the pace—Australia and New Zealand lands that breed men—Australians "very proud, individual men"—Geographical isolation a cause of independence—The "Anzacs'" idea of fighting—Sir Charles Birdwood—How he taught his troops discipline—Bean and Ross—Difference between Australians and New Zealanders—The Australian uniform and physique—A dollar and a half a day—General Birdwood and his men—Australian humor.

It was British troops exclusively which started the Grand Offensive if we except the Newfoundland battalion which alone had the honor of representing the heroism of North America on July 1st; for people in passing the Grand Banks which makes them think of Newfoundland are wont to regard it as a part of Canada, when it is a separate colony whose fishermen and frontiersmen were attached to a British division that went to Gallipoli with a British brigade and later shared the fate of British battalions in the attack on the Thiepval-Gommecourt sector.

On that famous day in Picardy the Newfoundlanders advanced into the smoke of the curtains of fire unflinchingly and kept on charging the machine guns. Survivors and the wounded who crept back at night across No Man's Land had no need to trumpet their heroism. All the army knew it. Newfoundland had set the pace for the other clans from oversea.

It was British troops, too, which took Contalmaison and Mametz, Bernafay and Trônes Woods and who carried out all the attack of July 15th, with the exception of the South African brigade which stormed Delville Wood with the tearing enthusiasm of a rush for a new diamond mine.

Whenever the troops from oversea are not mentioned you may be sure that it is the British, the home troops, who are doing the fighting, their number being about ten to one of the others with the one out of ten representing double the number of those who fought on either side in any great pitched battle in our Civil War. After the Newfoundlanders and South Africans, who were few but precious, the Australians, an army of themselves, came to take their part in the Somme battle.

I have never been in Australia or New Zealand, but this I know that when the war is over I am going. I want to see the land that breeds such men. They are free men if ever there were such; free whether they come from town or from bush. I had heard of their commonwealth ideas, their State-owned utilities, their socialistic inclinations, which might incline you to think that they were all of the same State-cut pattern of manhood; but I had heard, too, how they had restricted immigration of Orientals and limited other immigration by method if not by law, which was suggestive of a tendency to keep the breed to itself, as I understood from my reading.

Whenever I saw an Australian I thought: "Here is a very proud, individual man," but also an Australian, particularly an Australian. Some people thought that there was a touch of insolence in his bearing when he looked you straight in the eye as much as to say: "The best thing in the world is to be an upstanding member of the human race who is ready to prove that he is as good as any other. If you don't think so, well—" There was no doubt about the Australian being brave. This was as self-evident as that the pine is straight and the beech is hard wood.

The Australians came from a great distance. This you knew without geographical reference. Far away in their island continent they have been working out their own destiny, not caring for interference from the outside. To put it in strong language, there is a touch of the "I don't care a rap for anybody who does not care a rap for me" in their extreme moments of independence. It is refreshing that a whole population may have an island continent to themselves and carry on in this fashion.

They had had an introduction to universal service which was also characteristic of their democracy and helpful in time of war. The "Anzac" had caught the sense of its idea (before other English-speaking people) not to let others do your fighting for you but all "join in the scrum." Orientals might crave the broad spaces of a new land, in which event if they ever took Australia and New Zealand they would not be bothered by many survivors of the white population, because most of the Anzacs would be dead—this being particularly the kind of people the Anzacs are as I knew them in France, which was not a poor trial ground of their quality.

When they went to Gallipoli it was said that they had no discipline; and certainly at first discipline did irritate them as a snaffle bit irritates a high-spirited horse. "Little Kitch," as the stalwart Anzacs called the New Army Englishman, thought that they broke all the military commandments of the drill-grounds in a way that would be their undoing. I rather think that it might have been the undoing of Little Kitch, with his stubborn, methodical, phlegmatic, "stick-it" courage; but after the Australians had fought the Turk a while it was evident that they knew how to fight, and their general, Sir Charles Birdwood, supplied the discipline which is necessary if fighting power is not to be wasted in misplaced emotion.

Lucky Birdwood to command the Australians and lucky Australians to have him as commander! It was he who in choosing a telegraph code word made up "Anzac" for the Australian-New Zealand corps, which at once became the collective term for the combination. What a test he put them to and they put him to! He had to prove himself to them before he could develop the Anzacs into a war unit worthy of their fighting quality. Such is democracy where man judges man by standards, set, in this case, by Australian customs.

When he understood them he knew why he was fortunate. He was one of them and at the same time a stiff disciplinarian. They objected to saluting, but he taught them to salute in a way that did not make saluting seem the whole thing—this was what they resented—but a part of the routine. It was said that he knew every man in the corps by name, which shows how stories will grow around a commander who rises at five and retires at midnight and has a dynamic ubiquity in keeping in touch with his men. Such a force included some "rough customers" who might mistake war for a brawler's opportunity; but Sir Charles had a way with them that worked out for their good and the good of the corps.

Though they were of a free type of democracy, the Australian government, either from inherent sense or as the result of distance, as critics might say, or owing to General Birdwood's gift of having his way, did not handicap the Australians as heavily as they might have been handicapped under the circumstances by officers who were skilful in politics without being skilful in war.

As publicist the Australians had Bean, a trained journalist, a red-headed blade of a man who was an officer among officers and a man among men and held the respect of all by Australian qualities. If there could be only one chronicler allowed, then Bean's choice had the applause of a corps, though Bean says that Australia is full of just as good journalists who did not have his luck. The New Zealanders had Ross to play the same part for them with equal loyalty and he was as much of a New Zealander as Bean was an Australian.

For, make no mistake, though the Australians and the New Zealanders might seem alike to the observer as they marched along a road, they are not, as you will find if you talk with them. The New Zealanders have islands of their own, not to mention that the Tasmanians have one, too. Besides, the New Zealanders include a Maori battalion and of all aborigines of lands where the white races have settled in permanence to build new nations, the Maoris have best accustomed themselves to civilization and are the highest type—a fact which every New Zealander takes as another contributing factor to New Zealand's excellence. Quiet men the New Zealanders, bearing themselves with the pride of Guardsmen whose privates all belong to superior old families, and New Zealanders every minute of every hour of the day, though you might think that civil war was imminent if you started them on a discussion about home politics.

Give any unit of an army some particular, readily distinguishable symbol, be it only a feather in the cap or a different headgear, and that lot becomes set apart from the others in a fashion that gives them *esprit de corps*. With the Scots it is the kilt and the different plaids. All the varied uniforms of regiments of the armies of olden days had this object. Modern war requires neutral tones and its necessary machinelike homogeneity may look askance at too much rivalry among units as tending toward each one acting by itself rather than in co-operation with the rest.

All the forces at the front except the Anzacs were in khaki and wore caps when not wearing steel helmets in the trenches or on the firing-line. The Australians were in slate-colored uniform and they wore looped-up soft hats. The hats accentuated the manner, the height and the sturdiness of the men whose physique was unsurpassed at the British front, and practically all were smooth-shaven. For generations they had had adequate nutrition and they had the capacity to absorb it, which generations from the slums may lack even if the food is forthcoming.

There was no reason why every man in Australia should not have enough to eat and, whether bush or city dweller, he was fond of the open air where he might exercise the year around. He had blown his lungs; he had fed well and came of a daring pioneer stock. When an Anzac battalion under those hats went swinging along the road it seemed as if the men were taking the road along with them, such was their vigorous tread. On leave in London they were equally conspicuous. Sometimes they used a little vermilion with the generosity of men who received a dollar and a half a day as their wage. It was the first time, in many instances, that they had seen the "old town" and they had come far and to-morrow might go back to France for the last time.

My first view of them in the trenches after they came from Gallipoli was in the flat country near Ypres whose mushiness is so detested by all soldiers. They had been used to digging trenches in dry hillsides, where they might excavate caves with solid walls. Here they had to fill sandbags with mud and make breastworks, which were frequently breached by shell fire. At first, they had been poor diggers; but when democracy learns its lesson by individual experience it is incorporated in every man and no longer is a question of orders. Now they were deepening communication trenches and thickening parapet walls and were mud-plastered by their labor.

Having risen at General Birdwood's hour of five to go with him on inspection I might watch his methods, and it means something to men to have their corps commander thus early among them when a drizzly rain is softening the morass under foot. He stopped and asked the privates how they were in a friendly way and they answered with straight-away candor. Then he gave some directions about improvements with a we-are-all-working-together suggestiveness, but all the time he was the general. These privates were not without their Australian sense of humor, which is dry; and in answer to the inquiry about how he was one said:

"All right, except we'd like a little rum, sir."

In cold weather the distribution of a rum ration was at the disposition of a commander, who in most instances did not give it. This stalwart Australian evidently had not been a teetotaler.

"We'll give you some rum when you have made a trench raid and taken some prisoners," the general replied.

"It might be an incentive, sir!" said the soldier very respectfully.

"No Australian should need such an incentive!" answered the general, and passed on.

"Yes, sir!" was the answer of another soldier to the question if he had been in Gallipoli.

"Wounded?"

"Yes, sir."

"How?"

"I was examining a bomb, sir, to find out how it was made and it went off to my surprise, sir!"

There was not even a twinkle of the eye accompanying the response, yet I was not certain that this big fellow from the bush had been wounded in that way. I suspected him of a quiet joke.

"Throw them at the Germans next time," said the general.

"Yes, sir. It's safer!"

Returning after that long morning of characteristic routine, as we passed through a village where Australians were billeted one soldier failed to salute. When the general stopped him his hand shot up in approved fashion as he recognized his commander and he said contritely, with the touch of respect of a man to the leader in whom he believes:

"I did not see that it was you, sir!"

The general had on a mackintosh with the collar turned up, which concealed his rank.

"But you might see that it was an officer."

"Yes, sir."

"And you salute officers."

"Yes, sir."

Which he would hereafter now that it was General Birdwood's order, though this everlasting raising of your hand, as one Australian said, made you into a kind of human windmill when the world was so full of officers. Gradually all came to salute, and when an Australian salutes he does it in a way that is a credit to Australia.

After a period of fighting a tired division retired from the battle front and a fresh one took the place. Thus, following the custom of the circulation of troops by the armies of both sides, whether at Verdun or on the Somme, the day arrived when along the road toward the front came the Australian battalions, hardened and disciplined by trench warfare, keen-edged in spirit, and ready for the bold task which awaited them at Pozières. This time the New Zealanders were not along.

XVI

THE AUSTRALIANS AND A WINDMILL

The windmill upon the hill—Pozières—Its topography—Warlike intensity of the Australians—A "stiff job"—An Australian chronicler—Incentives to Australian efficiency—German complaint that the Australians came too fast—Clockwork efficiency—Man-to-man business—Sunburned, gaunt battalions from the vortex—The fighting on the Ridge—Mouquet Farm— A contest of individuality against discipline—"Advance, Australia!"—New Zealanders—South Africans.

When I think of the Australians in France I always think of a windmill. This is not implying that they were in any sense Quixotic or that they tilted at a windmill, there being nothing left of the windmill to tilt at when their capture of its ruins became the crowning labor of their first tour on the Somme front.

In their progress up that sector of the Ridge the windmill came after Pozières, as the ascent of the bare mountain peak comes after the reaches below the timber line. Pozières was beyond La Boisselle and Ovillers-la-Boisselle, from which the battle movement swung forward at the hinge of the point where the old first-line German fortifications had been broken on July 1st.

To think of Pozières will be to think of the Australians as long as the history of the Somme battle endures. I read an interview in a New York paper with the Chief of Staff of the German Army opposite the British in which he must have been correctly quoted, as his remarks passed the censorship. He said that the loss of Pozières was a blunder. I liked his frankness in laying the blame on a subordinate who, if he also had spoken, might have mentioned the presence of the Australians as an excuse, which, personally, I think is an excellent one.

Difficult as it now becomes to keep any sequence in the operations when, at best, chronology ceases to be illuminative of phases, it is well here to explain that the attack of July 15th had not gained the whole Ridge on the front ahead of the broad stretch of ruptured first line. Besides, the Ridge is not like the roof of a house, but a most illusive series of irregular knolls with small plateaus or valleys between, a sort of miniature broken tableland. The foothold gained on July 15th meant no broad command of vision down the slope to the main valley on the other side. Even a shoulder five or ten feet higher than the neighboring ground meant a barrier to artillery observation which shells would not blast away; and the struggle for such positions was to go on for weeks.

Pozières, then, was on the way to the Ridge and its possession would put the formidable defenses of Thiepval in a salient, thus enabling the British to strike it from the side as well as in front, which is the aim of all strategy whether it works in mobile divisions in an open field or is biting and tearing its way against field fortifications. Therefore, the Germans had good reason to hold Pozières, which protected first-line trenches that had required twenty months of preparation. Wherever they could keep the Briton or the Frenchman from forcing the fight into the open which made the contest an even one in digging, they were saving life and ammunition by nests of redoubts and dugouts.

The reason that the Australians wanted to take Pozières was not so tactical as human in their minds. It was the village assigned to them and they wished to investigate it immediately and get established in the property that was to be theirs, once they took it, to hold in trust for the inhabitants. I had a fondness for watching them as they marched up to the front looking unreal in their steel helmets which they wore in place of the broad-brimmed hats. There was a sort of warlike intensity about them which may come from the sunlight of an island continent reflecting the histrionic adaptability of appearances to the task in hand.

Their first objective was to be the main street. They had a "stiff job" ahead, as everybody agreed, and so had the British troops operating on their right.

"This objective business has a highly educated sound, which might limit martial enthusiasm," said one Australian. "As I understand it, that's the line where we stop no matter how good the going and which we must reach no matter how hard the going."

Precisely. An Australian battalion needed a warning in the first instance lest it might keep on advancing, which meant that commanders would not know where it was in the shell-smoke and it might get "squeezed" for want of support on the right and left, as I have explained elsewhere. Certainly, warning was unnecessary in the second instance about the hard going.

Bean has all the details of the taking of Pozières; he knows what every battalion did, and I was going to say what every soldier did. When the Australians were in he was in making notes and when they were out he was out writing up his notes. His was intimate war correspondence about the fellows who came from all the districts of his continent, his home folks. I am only expressing the impressions of one who had glimpses of the Australians while the battle was raging elsewhere.

Of course, skeptics had said that Gallipoli was one thing and the Somme another and the Australian man-to-man method might receive a shock from Prussian system; but, then, skeptics had said that the British could not make an army in two years. The Australians knew what was in the skeptics' minds, which was further incentive. They had a general whom they believed in and they did not admit that any man on earth was a better man than an Australian. And their staff? Of course, when it takes forty years to make a staff how could the Australians have one that could hold its own with the Germans? And this was what the Australians had to do, staff and man: beat the Germans.

When with clockwork promptness came the report that they had taken all of their objectives it showed that they were up to the standard of their looks and their staff signals were working well. They had a lot of prisoners, too, who complained that the Australians came on too fast. Meanwhile, they were on one side of the street and the Germans on the other, hugging débris and sniping at one another. Now the man-to-man business began to count. The Australian got across the street; he went after the other fellow; he made a still hunt of it. This battle had become a personal matter which pleased their sense of individualism; for it is not bred into Australians to be afraid if they are out alone after dark.

Having worked beyond their first objective, when they were given as their second the rest of the village they took it; and they were not "biffed" out of it, either. What was the use of yielding ground when you would have to make another charge in order to regain what had been lost? They were not that kind of arithmeticians, they said. They believed in addition not subtraction in an offensive campaign.

So they stuck, though the Germans made repeated daring counter-attacks and poured in shell fire from the guns up Thiepval way and off Bapaume way with hellish prodigality. For the German staff was evidently much out of temper about the "blunder" and for many weeks to come were to continue pounding Pozières. If they could not shake the Australian out of the village they meant to make him pay heavy taxes and to try to kill his reliefs and stop his supplies. How the Australians managed to get food and men up through the communication trenches under the unceasing inferno over that bare slope is tribute to their skill in slipping out and in between its blasts.

Not only were they able to hold, but they kept on attacking. Every day we heard that they had taken more ground and whenever we went out to have a look the German lines were always a little farther back. One day we were asking if the Australians were in the cemetery yet; the next day they were and the next they had more of it as they worked their way uphill, fighting from grave to grave; and the next day they had mastered all of it, thanks to a grim persistence which some had said would not comport with their highstrung temperament.

The windmill was a landmark crowning the Ridge; as fair a target as ever artillery ranged on—a gunner's delight. After having been knocked into splinters the splinters were spread about by high explosives which reduced the stone base to fragments.

Sunburned, gaunt battalions came out of the vortex for a turn of rest. With helmets battered by shrapnel bullets, after nights in the rain and broiling hot days, their faces grimy and unshaven, their clothes torn and spotted, they were still Australians who looked you in the eye with a sense of having proved their birthright as free men. Sometimes the old spirit incited by the situation got out of bonds. One night when a company rose up to the charge the company next in line called out, "Where are you going?" and on the reply, "We've orders to take that trench in front," the company that had no orders to advance exclaimed, "Here, we're going to join in the scrum!" and they did, taking more trench than the plan required.

The fierce period of the battle was approaching when fighting on the Ridge was to be a bloody, wrestling series of clinches. Now trenches could not be dug on that bold, treeless summit. As soon as an aeroplane spotted a line developing out of the field of shell-craters the guns filled the trench and then proceeded to pound it into the fashionable style for farming land on the Ridge.

Trenches out of the question, it became a war among shell-craters. Here a soldier ensconced himself with rifle and bombs or a machine gunner deepened the hole with his spade for the gun. This was "scrapping" to the Australians' taste. It called for individual nerve and daring on that shell-swept, pestled earth, creeping up to new positions or back for water and food by night, lying "doggo" by day and waiting for a counter-attack by the Germans, who were always the losers in this grim, stealthy advance.

In Mouquet Farm the Germans had dugouts whose elaborateness was realized only after they were taken. A battalion could find absolute security in them. Long galleries ran back to entrances in areas safe from shell fire. Overhead no semblance of farm buildings was left by British and Australian guns. When I visited the ruins later I could not tell how many buildings there had been; and Mouquet Farm was not the only strong point that the Germans had to fall back on, let it be said. In the underground tunnels and chambers the Germans gathered for their counter-attacks, which they attempted with something of their old precision and courage.

This was the opportunity of the machine gunners in shell-craters and the snipers and the curtain of artillery fire. Sometimes the Australians allowed the attack to get good headway. They even left gaps in their lines for the game to enter the net before they began firing; and again, when a broken German charge sought flight its remnants faced an impassable curtain of fire which fenced them in and they dropped into shell-craters and held up their hands, which was the only thing to do.

Soon the Germans learned, too, how to make the most of shell-craters. The harder the Australians fought the greater the spur to German pride not to be beaten by these supposedly undisciplined, untrained men. The Germans called for more guns and got them. Mouquet Farm became a fortress of machine guns. It was not taken by the Australians—their successors took what was left of it. The nearer they came to the crest which was their supreme goal the ghastlier and more concentrated grew the shell fire, as the German guns had only to range on the skyline. But this equally applied to Australian gunners as the Germans were crowded toward the summit where the débris of the windmill remained, till finally they had to fall back to the other side.

Then they tried sweeping over the Ridge from the cover of the reverse slope in counter-attacks, only to be whipped by machine gun fire, lashed by shrapnel and crushed by high explosives—themselves mixed with the ruins of the windmill. At last they gave up the effort. It was not in German discipline to make any more attempts.

The Australians had the windmill as much as anyone had it as, for a time, it was in No Man's Land where blasts of shells would permit of no occupation. But the symbol for which it stood was there in readiness as a jumping-off place for the sweep-down into the valley later on when the Canadians should take the place of the Australians; and before they retired they could look in triumph across at Thiepval and down on Courcelette and Martinpuich and past the valley to Bapaume.

The development of the campaign had given the Australians work suited to their bent when this war of machinery, attaining its supreme complexity on the Somme, left the human machine between walls of shell fire to fight it out individually against the human machine, in a contest of will, courage, audacity, alertness and resource, man to man. "Advance, Australia!" is the Australian motto; and the Australians advanced.

The New Zealanders had their part elsewhere and played it in the New Zealand way.

"They have never failed to take an objective set them," said a general after the taking of Flers, "and they have always gained their positions with slight losses."

Could there be higher praise? Success and thrift, courage and skill in taking cover! For the business of a soldier is to do his enemy the maximum of damage with the minimum to himself, as anyone may go on repeating. Probably the remark of the New Zealanders in answer to the commander's praise would be, "Thank you. Why not?" as if this were what the New Zealanders expected of themselves. They take much for granted about New Zealand, without being boastful.

"A blooming quiet lot that keeps to themselves," said a British soldier, "but likable when you get to know them."

You might depend upon the average New Zealand private for an interesting talk about social organization, municipal improvements, and human welfare under government direction. The standard of individual intelligence and education was high and it seemed to make good fighting men.

The Australians had had to grub their way foot by foot, and the South Africans on July 15th with veldt gallantry had swept into Delville Wood, which was to be a shambles for two months, and stood off with a thin line the immense forces of hastily gathered reserves which the Germans threw at this vital point which had been lost in a surprise attack.

All this on the way up to the Ridge. The New Zealanders were to play a part in the same movement as the Canadians after the Ridge was taken. They were in the big sweep down from the Ridge over a broad front. Across the open for about two miles they had to go, fair targets for shell fire; and they went, keeping their order as if on parade, working out each evolution with soldierly precision including coöperation with the "tanks." They were at their final objective on schedule time, accomplishing the task with amazingly few casualties and so little fuss that it seemed a kind of skilful field-day manoeuver. All that they took they held and still held it when the mists of autumn obscured artillery observation and they were relieved from the quagmire for their turn of rest.

XVII

THE HATEFUL RIDGE

Grinding of courage of three powerful races—A ridge that will be famous—
Germans on the defensive—Efforts to maintain their *morale*—Gas shells—
Summer heat, dust and fatigue—Prussian hatred of the British—Dead
bodies strapped to guns—Guillemont a granulation of bricks and mortar and
earth—"We've only to keep at them, sir"—Stalking machine guns—Machine
guns in craters—British cheerfulness—The war will be over when it is
won—Soldiers talk shop—An incident of brutal militarism—Simple rules
for surviving shell fire—A "happy home" with a shell arriving every
minute—Business-like monotony of the battle—Insignificance of one man
among millions—A victory of position, of will, of *morale*!

Sometimes it occurred to one to consider what history might say about the
Ridge and also to wonder how much history, which pretends to know all,
would really know. Thus, one sought perspective of the colossal significance
of the uninterrupted battle whose processes numbed the mind and to
distinguish the meaning of different stages of the struggle. Nothing had so
well reflected the character of the war or of its protagonists, French, British
and German, as this grinding of resources, of courage, and of will of three
powerful races.

We are always talking of phases as the result of natural human speculation
and tendency to set events in groups. Observers also may gratify this
inclination as well as the contemporaneous military expert writing from his
maps. It is historically accepted, I think, that the first decisive phase was the
battle of the Marne when Paris was saved. The second was Verdun, when
the Germans again sought a decision on the Western front by an offensive
of sledgehammer blows against frontal positions; and, perhaps, the third
came when on the Ridge the British and the French kept up their grim,
insistent, piecemeal attacks, holding the enemy week in and week out on the
defensive, aiming at mastery as the scales trembled in the new turn of the
balance and initiative passed from one side to the other in the beginning of
that new era.

This scarred slope with its gentle ascent, this section of farming land with its
woods growing more ragged every day from shell fire, with its daily and
nightly thunders, its trickling procession of wounded and prisoners down the
communication trenches speaking the last word in human bravery, industry,
determination and endurance—this might one day be not only the
monument to the positions of all the battalions that had fought, its copses,
its villages, its knolls famous to future generations as is Little Round Top
with us, but in its monstrous realism be an immortal expression, unrealized

by those who fought, of a commander's iron will and foresight in gaining that supremacy in arms, men and material which was the genesis of the great decision.

The German had not yielded his offensive at Verdun after the attack of July 1st. At least, he still showed the face of initiative there while he rested content that at the same time he could maintain his front intact on the Somme. The succeeding attack of July 15th broke his confidence with its suggestion that the confusion in his lines would be too dangerous if it happened over a broader front for him to consider anything but the defensive. Thus, the Allied offensive had broken his offensive.

Now he began drawing away his divisions from the Verdun sector, bringing guns to answer the British and French fire and men whose prodigal use alone could enforce his determination to maintain *morale* and prevent any further bold strokes such as that of July 15th.

His sausage balloons began to reappear in the sky as the summer wore on; he increased the number of his aeroplanes; more of his five-point-nine howitzers were sending their compliments; he stretched out his shell fire over communication trenches and strong points; mustered great quantities of lachrymatory shells and for the first time used gas shells with a generosity which spoke his faith in their efficacy. The lachrymatory shell makes your eyes smart, and the Germans apparently considered this a great auxiliary to high explosives and shrapnel. Was it because of the success of the first gas attack at Ypres that they now placed such reliance in gas shells? The shell when it lands seems a "dud," which is a shell that has failed to explode; then it blows out a volume of gas.

"If one hit right under your nose," said a soldier, "and you hadn't your gas mask on, it might kill you. But when you see one fall you don't run to get a sniff in order to accommodate the Boche by asphyxiating yourself."

Another soldier suggested that the Germans had a big supply on hand and were working off the stock for want of other kinds. The British who by this time were settled in the offensive joked about the deluge of gas shells with a gallant, amazing humor. Going up to the Ridge was going to their regular duty. They did not shirk it or hail it with delight. They simply went, that was all, when it was a battalion's turn to go.

July heat became August heat as the grinding proceeded. The gunners worked in their shirts or stripped to the waist. Sweat streaks mapped the faces of the men who came out of the trenches. Stifling clouds of dust hung over the roads, with the trucks phantom-like as they emerged from the gritty mist and their drivers' eyes peered out of masks of gray which clung to their faces. A fall of rain came as a blessing to Briton and German alike. German prisoners worn with exhaustion had complexions the tint of their uniforms. If the British seemed weary sometimes, one had only to see the prisoners to realize that the defensive was suffering more than the offensive. The fatigue of some of the men was of the kind that one week's sleep or a month's rest will not cure; something fixed in their beings.

It was a new kind of fighting for the Germans. They smarted under it, they who had been used to the upper hand. In the early stages of the war their artillery had covered their well-ordered charges; they had been killing the enemy with gunfire. Now the Allies were returning the compliment; the shoe was on the other foot. A striking change, indeed, from "On to Paris!" the old battle-cry of leaders who had now come to urge these men to the utmost of endurance and sacrifice by telling them that if they did not hold against the relentless hammering of British and French guns what had been done to French villages would be done to their own.

Prisoners spoke of peace as having been promised as close at hand by their officers. In July the date had been set as Sept. 1st. Later, it was set as Nov. 1st. The German was as a swimmer trying to reach shore, in this case peace, with the assurance of those who urged him on that a few more strokes would bring him there. Thus have armies been urged on for years.

Those fighting did not have, as had the prisoners, their eyes opened to the vast preparations behind the British lines to carry on the offensive. Mostly the prisoners were amiable, peculiarly unlike the proud men taken in the early days of the war when confidence in their "system" as infallible was at its height. Yet there were exceptions. I saw an officer marching at the head of the survivors of his battalion along the road from Montauban one day with his head up, a cigar stuck in the corner of his mouth at an aggressive angle, his unshaven chin and dusty clothes heightening his attitude of "You go to ———, you English!"

The hatred of the British was a strengthening factor in the defense. Should they, the Prussians, be beaten by New Army men? No! Die first! said Prussian officers. The German staff might be as good as ever, but among the mixed troops—the old and the young, the hollow-chested and the square-shouldered, mouth-breathers with spectacles and bent fathers of families, vigorous boys in their late 'teens with the down still on their cheeks and hardened veterans survivors of many battles east and west—they were reverting appreciably to natural human tendencies despite the iron discipline.

It was Skobeloff, if I recollect rightly, who said that out of every hundred men twenty were natural fighters, sixty were average men who would fight under impulse or when well led, and twenty were timid; and armies were organized on the basis of the sixty average to make them into a whole of even efficiency in action. The German staff had supplied supreme finesse to this end. They had an army that was a machine; yet its units were flesh and blood and the pounding of shell fire and the dogged fighting on the Ridge must have an effect.

It became apparent through those two months of piecemeal advance that the sixty average men were not as good as they had been. The twenty "funk-sticks," in army phrase, were given to yielding themselves if they were without an officer, but the twenty natural fighters—well, human psychology does not change. They were the type that made the professional armies of other days, the brigands, too, and also those of every class of society to whom patriotic duty had become an exaltation approaching fanaticism. More fighting made them fight harder.

Such became members of the machine gun corps, which took an oath never to surrender, and led bombing parties and posted themselves in shell-craters to face the charges while shells fell thick around them, or remained up in the trench taking their chances against curtains of fire that covered an infantry charge, in the hope of being able to turn on their own bullet spray for a moment before being killed. Sometimes their dead bodies were found strapped to their guns, more often probably by their own request, as an insurance against deserting their posts, than by command.

Shell fire was the theatricalism of the struggle, the roar of guns its thunder; but night or day the sound of the staccato of that little arch devil of killing, the machine gun, coming from the Ridge seemed as true an expression of what was always going on there as a rattlesnake's rattle is of its character. Delville and High Woods and Guillemont and Longueval and the Switch Trench—these are symbolic names of that attrition, of the heroism of British persistence which would not take No for answer.

You might think that you had seen ruins until you saw those of Guillemont after it was taken. They were the granulation of bricks and mortar and earth mixed by the blasts of shell fire which crushed solids into dust and splintered splinters. Guillemont lay beyond Trônes Wood across an open space where the German guns had full play. There was a stone quarry on the outskirts, and a quarry no less than a farm like Waterlot, which was to the northward, and Falfemont, to the southward and flanking the village, formed shelter. It was not much of a quarry, but it was a hole which would be refuge for reserves and machine guns. The two farms, clear targets for British guns, had their deep dugouts whose roofs were reinforced by the ruins that fell upon them against penetration even by shells of large caliber. How the Germans fought to keep Falfemont! Once they sent out a charge with the bayonet to meet a British charge between walls of shell fire and there through the mist the steel was seen flashing and vague figures wrestling.

Guillemont and the farms won and Ginchy which lay beyond won and the British had their flank on high ground. Twice they were in Guillemont but could not remain, though as usual they kept some of their gains. It was a battle from dugout to dugout, from shelter to shelter of any kind burrowed in débris or in fields, with the British never ceasing here or elsewhere to continue their pressure. And the débris of a village had particular appeal; it yielded to the spade; its piles gave natural cover.

A British soldier returning from one of the attacks as he hobbled through Trônes Wood expressed to me the essential generalship of the battle. He was outwardly as unemotional as if he were coming home from his day's work, respectful and good-humored, though he had a hole in both arms from machine gun fire, a shrapnel wound in the heel, and seemed a trifle resentful of the added tribute of another shrapnel wound in his shoulder after he had left the firing-line and was on his way to the casualty clearing station. Insisting that he could lift the cigarette I offered him to his lips and light it, too, he said:

"We've only to keep at them, sir. They'll go."

So the British kept at them and so did the French at every point. Was Delville Wood worse than High Wood? This is too nice a distinction in torments to be drawn. Possess either of them completely and command of the Ridge in that section was won. The edge of a wood on the side away from your enemy was the easiest part to hold. It is difficult to range artillery on it because of restricted vision, and the enemy's shells aimed at it strike the trees and burst prematurely among his own men. Other easy, relatively easy, places to hold are the dead spaces of gullies and ravines. There you were out of fire and there you were not; there you could hold and there you could not. Machine gun fire and shell fire were the arbiters of topography more dependable than maps.

Why all the trees were not cut down by the continual bombardments of both sides was past understanding. There was one lone tree on the skyline near Longueval which I had watched for weeks. It still had a limb, yes, the luxury of a limb, the last time that I saw it, pointing with a kind of defiance in its immunity. Of course it had been struck many times. Bits of steel were imbedded in its trunk; but only a direct hit on the trunk will bring down a tree. Trees may be slashed and whittled and nicked and gashed and still stand; and when villages have been pulverized except for the timbering of the houses, a scarred shade tree will remain.

Thus, trees in Delville Wood survived, naked sticks among fallen and splintered trunks and upturned roots. How any man could have survived was the puzzling thing. None could if he had remained there continuously and exposed himself; but man is the most cunning of animals. With gas mask and eye-protectors ready, steel helmet on his head and his faithful spade to make himself a new hole whenever he moved, he managed the incredible in self-protection. Earth piled back of a tree-trunk would stop bullets and protect his body from shrapnel. There he lay and there a German lay opposite him, except when attacks were being made.

Not getting the northern edge of the woods the British began sapping out in trenches to the east toward Ginchy, where the map contours showed the highest ground in that neighborhood. New lines of trenches kept appearing on the map, often with group names such as Coffee Alley, Tea Lane and Beer Street, perhaps. Out in the open along the irregular plateau the shells were no more kindly, the bombing and the sapping no less diligent all the way to the windmill, where the Australians were playing the same kind of a game. With the actual summit gained at certain points, these had to be held pending the taking of the whole, or of enough to permit a wave of men to move forward in a general attack without its line being broken by the resistance of strong points, which meant confusion.

Before any charge the machine guns must be "killed." No initiative of pioneer or Indian scout surpassed that exhibited in conquering machine gun positions. When a big game hunter tells you about having stalked tigers, ask him if he has ever stalked a machine gun to its lair.

As for the nature of the lair, here is one where a Briton "dug himself in" to be ready to repulse any counter-attack to recover ground that the British had just won. Some layers of sandbags are sunk level with the earth with an excavation back of them large enough for a machine gun standard and to give the barrel swing and for the gunner, who back of this had dug himself a well four or five feet deep of sufficient diameter to enable him to huddle at the bottom in "stormy weather." He was general and army, too, of his little establishment. In the midst of shells and trench mortars, with bullets whizzing around his head, he had to keep a cool aim and make every pellet which he poured out of his gun muzzle count against the wave of men coming toward him who were at his mercy if he could remain alive for a few minutes and keep his head.

He must not reveal his position before his opportunity came. All around where this Briton had held the fort there were shell-craters like the dots of close shooting around a bull's-eye; no tell-tale blood spots this time, but a pile of two or three hundred cartridge cases lying where they had fallen as they were emptied of their cones of lead. Luck was with the occupant, but not with another man playing the same game not far away. Broken bits of gun and fragments of cloth mixed with earth explained the fate of a German machine gunner who had emplaced his piece in the same manner.

Before a charge, crawl up at night from shell-crater to shell-crater and locate the enemy's machine guns. Then, if your own guns and the trench mortars do not get them, go stalking with supplies of bombs and remember to throw yours before the machine gunner, who also has a stock for such emergencies, throws his. When a machine gun begins rattling into a company front in a charge the men drop for cover, while officers consider how to draw the devil's tusks. Arnold von Winkelried, who gathered the spears to his breast to make a path for his comrades, won his glory because the fighting forces were small in his day. But with such enormous forces as are now engaged and with heroism so common, we make only an incident of the officer who went out to silence a machine gun and was found lying dead across the gun with the gunner dead beside him.

Those whose business it was to observe, the six correspondents, Robinson, Thomas, Gibbs, Philips, Russell and myself, went and came always with a sense of incapacity and sometimes with a feeling that writing was a worthless business when others were fighting. The line of advance on the big map at our quarters extended as the brief army reports were read into the squares every morning by the key of figures and numerals with a detail that included every little trench, every copse, every landmark, and then we chose where we would go that day. At corps headquarters there were maps with still more details and officers would explain the previous day's work to us. Every wood and village, every viewpoint, we knew, and every casualty clearing station and prisoners' inclosure. At battalion camps within sight of the Ridge and within range of the guns, where their blankets helped to make shelter from the sun, you might talk with the men out of the fight and lunch and chat with the officers who awaited the word to go in again or perhaps to hear that their tour was over and they could go to rest in Ypres sector, which had become relatively quiet.

They had their letters and packages from home before they slept and had written letters in return after waking; and there was nothing to do now except to relax and breathe, to renew the vitality that had been expended in the fierce work where shells were still threshing the earth, which rose in clouds of dust to settle back again in enduring passive resistance.

There was much talk early in the war about British cheerfulness; so much that officers and men began to resent it as expressing the idea that they took such a war as this as a kind of holiday, when it was the last thing outside of Hades that any sane man would choose. It was a question in my own mind at times if Hades would not have been a pleasant change. Yet the characterization is true, peculiarly true, even in the midst of the fighting on the Ridge. Cheerfulness takes the place of emotionalism as the armor against hardship and death; a good-humored balance between exhilaration and depression which meets smile with smile and creates an atmosphere superior to all vicissitudes. Why should we be downhearted? Why, indeed, when it does no good. Not "Merrie England!" War is not a merry business; but an Englishman may be cheerful for the sake of self and comrades.

Of course, these battalions, officers and men, would talk about when the war would be over. Even the Esquimaux must have an opinion on the subject by this time. That of the men who make the war, whose lives are the lives risked, was worth more, perhaps, than that of people living thousands of miles away; for it is they who are doing the fighting, who will stop fighting. To them it would be over when it was won. The time this would require varied with different men—one year, two years; and again they would turn satirical and argue whether the sixth or the seventh year would be the worst. And they talked shop about the latest wrinkles in fighting; how best to avoid having men buried by shell-bursts; the value of gas and lachrymatory shells; the ratio of high explosives to shrapnel; methods of "cleaning out" dugouts or "doing in" machine guns, all in a routine that had become an accepted part of life like the details of the stock carried and methods of selling in a department store.

Indelible the memories of these talks, which often brought out illustrations of racial temperament. One company was more horrified over having found a German tied to a trench *parados* to be killed by British shell fire as a field punishment than by the horrors of other men equally mashed and torn, or at having crawled over the moist bodies of the dead, or slept among them, or been covered with spatters of blood and flesh—for that incident struck home with a sense of brutal militarism which was the thing in their minds against which they were fighting.

With steel helmets on and gas masks over our shoulders, we would leave our car at the dead line and set off to "see something," when now the fighting was all hidden in the folds of the ground, or in the woods, or lost on the horizon where the front line of either of these two great armies, with their immense concentration of men and material and roads gorged with transport and thousands of belching guns, was held by a few men with machine guns in shell-craters, their positions sometimes interwoven. Old hands in the Somme battle become shell-wise. They are the ones whom the French call "varnished," which is a way of saying that projectiles glance off their anatomy. They keep away from points where the enemy will direct his fire as a matter of habit or scientific gunnery, and always recollect that the German has not enough shells to sow them broadcast over the whole battle area.

It is not an uncommon thing for one to feel quite safe within a couple of hundred yards of an artillery concentration. That corner of a village, that edge of a shattered grove, that turn in the highway, that sunken road—keep away from them! Any kind of trench for shrapnel; lie down flat unless a satisfactory dugout is near for protection from high explosives which burst in the earth. If you are at the front and a curtain of fire is put behind you, wait until it is over or go around it. If there is one ahead, wait until another day—provided that you are a spectator. Always bear in mind how unimportant you are, how small a figure on the great field, and that if every shell fired had killed one soldier there would not be an able-bodied man in uniform left alive on the continent of Europe. By observing these simple rules you may see a surprising amount with a chance of surviving.

One day I wanted to go into the old German dugouts under a formless pile of ruins which a British colonel had made his battalion headquarters; but I did not want to go enough to persist when I understood the situation. Formerly, my idea of a good dugout—and I always like to be within striking distance of one—was a cave twenty feet deep with a roof of four or five layers of granite, rubble and timber; but now I feel more safe if the fragments of a town hall are piled on top of this.

The Germans were putting a shell every minute with clockwork regularity into the colonel's "happy home" and at intervals four shells in a salvo. You had to make a run for it between the shells, and if you did not know the exact location of the dugout you might have been hunting for it some time. Runners bearing messages took their chances both going and coming and two men were hit. The colonel was quite safe twenty feet underground with the matting of débris including that of a fallen chimney overhead, but he was a most unpopular host. The next day he moved his headquarters and not having been considerate enough to inform the Germans of the fact they kept on methodically pounding the roof of the untenanted premises.

After every battlefield "promenade" I was glad to step into the car waiting at the "dead line," where the chauffeurs frequently had had harder luck in being shelled than we had farther forward. Yet I know of no worse place to be in than a car when you hear the first growing scream which indicates that yours is the neighborhood selected by a German battery or two for expending some of its ammunition. When you are in danger you like to be on your feet and to possess every one of your faculties. I used to put cotton in my ears when I walked through the area of the gun positions as some protection to the eardrums from the blasts, but always took it out once I was beyond the big calibers, as an acute hearing after some experience gave you instant warning of any "krump" or five-point-nine coming in your direction, advising you which way to dodge and also saving you from unnecessarily running for a dugout if the shell were passing well overhead or short.

I was glad, too, when the car left the field quite behind and was over the hills in peaceful country. But one never knew. Fifteen miles from the front line was not always safe. Once when a sudden outburst of fifteen-inch naval shells sent the people of a town to cover and scattered fragments over the square, one cut open the back of the chauffeur's head just as we were getting into our car.

"Are you going out to be strafed at?" became an inquiry in the mess on the order of "Are you going to take an afternoon off for golf to-day?" The only time I felt that I could claim any advantage in phlegm over my comrades was when I slept through two hours of aerial bombing with anti-aircraft guns busy in the neighborhood, which, as I explained, was no more remarkable than sleeping in a hotel at home with flat-wheeled surface cars and motor horns screeching under your window. A subway employee or a traffic policeman in New York ought never to suffer from shell-shock if he goes to war.

The account of personal risk which in other wars might make a magazine article or a book chapter, once you sat down to write it, melted away as your ego was reduced to its proper place in cosmos. Individuals had never been so obscurely atomic. With hundreds of thousands fighting, personal experience was valuable only as it expressed that of the whole. Each story brought back to the mess was much like others, thrilling for the narrator and repetition for the polite listener, except it was some officer fresh from the communication trench who brought news of what was going on in that day's work.

Thus, the battle had become static; its incidents of a kind like the product of some mighty mill. The public, falsely expecting that the line would be broken, wanted symbols of victory in fronts changing on the map and began to weary of the accounts. It was the late Charles A. Dana who is credited with saying: "If a dog bites a man it is not news, but if a man bites a dog it is."

Let the men attack with hatchets and in evening dress and this would win all the headlines in the land because people at their breakfast tables would say: "Here is something new in the war!" Men killing men was not news, but a battalion of trained bloodhounds sent out to bite the Germans would have been. I used to try to hunt down some of the "novelties" which received the favor of publication, but though they were well known abroad the man in the trenches had heard nothing about them.

Bullets, shells, bayonets and bombs remained the tried and practical methods there on the Ridge with its overpowering drama, any act of which almost any day was greater than Spionkop or Magersfontein which thrilled a world that was not then war-stale; and ever its supreme feature was that determination which was like a kind of fate in its progress of chipping, chipping at a stone foundation that must yield.

The Ridge seeped in one's very existence. You could see it as clearly in imagination as in reality, with its horizon under shell-bursts and the slope with its maze of burrows and its battered trenches. Into those calm army reports association could read many indications: the telling fact that the German losses in being pressed off the Ridge were as great if not greater than the British, their sufferings worse under a heavier deluge of shell fire, the increased skill of the offensive and the failure of German counter-attacks after each advance.

No one doubted that the Ridge would be taken and taken it was, or all of it that was needed for the drive that was to clean up any outstanding points, with its sweep down into the valley. A victory this, not to be measured by territory; for in one day's rush more ground was gained than in two months of siege. A victory of position, of will, of *morale*! Sharpening its steel and wits on enemy steel and wits in every kind of fighting, the New Army had proved itself in the supreme test of all qualities.

XVIII

A TRULY FRENCH AFFAIR

A French lieutenant arm-in-arm with two privates—A luncheon at the front—French regimental officers—Three and four stripes on the sleeves for the number of wounds—Over the parapet twenty-three times—Comradeship of soldiers—Monsieur Élan again—Baby *soixante-quinze*—An incident truly French.

This was another French day, an ultra French day, with Monsieur Élan playfully inciting human nature to make holiday in the sight of bursting shells. There had been many other luncheons with generals and staffs in their chateaux which were delightful and illuminating occasions, but this had a distinction of its own not only in its companionship but in its surroundings.

Mon lieutenant who invited me warned me to eat a light breakfast in order to leave room for adequate material appreciation of the hospitality of his own battalion, in which he had fought in the ranks earning promotion and his *croix de guerre* in a way that was more gratifying to him than the possession of a fortune, chateaux and high-powered cars. I have seen him in the streets of our town "hiking" along with the French marching step arm-in-arm with two French privates, though he was an officer. He introduced them as from "my battalion!" with as much pride as if they were Generals Joffre and Castelnau.

What a setting for a "swell repast," as he jokingly called it! A table made of boxes with boxes for seats and plates of tin, under apple trees looking down into a valley where the transport and blue-clad regiments were winding their way past the eddies of men of the battalion in a rest camp, with the *soixante-quinze* firing from the slopes beyond at intervals and a German battery trying to reach a British sausage balloon hanging lazily in the still air against the blue sky and never getting it. A flurry of figures after some "krumps" had burst at another point meant that some men had been killed and wounded.

As the colonel and the second in command were not present there was no restraint of seniority on the festivity, though I think that seniority knowing what was going on might have felt lonely in its isolation. We had many courses, soup, fish, entrée and roast, salad and cheese which was cheese in a land where they eat cheese, and luscious grapes and pears; everything that the market afforded served in sight of the front line. Why not? France thinks that nothing is too good for her fighters. If ever man ought to have the best it is when to-morrow he returns to the firing-line and hard rations—when to-morrow he may die for France.

The senior captain presided. He was a man of other wars, burned by the suns of Morocco, with a military moustache that gave effect to his spirited manner. When my friend, the lieutenant, joined the regiment as a private he was smooth-shaven and his colonel asked him whether he was a priest or a bookmaker, or meant to be a soldier. Next morning he allowed nature to have her way on his upper lip, the colonel's hint being law in all things to those who served under him.

Every officer had his *croix de guerre* in this colonial battalion with its ranks open to all comers of all degrees and promotion for those who could earn it in face of the machine guns where the New Army privates were earning theirs. One officer with the chest of Hercules, who looked equal to the fiercest Prussian or the tallest Pomeranian and at least one additional small Teuton for good measure, mentioned that he had been in Peking. I asked him if he knew some officer friends of mine who had been there at the same time. He replied that he had been a private then, and he liked the American Y.M.C.A.

His breast was a panoply of medals. Among them was the Legion of Honor, while his *croix de guerre* had all the stars, bronze, silver and gold, and two palms, as I remember, which meant that twice some deed of his out in the inferno had won official mention for him all the way up from the battalion through brigade, division and corps to the supreme command. The American Y.M.C.A. in Peking ought to be proud of his good opinion.

The architect, tall, well built, smiling and fair-haired, with an intellectual face, sat opposite the little dealer in precious stones who had traveled the world around in his occupation. There was an artist, too, who held an argument with the architect on art which *mon capitaine* considered meretricious and hair-splitting, his conviction being that they were only airing a wordy pretentiousness and really knew little more of what they were talking about than he. In politics we had a Republican, a Socialist and a Royalist, who also were babbling without capturing any dugouts, according to *mon capitaine* who was simply a soldier. It was clear that the Socialist and the Royalist were both popular, as well as my friend, though he had been promoted to the staff.

Another present was the "Admiral," a naval officer, commanding the monstrous guns of twelve to seventeen inches mounted on railway trucks, who wrote sonnets between directing two-thousand-pound projectiles on their errands of mashing German dugouts. He did not like gunnery where he did not see his target naval fashion, but he had done so well that he was kept at it. His latest sonnet was to an abstract girl somewhere in France which the Socialist, who was a man of critical judgment in everything and of a rollicking disposition, praised very highly and read aloud with the elocution of a Coquelin.

While others had as many as three and four gold stripes on their sleeves to indicate the number of their wounds, the Socialist had been over the parapet twenty-three times in charges without being hit, which he took as a sure sign that his was the right kind of politics, the Royalist and the Republican disagreeing and *mon capitaine* saying that politics were a mere matter of taste and being wounded a matter of luck. Thereupon, the Socialist undertook a brief oration rich with humor, relieving it of too much of the seriousness of the tribune in the Chamber of Deputies, where he will probably thunder out his periods one of these days if he contrives to keep on going over the parapet without being hit.

A man was what he was as a man and nothing more in that distinguished company which had gained its distinction by extinguishing Germans. Comradeship made all differences of opinion, birth and wealth only the excuse for banter in this variation of type from the tall architect with his charming manner to the matter-of-fact expert in diamonds and opals, from the big private of colonial regulars who had won his shoulder straps to the fellow with the blue blood of aristocratic France in his veins. The architect I particularly remember, for he was killed in the next charge, and the dealer in precious stones, for a shell-burst in the face would never allow his eyes to see the flash of a diamond again.

But let youth eat, drink and be merry in the shadow of the fortunes of war which might claim some of them to-morrow, making vacancies for promotion of privates down in the camp. Where Cheeriness was the handmaiden of *morale* with the British, Monsieur Élan was with the French. Everybody talked not only with his lips but with his hands and shoulders, in that absence of self-consciousness which gives grace to free expression. They spoke of their homes at one juncture with a sober and lingering desire and a catch in the throat and they touched on the problems after the war, which they would win or fight on forever, concluding that the men from the trenches who would have the say would make a new and better France and sweep aside any interference with the march of their numbers and patriotism.

We ate until capacity was reached and loitered over the black coffee, with the private who had produced all the courses out of the dugout with the magic of the rabbit out of a hat sharing in the conversation at times without breaking the bonds of discipline. Finally, the cook was brought forth, too, to receive his meed of praise as the real magician. Then we went to pay our respects to the colonel and the second in command. A sturdy little man the colonel, a regular from his neat fatigue cap to the soles of his polished boots, but with a human twinkle through his eyeglasses reflecting much wisdom in the handling of men of all kinds, which, no doubt, was why he was in command of this battalion.

Afterward, we visited the men lounging in their quarters or forming a smiling group, each one ready with quick responses when spoken to, men of all kinds from Apaches of Paris to the sons of princes, perhaps, while the Washington Post March was played for the American. Later, across the road we saw the then new baby *soixante-quinze* guns for trench work, which were being wheeled about with a merry appreciation of the fact that a battery of father *soixante-quinze* was passing by at the time.

Finally, came an incident truly French and delightful in its boyishness, as *mon capitaine* hinted that I should ask *mon colonel* if he would permit *mon capitaine* to go into town and have dinner with my friend and the admiral and myself, returning in my friend's car in time to proceed to the firing-line with the battalion to-morrow. Accordingly I spoke to the colonel and the twinkle of his eye as he gave consent indicated, perhaps, that he knew who had put me up to it. *Mon capitaine* had his dinner and a good one, too, and was back at dawn ready for battle.

It is not that France has changed; only that some people who ought to have known better have changed their opinions formed about her after '70 when, in the company of other foreigners, they went to see the sights of Paris.

XIX

ON THE AERIAL FERRY

The "Ferry-Pilot's" office—Everybody is young in the Royal Flying Corps—Any kind of aeroplane to choose from—A flying machine new from the factory—"A good old 'bus"—Twenty planes a day from England to France—England seen from the clouds—An aerial guide-post—Stopping places—The channel from 4,000 feet aloft—Out of sight in the clouds midway between England and France—Tobogganing from the clouds—France from the air—A good flight.

Personal experience now intrudes in answer to the question whence come all the aeroplanes that take the place of those lost or worn out, which was made clear when I was in London for a few days' change from the fighting on the Ridge through a request to a general at the War Office for permission to fly back to the front.

"Why not?" he said. "When are you going?"

"Monday."

He called up another general on the telephone and in a few words the arrangements were made.

"And my baggage?" I suggested.

"How much of it?"

"A suit case."

"The machine ought to manage that considering that it carries one hundred and fifty pounds in bombs."

On Monday morning at the appointed hour I was walking past a soldierly line of planes flanking an aerodrome field scattered with others that had just alighted or were about to rise and inquiring my way to the "Ferry-Pilot's" office. I found it, identified by a white-lettered sign on a blackboard, down the main street of temporary buildings occupied by the aviators as quarters.

"Yes, all right," said the young officer sitting at the desk, "but we are making no crossings this morning. There is a storm over the channel."

Weather forecasts, which had long ago disappeared from the English newspapers lest they give information to Zeppelins, had become the privilege of those who travel by air or repulsed aerial raids.

"It may clear up this afternoon," he added. "Why not go up to the mess and make yourself comfortable, and return about three? Perhaps you may go then."

At three I was back in his office, where five or six young aviators were waiting for their orders as jockeys might wait their turn to take out horses. Everybody is young in the Royal Flying Corps and everybody thinks and talks in the terms of youth.

"You can push off at once!" said the officer at the desk.

Of course I must have a pass, which was a duplicate in mimeograph with my name as passenger in place of "machine gunner;" or, to put it another way, I was one joy-rider who must be officially delivered from an aerodrome in England to an aerodrome in France. Youth laughed when I took that view. Had I ever flown before? Oh, yes, a fact that put the situation still more at ease.

"What kind of a 'bus would you like?" asked the master pilot. "We have all kinds going over to-day. Take your choice."

I went out into the field to choose my steed and decided upon a big "pusher," where both aviator and passenger sit forward with the propeller and the roar of the motor behind them. She had been flown down across England from the factory the day before and, tried out, was ready for the channel passage.

"You'll take her over," said the master pilot to one of the group waiting their turn.

Then it occurred to somebody that another official detail had been overlooked, and I had to give my name and address and next of kin to complete formalities which should impress novices, while youth looked on smilingly at forty-three which was wise if not reckless. They put me in an aviator's rig with the addition of a life-belt in case we should get a ducking in the channel and I climbed up into my position for the long run, a roomy place in the semi-circular bow of the beast which was ordinarily occupied by a machine gun and gunner.

"She's a good old 'bus, very steady. You'll like her," said one of the group of youngsters looking on.

There were no straps, these being quite unnecessary, but also there was no seat.

"What is *à la mode*?" I asked.

"Stand up if you like!"

"Or sit on the edge and let your feet hang over!"

We were all laughing, for the aviation corps is never gloomy. It rises and alights and fights and dies smilingly.

"I like your hospitality, but not having been trained to trapeze work I'll play the Turk," I replied, squatting with legs crossed; and in this position I was able to look over the railing right and left and forward. The world was mine.

Flight being no new thing in the year 1916, I shall not indulge in any rhetoric. The pertinence of the experience was entirely in the fact that I was taking the aerial ferry which sent twenty planes a day to France on an average and perhaps fifty when the weather had held up traffic the previous day. I was to buffet the clouds instead of the waves on a crowded steamer and have a glimpse behind the curtains of military secrecy of the wonders of resource and organization, which are a commonplace to the wonder-workers themselves.

It was to be a straight, business flight, a matter of routine, a flight without any loitering on the way or covering unnecessary distance to reach the destination. There would be risks enough for the plane when it crossed into the enemy's area with its machine gun in position. The gleam of two lines of steel of a railroad set our course. After we had risen to a height of three or four thousand feet an occasional dash of rain whipped your face, and again the soft mist of a cloud.

It was real English weather, overcast; and England plotted under your eye, a vast garden with its hedges, fields and quiet villages, had never been so fully realized in its rich greens. We overtook trains going in our direction and passed trains going in the opposite direction under their trailing spouts of steam. Only an occasional encampment of tents suggested that the land was at war. The soft light melted the different tones of the landscape together in a dreamy whole and always the impression was of a land loved for its hedges, its pastures and its island seclusion, loved as a garden. In order to hold it secure this plane was flying and the great army in France was fighting.

After forty minutes of the exhilaration of flight which never grows stale, the pilot thumped one of the wings which gave out the sound of a drumhead to attract my attention and indicated an immense white arrow on a pasture pointing toward the bank of mist that hid the channel. This was the guide-post of the aerial ferry. He wheeled around it in order to give me a better view, which was his only departure from routine before, on the line of the arrow's pointing, he took his course, leaving the railroad behind, while ahead the green carpet seemed to end in a vaporish horizon.

Usually as they rose for the channel crossing pilots ascended to a height of ten thousand feet, in order that they should have range in case of engine trouble for a long glide which might permit them to reach shore, or, if they must alight in the sea, to descend close to a vessel. In both England and France along the established aerial pathway are certain way stations fit to give rubber tires a soft welcome, with gasoline in store if a fresh supply is required.

It was the pride of my pilot, who had formerly been in the navy and had come from South Africa to "do his bit," that in twenty crossings he had never had to make a stop. To-day the clouds kept us down to an altitude of only four thousand feet.

Hills and valleys do not exist, all landscape being flat to the aviator's eye, as we know; but against reason some mental kink made me feel that this optical law should not apply to the chalk cliffs when we came to the coast, where only the green sward which crowns them was visible and beyond this a line of gray, the beach, which had an edge of white lace that was moving—the surf.

Soldiers who were returning from leave in the regular way were having a jumpy passage, as one knew by the whitecaps that looked like tiny white flowers on a pewter cloth; only if you looked steadily at one it disappeared and others appeared in its place. Otherwise, the channel in a heavy sea was as still as a painted ocean with painted ships which, however fast they were moving, were making no headway to us traveling as smoothly in our 'bus as a motor boat on a glassy lake.

I looked at my watch as we crossed the lace edging on the English side and again as we crossed it on the French side. The time elapsed was seventeen and a half minutes, which is not rapid going, even for the broader part of the channel which we chose. The fastest plane, I am told, has made it at the narrowest point in eight and a half minutes. Not going as high as usual, the pilot did not speed his motor, as the lower the altitude the more uncomfortable might be the result of engine trouble to his passenger.

Now, however, we were rising midway of the crossing into the gray bank overhead; one second the channel floor was there and the next it was not. Underneath us was mist and ahead and behind and above us only mist, soft and cool against the face. We were wholly out of sight of land and water, above the clouds, detached from earth, lost in the sky between England and France.

This was the great moment to me. I was away from the sound of the guns; from the headlines of newspapers announcing the latest official bulletins; from prisoners' camps and casualty clearing stations; from dugouts and trenches and the Ridge. Here was real peace, the peace of the infinite—and no one could ask you when you thought the war would be over. You were nobody, yet again you were the whole population of the world, you and the aviator and the plane, perfectly helpless in one sense and in another gloriously secure. Even he seemed a part of the machine carrying you swiftly on, without any sense of speed except the driving freshness of the air in your face. I felt that I should not mind going on forever. Time was unlimited. There was only space and the humming of the motor and the faintly gleaming circle of light of the propeller and those two rigid wings with their tracery of braces.

We were not long out of sight of land and water, but long enough to make one wish to fly over the channel again, the next time at ten thousand feet, when it was a gleaming swath hidden at times by patches of luminous nimbus.

The engine stopped. There was the silence of the clouds, cushioned silence, cushioned by the mist. Next, we were on a noiseless toboggan and when we came to the end of a glide of a thousand feet or more, France loomed ahead with its lacework of surf and an expanse of chalk cliffs at an angle and landscape rising out of the haze. A few minutes more and the salt thread that kept Napoleon out of England and has kept Germany out of England was behind us. We were over the Continent of Europe.

I had never before understood the character of both England and France so well. England was many little gardens correlated by roads and lanes; France was one great garden. Majestic in their suggestion of spaciousness were those broad stretches of hedgeless, fenceless fields, their crop lines sharply drawn as are all lines from a plane, fields between the plots of woodland and the villages and towns, revealing a land where all the soil is tilled.

Soon we were over camps that I knew and long, straight highways that I had often traveled in my comings and goings. But how empty seemed the roads where you were always passing motor trucks and guns! Long, gray streaks with occasional specks which, as you rose to a greater height, were lost like scattered beads melting into a ribbon! Reserve trenches that I had known, too, were white tracings on a flat surface in their standard contour of traverses. There was the chateau where I had lived for months. Yes, I could identify that, and there the town where we went to market.

We flew around the tower of a cathedral low enough to see the people moving in the streets, and then, in a final long glide, after an hour and fifty minutes in the air, the rubber wheels touched earth, rose and touched it again before the steady old 'bus slowed down not far from another plane that had arrived only a few minutes previously. When a day of good weather follows a day of bad and the arrivals are frequent, planes are flopping about this aerodrome like so many penguins before they are marshaled by the busy attendants in line along the edge of the field or under the shelter of hangars.

We had had none of those thrilling experiences which are supposed to happen to aerial joy-riders, but had made a perfectly safe, normal trip, which, I repeat, was the real point of this wonderful business of the aerial ferry. I went into the office and officially reported my arrival at the same time that the pilot reported delivery of his plane.

"Good-night," he said. "I'm off to catch the steamer to bring over another 'bus to-morrow."

Waiting near by was my car and soldier chauffeur, who asked, in his quiet English way, if I had had "a good flight, sir;" and soon I was back in the atmosphere of the army as the car sped along the road, past camps, villages and motor trucks, until in the moonlight, as we came over a hill, the cathedral tower of Amiens appeared above the dark mass of the town against the dim horizon.

XX

THE EVER MIGHTY GUNS

A thousand guns at the master's call—Schoolmaster of the guns—More and more guns but never too many—The gunner's skill which has life and death at stake—"Grandmother" first of the fifteen-inch howitzers—Soldier-mechanics—War still a matter of missiles—Improvements in gunnery—Third rail of the battlefield—The game of guns checkmating guns—A Niagara of death—A giant tube of steel painted in frog patches.

How reconcile that urbane gunner-general, a genius among experts you were told, as the master of a thunderous magic which shot its deadly lightnings over the German area! Let him move a red pin on the map and a tractor was towing a nine-inch gun to a new position; a black pin and a battery of eighteen pounders took the road. A thousand guns answered his call with a hundred thousand shells when it pleased him. I stood in awe of him, for chaos seemed to be doing his bidding at the end of a pushbutton.

Whirlwind curtains of fire and creeping and leaping curtains were his familiar servants, and he set the latest fashion by his improvements. Had the French or the Germans something new? This he applied. Had he something new? He passed on the method to the French and gave the Germans the benefit of its results.

Observers seated in the baskets of observation balloons, aeroplanes circling low in risk of anti-aircraft fire, men sitting in tree-tops and others in front-line trenches spotting the fall of shells were the eyes for the science he was working out on his map. Those nests and lines of guns that seemed to be simply sending shells into the blue from their hiding-places played fortissimo and pianissimo under his baton. He correlated their efforts, gave them purpose and system in their roaring traffic of projectiles.

Where Sir Douglas Haig was schoolmaster of the whole, he was schoolmaster of the guns. After the grim days of the salient, when he worked with relics from fortresses and anything that could be improvised against the German artillery, came the latest word in black-throated, fiery-tongued monsters from England where the new gunners had learned their ABC's and he and his assistants were to teach them solid geometry and calculus and give them a toilsome experience, which was still more useful.

His host kept increasing as more and more guns arrived, but never too many. There cannot be too many. Plant them as thick as trees in a forest for a depth of six or eight miles and there would not be enough by the criterion of the infantry, to whom the fortunes of war increasingly related to the nature of the artillery support. He must have smiled with the satisfaction of a farmer over a big harvest yield that filled the granary as the stack of shells at an ammunition depot spread over the field, and he could go among his guns with the pride of a landowner among his flocks. He knew all the diseases that guns were heir to and their weaknesses of temperament. A gun doctor was part of the establishment. This specialist went among the guns and felt of their pulses and listened to accounts of their symptoms and decided whether they could be cared for at a field hospital or would have to go back to the base.

Temperament? An old eight-inch howitzer which has helped in a dozen curtains of fire and blown in numerous dugouts may be a virtuoso for temperament. Many things enter into mastery of the magic of the thunders, from clear eyesight of observers who see accurately to precision of gunner's skill, of powder, of fuse, of a hundred trifles which can never be too meticulously watched. The erring inspector of munitions far away oversea by an oversight may cost the lives of many soldiers or change the fate of a charge.

Comparable only with the surgeon's skill in the skill which has life and death as the stake of its result is the gunner's. The surgeon is trying to save one life which a slip of the knife may destroy; the gunner is trying both to save and to take life. In the gunner's skill life that is young and sturdy, muscles that are hardened by exercise and drill, manhood in its pink, must place its trust. A little carelessness or the slightest error and monsters with their long, fiery reach may strike you in the back instead of the enemy in front, and instead of dead and wounded and capitulation among smashed dugouts and machine gun positions you may be received by showers of bombs. No wonder that gunners work hard! No wonder that discipline is tightened by the screw of fearful responsibility!

At the front we had a sort of reverence for Grandmother, the first of the fifteen-inch howitzers to arrive as the belated answer of "prepared England" who "forced the war" on "unprepared Germany" to the famous forty-two centimeters that pounded Liège and Maubeuge. Gently Grandmother with her ugly mouth and short neck and mammoth supporting ribs of steel was moved and nursed; for she, too, was temperamental. Afterward, Grandfather came and Uncle and Cousin and Aunt and many grown sons and daughters, until the British could have turned the city of Lille into ruins had they chosen; but they kept their destruction for the villages on the Somme, which represent a property loss remarkably small, as the average village could be rebuilt for not over two hundred thousand dollars.

Other children of smaller caliber also arrived in surprising numbers. Make no mistake about that nine-inch howitzer, which appears to be only a monstrous tube of steel firing a monstrous shell, not being a delicately adjusted piece of mechanism. The gunner, his clothes oil-soaked, who has her breech apart pays no attention to the field of guns around him or the burst of a shell a hundred yards away, no more than the man with a motor breakdown pays to passing traffic. Is he a soldier? Yes, by his uniform, but primarily a mechanic, this man from Birmingham, who is polishing that heavy piece of steel which, when it locks in the breech, holds the shell fast in place and allows all the force of the explosion to pass through the muzzle, while the recoil cylinder takes up the shock as nicely as on a battleship, with no tremble of the base set in the débris of a village. He shakes his head, this preoccupied mechanician. It may be necessary to call in the gun doctor. His "how" has been in service a long time, but is not yet showing the signs of general debility of the eight-inch battery near by. They have fired three times their allowance and are still good for sundry purposes in the gunner-general's play of red and black pins on his map. The life of guns has surpassed all expectations; but the smaller calibers forward and the *soixante-quinze* must not suffer from general debility when they lay on a curtain of fire to cover a charge.

War is still a matter of projectiles, of missiles thrown by powder, whether cannon or rifle, as it was in Napoleon's time, the change being in range, precision and destructive power. The only new departure is the aeroplane, for the gas attack is another form of the Chinese stink-pot and our old mystery friend Greek fire may claim antecedence to the *Flammenwerfer*. The tank with its machine guns applied the principle of projectiles from guns behind armor. Steel helmets would hardly be considered an innovation by mediæval knights. Bombs and hand grenades and mortars are also old forms of warfare, and close-quarter fighting with the bayonet, as was evident to all practical observers before the war, will endure as long as the only way to occupy a position is by the presence of men on the spot and as long as the defenders fight to hold it in an arena free of interference by guns which must hold their fire in fear of injury to your own soldiers as well as to the enemy.

With all the inventive genius of Europe applied in this war, the heat ray or any other revolutionary means of killing which would make guns and rifles powerless has not been developed. It is still a question of throwing or shooting projectiles accurately at your opponent, only where once it was javelin, or spear, or arrow, now it is a matter of shells for anywhere from one mile to twenty miles; and the more hits that you could make with javelins or arrows and can make with shells the more likely it is that victory will incline to your side. Where flights of arrows hid the sun, barrages now blanket the earth.

The improvement in shell fire is revolutionary enough of itself. Steadily the power of the guns has increased. What they may accomplish is well illustrated by the account of a German battalion on the Somme. When it was ten miles from the front a fifteen-inch shell struck in its billets just before it was ordered forward. On the way luck was against it at every stage of progress and it suffered in turn from nine-inch, eight-inch and six-inch shells, not to mention bombs from an aviator flying low, and afterward from eighteen pounders. When it reached the trenches a preliminary bombardment was the stroke of fate that led to the prompt capitulation of some two hundred survivors to a British charge. The remainder of the thousand men was practically all casualties from shell-bursts, which, granting some exaggeration in a prisoner's tale, illustrates what killing the guns may wreak if the target is under their projectiles.

The gunnery of 1915 seems almost amateurish to that of 1916, a fact hardly revealed to the public by its reading of bulletins and of such a quantity of miscellaneous information that the significance of it becomes obscure. At the start of the war the Germans had the advantage of many mobile howitzers and immense stores of high explosive shells, while the French were dependent on their *soixante-quinze* and shrapnel; and at this disadvantage the brilliancy of their work with this wonderful field gun on the Marne and in Lorraine was the most important contributory factor in saving France next to the vital one of French courage and organization. The Allies had to follow the German suit with howitzers and high explosive shells and the cry for more and more guns and more and more munitions for the business of blasting your enemy and his positions to bits became universal.

The first barrage, or curtain of fire, ever used to my knowledge was a feeble German effort in the Ypres salient in the autumn of 1914, though the French drum fire distributed over a certain area had, in a sense, a like effect. To make certain of clearness about fundamentals familiar to those at the front but to the general public only a symbol for something not understood, a curtain of fire is a swath of fragments and bullets from bursting projectiles which may stop a charge or prevent reserves from coming to the support of the front line. It is a barrier of death, the third rail of the battlefield. From the sky shrapnel descend with their showers of bullets, while the high explosives heave up the earth under foot. Shrapnel largely went out of fashion in the period when high explosives smashed in trenches and dugouts; but the answer was deeper dugouts too stoutly roofed to permit of penetration and shrapnel returned to play a leading part again, as we shall see in the description of a charge under an up-to-date curtain of fire in another chapter.

Counter-battery work is another one of the gunner-general's cares, which requires, as it were, the assistance of the detective branch. Before you can fight you must find the enemy's guns in their hiding-places or take a chance on the probable location of his batteries, which will ordinarily seek every copse, every sunken road and every reverse slope. The interesting captured essay on British fighting methods, by General von Arnim, the general in command of the Germans opposite the British on the Somme, with its minutiæ of directions indicative of how seriously he regarded the New Army, mentioned the superior means of reporting observations to the guns used by British aeroplanes and warned German gunners against taking what had formerly been obvious cover, because British artillery never failed to concentrate on those spots with disastrous results.

Where aeroplanes easily detect lines, be they roads or a column of infantry, as I have said, a battery in the open with guns and gunners the tint of the landscape is not readily distinguishable at the high altitude to which anti-aircraft gunfire restricts aviators. When a concentration begins on a battery, either the gunners must go to their dugouts or run beyond the range of the shells until the "strafe" is over. If A could locate all of B's guns and had two thousand guns of his own to keep B's two thousand silenced by counter-battery work and two thousand additional to turn on B's infantry positions, it would be only a matter of continued charges under cover of curtains of fire until the survivors, under the gusts of shells with no support from their own guns, would yield against such ghastly, hopeless odds.

Such is the power of the guns—and such the game of guns checkmating guns—in their effort to stop the enemy's curtains of fire while maintaining their own that the genius who finds a divining rod which, from a sausage balloon, will point out the position of every enemy battery has fame awaiting him second only to that of the inventor of a system of distilling a death-dealing heat ray from the sun.

And the captured gun! It is a prize no less dear to the infantry's heart to-day than it was a hundred years ago. Our battalion took a battery! There is a thrill for every officer and man and all the friends at home. Muzzle cracked by a direct hit, recoil cylinder broken, wheels in kindling wood, shield fractured—there you have a trophy which is proof of accuracy to all gunners and an everlasting memorial in the town square to the heroism of the men of that locality.

In the gunners' branch of the corps or division staff (which may be next door to the telephone exchange where "Hello!" soldiers are busy all day keeping guns, infantry, transport, staff and units, large and small, in touch) the visitor will linger as he listens to the talk of shop by these experts in mechanical destruction. Generic discussions about which caliber of gun is most efficient for this and that purpose have the floor when the result of a recent action does not furnish a fresher topic. There are faddists and old fogies of course, as in every other band of experts. The reports of the infantry out of its experience under shell-bursts, which should be the gospel, may vary; for the infantry think well of the guns when the charge goes home with casualties light and ill when the going is bad.

Every day charts go up to the commanders showing the expenditure of ammunition and the stock of different calibers on hand; for the army is a most fastidious bookkeeper. Always there must be immense reserves for an emergency, and on the Somme a day's allowance when the battle was only "growling" was a month's a year previous. Let the general say the word and fifty thousand more shells will be fired on Thursday than on Wednesday. He throws off and on the switch of a Niagara of death. The infantry is the Oliver Twist of incessant demand. It would like a score of batteries turned on one machine gun, all the batteries in the army against a battalion front, and a sheet of shells in the air night and day, as you yourself would wish if you were up in the firing-line.

Guardians of the precious lives of their own men and destroyers of the enemy's, the guns keep vigil. Every night the flashes on the horizon are a reminder to those in the distance that the battle never ends. Their voices are like none other except guns; the flash from their muzzles is as suggestive as the spark from a dynamo, which says that death is there for reaching out your hand. Something docile is in their might, like the answering of the elephant's bulk to the mahout's command, in their noiseless elevation and depression, and the bigger they are the smoother appears their recoil as they settle back into place ready for another shot. The valleys where the guns hide play tricks with acoustics. I have sat on a hill with a dozen batteries firing under the brow and their crashes were hardly audible.

"Only an artillery preparation, sir!" said an artilleryman as we started up a slope stiff with guns, as the English say, all firing. You waited your chance to run by after a battery had fired and were on the way toward the next one before the one behind sent another round hurtling overhead.

The deep-throated roar of the big calibers is not so hard on the ears as the crack of the smaller calibers. Returning, you go in face of the blasts and then, though it rarely happens, you have in mind, if you have ever been in front of one, the awkward possibility of a premature burst of a shell in your face. Signs tell you where those black mouths which you might not see are hidden, lest you walk straight into one as it belches flame. When you have seen guns firing by thousands as far as the eye can reach from a hill; when you have seen every caliber at work and your head aches from the noise, the thing becomes overpowering and monotonous. Yet you return again, drawn by the uncanny fascination of artillery power.

Riding home one day after hours with the guns in an attack, I saw for the first time one of the monster railroad guns firing as I passed by on the road. Would I get out to watch it? I hesitated. Yes, of course. But it was only another gun, a giant tube of steel painted in frog patches to hide it from aerial observation; only another gun, though it sent a two-thousand-pound projectile to a target ten miles away, which a man from a sausage balloon said was "on."

XXI

BY THE WAY

The River Somme—Amiens cathedral—Sunday afternoon promenaders—Women, old men and boys—A prosperous old town—Madame of the little Restaurant des Huîtres—The old waiter at the hotel—The stork and the sea-gull—Distinguished visitors—Horses and dogs—Water carts—Gossips of battle—The donkeys.

What contrasts! There was none so pleasant as that when you took the river road homeward after an action. Leaving behind the Ridge and the scarred slope and the crowding motor trucks in their cloud of dust, you were in a green world soothing to eyes which were painful from watching shell-blasts. Along the banks of the Somme on a hot day you might see white figures of muscle-armored youth washed clean of the grime of the firing-line in the exhilaration of minutes, seconds, glowingly lived without regard to the morrow, shaking drops of water free from white skins, under the shade of trees untouched by shell fire, after a plunge in cool waters. Then from a hill where a panorama was flung free to the eye, the Somme at your feet held islands of peace in its shining net as it broke away from confining green walls and wound across the plain toward Amiens.

The Somme is kindly by nature with a desire to embrace all the country around, and Amiens has trained its natural bent to man's service.

It gave softer springs than those of any ambulance for big motor scows that brought the badly wounded down from the front past the rich market gardens that sent their produce in other boats to market. Under bridges its current was divided and subdivided until no one could tell which was Somme and which canal, busy itself as the peasants and the shopkeepers doing a good turn to humankind, grinding wheat in one place and in another farther on turning a loom to weave the rich velvets for which Amiens is famous, and between its stages of usefulness supplying a Venetian effect where balconies leaned across one of its subdivisions, an area of old houses on crooked, short streets at their back huddled with a kind of ancient reverence near the great cathedral.

At first you might be discriminative about the exterior of Amiens cathedral, having in mind only the interior as being worth while. I went inside frequently and the call to go was strongest after seeing an action. Standing on that stone floor where princes and warriors had stood through eight hundred years of the history of France, I have seen looking up at the incomparable nave with its majestic symmetry, French *poilus* in their faded blue, helmets in hand and perhaps the white of a bandage showing, spruce generals who had a few hours away from their commands, dust-laden dispatch riders, boyish officers with the bit of blue ribbon that they had won for bravery on their breasts and knots of privates in worn khaki. The man who had been a laborer before he put on uniform was possessed by the same awe as the one who had been favored by birth and education. A black-robed priest passing with his soft tread could not have differed much to the eye from one who was there when the Black Prince was fighting in France or the soldiers of Joan or of Condé came to look at the nave.

The cathedral and the Somme helped to make you whole with the world and with time. After weeks you ceased to be discriminative about the exterior. The cathedral was simply the cathedral. Returning from the field, I knew where on every road I should have the first glimpse of its serene, assertive mass above the sea of roofs—always there, always the same, immortal; while the Ridge rocked with the Allied gun-blasts that formed the police line of fire for its protection.

I liked to walk up the canal tow-path where the townspeople went on Sunday afternoons for their promenade, the blue of French soldiers on leave mingling with civilian black—soldiers with wives or mothers on their arms, safe for the time being. One scene reappears to memory as I write: A young fellow back from the trenches bearing his sturdy boy of two on his shoulder and the black-eyed young mother walking beside him, both having eyes for nothing in the world except the boy.

The old fishermen would tell you as they waited for a bite that the German was *fichu*, their faith in the credit of France unimpaired as they lived on the income of the savings of their industry before they retired. You asked gardeners about business, which you knew was good with that ever-hungry and spendthrift British Army "bulling" the market. One day while taking a walk, Beach Thomas and I saw a diver preparing to go down to examine the abutment of a bridge and we sat down to look on with a lively interest, when we might have seen hundreds of guns firing. It was a change. Nights, after dispatches were written, Gibbs and I, anything but gory-minded, would walk in the silence, having the tow-path to ourselves, and after a mutual agreement to talk of anything but the war would revert to the same old subject.

On other days when only "nibbling" was proceeding on the Ridge you might strike across country over the stubble, flushing partridges from the clover. And the women, the old men and the boys got in all the crops. How I do not know, except by rising early and keeping at it until dark, which is the way that most things worth while are accomplished in this world. Those boys from ten to sixteen who were driving the plow for next year's sowing had become men in their steadiness.

Amiens was happy in the memory of the frustration of what might have happened when her citizens looked at the posters, already valuable relics, that had been put up by von Kluck's army as it passed through on the way to its about-face on the Marne. The old town, out of the battle area, out of the reach of shells, had prospered exceedingly. Shopkeepers, particularly those who sold oysters, fresh fish, fruits, cheese, all delicacies whatsoever to victims of iron rations in the trenches, could retire on their profits unless they died from exhaustion in accumulating more. They took your money so politely that parting with it was a pleasure, no matter what the prices, though they were always lower for fresh eggs than in New York.

We came to know all with the intimacy that war develops, but for sheer character and energy the blue ribbon goes to Madame of the little Restaurant des Huîtres. She needed no gallant husband to make her a marshal's wife, as in the case of Sans-Gêne, for she was a marshal herself. She should have the *croix de guerre* with all the stars and a palm, too, for knowing how to cook. A small stove which was as busy with its sizzling pans as a bombing party stood at the foot of a cramped stairway, whose ascent revealed a few tables, with none for two and everybody sitting elbow to elbow, as it were, in the small dining-room. There were dishes enough and clean, too, and spotless serviettes, but no display of porcelain and silver was necessary, for the food was a sufficient attraction. Madame was all for action. If you did not order quickly she did so for you, taking it for granted that a wavering mind indicated a palate that called for arbitrary treatment.

She had a machine gun tongue on occasion. If you did not like her restaurant it was clear that other customers were waiting for your place, and generals capitulated as promptly as lieutenants. A camaraderie developed at table under the spur of her dynamic presence and her occasional artillery concentrations, which were brief and decisive, for she had no time to waste. Broiled lobster and sole, oysters, filets and chops, sizzling fried potatoes, crisp salads, mountains of forest strawberries with pots of thick cream and delectable coffee descended from her hands, with no mistake in any orders or delay in the prompt succession of courses, on the cloth before you by some legerdemain of manipulation in the narrow quarters to the accompaniment of her repartee. It was past understanding how she accomplished such results in quantity and quality on that single stove with the help of one assistant whom, apparently, she found in the way at times; for the assistant would draw back in the manner of one who had put her finger into an electric fan as her mistress began a manipulation of pots and pans.

If Madame des Huîtres should come to New York, I wonder—yes, she would be overwhelmed by people who had anything like a trench appetite. Soon she would be capitalized, with branches des Huîtres up and down the land, while she would no longer touch a skillet, but would ride in a limousine and grow fat, and I should not like her any more.

People who could not get into des Huîtres or were not in the secret which, I fear, was selfishly kept by those who were, had to dine at the hotel, where a certain old waiter—all young ones being at the front—though called mad could be made the object of method if he had not method in madness. When he seemed about to collapse with fatigue, tell him that there had been a big haul of German prisoners on the Ridge and the blaze of delight in his dark eyes would galvanize him. If he should falter again, a shout of, "*Vive l'Entente cordiale! En avant!*" would send him off with coat-tails at right angles to his body as he sprang into the midst of the riot of waiters outside the kitchen door, from which he would emerge triumphantly bearing the course that was next in order. Nor would he allow you to skip one. You must take them all or, as the penalty of breaking up the system, you went hungry.

Outside in the court where you went for coffee and might sometimes get it if you gave the head waiter good news from the front, a stork and a sea-gull with clipped wings posed at the fountain. What tales of battle were told in sight of this incongruous pair whose antics relieved the strain of war! When the stork took a step or two the gull plodded along after him and when the gull moved the stork also moved, the two never being more than three or four feet apart. Yet each maintained an attitude of detachment as if loath to admit the slightest affection for each other. Foolish birds, as many said and laughed at them; and again, heroes out of the hell on the Ridge and wholly unconscious of their heroism said that the two had the wisdom of the ages, particularly the stork, though expert artillery opinion was that the practical gull thought that only his own watchfulness kept the wisdom of the ages from being drowned in the fountain in an absent-minded moment, though the water was not up to a stork's ankle-joint. More nonsense, when the call was for reaction from the mighty drama, was woven around these entertainers by men who could not go to plays than would be credible to people reading official bulletins; woven by dining parties of officers who when dusk fell went indoors and gathered around the piano before going into a charge on the morrow.

At intervals men in civilian clothes, soft hats, gaiters over everyday trousers, golf suits, hunting suits, appeared at the hotel or were seen stalking about captured German trenches, their garb as odd in that ordered world of khaki as powdered wig, knee-breeches and silver buckles strolling up Piccadilly or Fifth Avenue. Prime ministers, Cabinet members, great financiers, potentates, journalists, poets, artists of many nationalities came to do the town. They saw the Ridge under its blanket of shell-smoke, the mighty columns of transport, all the complex, enormous organization of that secret world, peeked into German dugouts, and in common with all observers estimated the distance of the nearest shell-burst from their own persons.

Many were amazed to find that generals worked in chateaux over maps, directing by telephone, instead of standing on hilltops to give their commands, and that war was a systematic business, which made those who had been at the front writing and writing to prove that it was wonder if nobody read what they wrote. An American who said that he did not see why all the trucks and horses and wagons and men did not lose their way was suggestive of the first vivid impressions which the "new eye" brought to the scene. Another praised my first book for the way it had made life at the front clear and then proceeded to state his surprise at finding that trenches did not run straight, but in traverses, and that soldiers lived in houses instead of tents and gunners did not see their targets. Now he had seen this mighty army at work for himself. It is the only way. I give up hope of making others see it.

So grim the processes of fighting, so lacking in picturesqueness, that one welcomed any of the old symbols of war. I regretted yet rejoiced that the horse was still a factor. It was good to think that the gasoline engine had saved the sore backs of the pack animals of other days, removed the horror of dead horses beside the road and horses driven to exhaustion by the urgency of fierce necessity, and that a shell in the transport meant a radiator smashed instead of flesh torn and scattered. Yet the horse was still serving man at the front and the dog still flattering him. I have seen dogs lying dead on the field where the mascot of a battalion had run along with the men in a charge; dogs were found in German dugouts, and one dog adopted by a corps staff had refused to leave the side of his fallen master, a German officer, until the body was removed.

The horse brought four-footed life into the dead world of the slope, patiently drawing his load, mindless of gun-blasts and the shriek of shell-fragments once he was habituated to them. As he can pass over rough ground, he goes into areas where no motor vehicle except the tanks may go. He need not wait on the road-builders before he takes the eighteen pounders to their new positions or follows them with ammunition. Far out on the field I have seen groups of artillery horses waiting in a dip in the ground while their guns were within five hundred yards of the firing-line, and winding across dead fields toward an isolated battery the caisson horses trotting along with shells bursting around them.

Upon August days when the breeze that passed overhead was only tantalization to men in communication trenches carrying up ammunition and bombs, when dugouts were ovens, when the sun made the steel helmet a hot skillet-lid over throbbing temples, the horse-drawn water carts wound up the slope to assuage burning thirst and back again, between the gates of hell and the piping station, making no more fuss than a country postman on his rounds.

Practically all the water that the fighters had, aside from what was in their canteens, must be brought up in this way, for the village wells were filled with the remains of shell-crushed houses. Gossips of battle the water men, they and the stretcher-bearers both non-combatants going and coming under the shells up to the battle line, but particularly so the water men, who passed the time of day with every branch, each working in its own compartment. When the weather was bad the water man's business became slack and the lot of the stretcher-bearer grew worse in the mud. What stories the stretcher-bearers brought in of wounded blown off litters by shells, of the necessity of choosing the man most likely to survive when only one of two could be carried, of whispered messages from the dying, and themselves keeping to their work with cheery British phlegm; and the water men told of new gun positions, of where the shells were thickest, of how the fight was going.

It irritated the water men, prosaic in their disregard of danger, to have a tank hit on the way out. If it were hit on the way back when it was empty this was of less account, for new tanks were waiting in reserve. Tragedy for them was when a horse was killed and often they returned with horses wounded. It did not occur to the man that he might be hit; it was the loss of a horse or a tank that worried him. One had his cart knocked over by a salvo of shells and set upright by the next, whereupon, according to the account, he said to his mare: "Come on, Mary, I always told you the Boches were bad shots!" But there are too many stories of the water men to repeat without sifting.

We must not forget the little donkeys which the French brought from Africa to take the place of men in carrying supplies up to the trenches. Single file they trotted along on their errand and they had their own hospitals for wounded. It is said that when curtains of fire began ahead they would throw forward their long ears inquiringly and hug close to the side of the trench for cover and even edge into a dugout with the men, who made room for as much donkey as possible, or when in the open they would seek the shelter of shell-craters. Lest their perspicacity be underrated, French soldiers even credited the wise elders among them with the ability to distinguish between different calibers of shells.

XXII

THE MASTERY OF THE AIR

"Nose dives" and "crashers"—The most intense duels in history—Aviators the pride of nations—Beauchamp—The D'Artagnan of the air—Mastery of the air—The aristocrat of war, the golden youth of adventure—Nearer immortality than any other living man can be—The British are reckless aviators—Aerial influence on the soldier's psychology—Varieties of aeroplanes—Immense numbers of aeroplanes in the battles in the air.

Wing tip touching wing tip two phantoms passed in the mist fifteen thousand feet above the earth and British plane and German plane which had grazed each other were lost in the bank of cloud. The dark mass which an aviator sees approaching when he is over the battlefield proves to be a fifteen-inch shell at the top of its parabola which passes ten feet over his head. A German aviator thinking he is near home circles downward on an overcast day toward a British aerodrome to find out his mistake too late, and steps out of his machine to be asked by his captors if he won't come in and have tea. Thus, true accounts that come to the aviators' mess make it unnecessary to carry your imagination with you at the front.

They talk of "nose dives" and "crashers," which mean the way an enemy's plane was brought down, and although they have no pose or theatricalism the consciousness of belonging to the wonder corps of modern war is not lacking. One returns from a flight and finds that a three-inch anti-aircraft gun-shell has gone through the body of his plane.

"So that was it! Hardly felt it!" he said.

If the shell had exploded? Oh, well, that is a habit of shells; and in that case the pilot would be in the German lines unrecognizable among the débris of his machine after a "crasher."

Where in the old West gunmen used to put a notch on their revolver handle for every man killed, now in each aviator's record is the number of enemy planes which he has brought down. When a Frenchman has ten his name goes into the official bulletin. Everything contributes to urge on the fighting aviator to more and more victims till one day he, too, is a victim. Never were duels so detached or so intense. No clashing of steel, no flecks of blood, only two men with wings. While the soldier feels his weapon go home and the bomber sees his bomb in flight, the aviator watches for his opponent to drop forward in his seat as the first sign that he has lost control of his plane and of victory, and he does not hear the passing of the bullets that answer those from his own machine gun. One hero comes to take the place of another who has been lost. A smiling English youth was embarrassed when asked how he brought down the great Immelmann, most famous of German aviators.

Nelson's "Death or Westminster Abbey" has become paraphrased to "Death or the *communiqué*." At twenty-one, while a general of division is unknown except in the army an aviator's name may be the boast of a nation. In him is expressed the national imagination, the sense of hero-worship which people love to personify. The British aviation corps stuck to anonymity until the giving of a Victoria Cross one day revealed that Lieutenant Ball had brought down his twenty-sixth German plane.

Soon after the taking of Fort Douaumont when I was at Verdun, Beauchamp, blond, blue-eyed and gentle of manner, who had thrilled all France by bombing Essen, said, "Now they will expect me to go farther and do something greater;" and I was not surprised to learn a month later that he had been killed. Something in the way he spoke convinced me that he foresaw death and accepted it as a matter of course; and he realized, too, the penalty of being a hero. He had flown over Essen and dropped his bombs and seen them burst, which was all of his story.

The public thrill over such exploits is the greater because of their simplicity. An aviator has no experiences on the road; he cannot stop to talk to anyone. There is flight; there is a lever that releases a bomb; there is a machine gun. He may not indulge in psychology, which would be wool-gathering, when every faculty is objectively occupied. He is strangely helpless, a human being borne through space by a machine, and when he returns to the mess he really has little to tell except as it relates to mechanism and technique.

The Royal Flying Corps, which is the official name, never wants for volunteers. Ever the number of pilots is in excess of the number of machines. Young men with embroidered wings on their breasts, which prove that they have qualified, waited on factories to turn out wings for flying. Flight itself is simple, but the initiative equal to great deeds is another thing. Here you revert to an innate gift of the individual who, finding in danger the zest of a glorious, curiosity, the intoxication of action, clear eye, steady hand answering lightning quickness of thought, becomes the D'Artagnan of the air. There is no telling what boyish neophyte will show a steady hand in daring the supreme hazards with light heart, or what man whom his friends thought was born for aviation may lack the touch of genius.

Far up in the air there is an imaginary boundary line which lies over the battle line; and there is another which may be on your side or on the other side of the battle line. It is the location of the second line that tells who has the mastery of the air. A word of bare and impressive meaning this of mastery in war, which represents force without qualification; that the other man is down and you are up, the other fends and you thrust. More glorious than the swift rush of destroyer to a battleship that of the British planes whose bombs brought down six German sausage balloons in flames before the Grand Offensive began.

I need never have visited an aerodrome on the Somme to know whether Briton and Frenchman or German was master of the air. The answer was there whenever you looked in the heavens in the absence of iron crosses on the hovering or scudding or turning plane wings and the multiplicity of bull's-eyes; in the abandoned way that both British and French pickets flew over the enemy area, as if space were theirs and they dared any interference. If you saw a German plane appear you could count three or four Allied planes appearing from different directions to surround it. The German had to go or be caught in a cross fire, and manoeuvered to his death.

Mastery of the air is another essential of superiority for an offensive; one of the vital features in the organized whole of an attack. As you press men and guns forward enemy planes must not locate your movements. Your planes with fighting planes as interference must force a passage for your observers to spot the fall of shells on new targets, to assist in reporting the progress of charges and to play their proper auxiliary part in the complex system of army intelligence.

Before the offensive new aerodromes began to appear along the front at the same time that new roads were building. An army that had lacked both planes and guns at the start now had both. Every aviator knew that he was expected to gain and hold the mastery; his part was set no less than that of the infantry. Where should "the spirit that quickeneth" dwell if not with the aviators? No weary legs hamper him; he does not have to crawl over the dead or hide in shell-craters or stand up to his knees in mire. He is the pampered aristocrat of war, the golden youth of adventure.

He leaves a comfortable bed, with bath, a good breakfast, the comradeship of a pleasant mess, the care of servants, to mount his steed. When he returns he has only to step out of his seat. Mechanics look after his plane and refreshment and shade in summer and warmth in winter await alike the spoiled child of the favored, adventurous corps who has not the gift and never quite dares the great hazards as well as the one who dares them to his certain end. All depends on the man.

Rising ten or fifteen thousand feet, slipping in and out of clouds, the aviator breathes pure ozone on a dustless roadway, the world a carpet under him; and though death is at his elbow it is no grimy companion like death in the trenches. He is up or he is down, and when he is up the thrill that holds his faculties permits of no apprehensions. There is no halfway business of ghastly wounds which foredoom survival as a cripple. Alive, he is nearer immortality than any other living man can be; dead, his spirit leaves him while he is in the heavens. Death comes splendidly, quickly, and until the last moment he is trying to keep control of his machine. It is not for him to envy the days of cavalry charges. He does not depend upon the companionship of other men to carry him on, but is the autocrat of his own fate, the ruler of his own dreams. All hours of daylight are the same to him. At any time he may be called to flight and perhaps to die. The glories of sunset and sunrise are his between the sun and the earth.

You expect the British to be cool aviators, but with their phlegm, as we have seen, goes that singular love of risk, of adventure, which sends them to shoot tigers and climb mountains. Indeed, the Englishman's phlegm is a sort of leash holding in check a certain recklessness which his seeming casualness conceals. After it had become almost a law that no aviator should descend lower than twelve thousand feet, British aviators on the Somme descended to three hundred, emptied their machine guns into the enemy, and escaped the patter of rifle fire which the surprised German soldiers had hardly begun before the plane at two miles a minute or more was out of range.

When Lord Kitchener was inspecting an aerodrome in France in 1914 he said: "One day you will be flying and evoluting in squadrons like the navy;" and the aviators, then feeling their way step by step, smiled doubtfully, convinced that "K" had an imagination. A few months later the prophecy had come true and the types of planes had increased until they were as numerous as the types of guns.

The swift falcon waiting fifteen thousand feet up for his prey to add another to his list in the *communiqué* is as distinct from the one in which I crossed the channel as the destroyer is from the cruiser and from some still bigger types as is the cruiser from a battleship. While the enemy was being fought down, bombs were dropped not by pounds but by tons on villages and billets, on ammunition dumps and rail-heads, adding their destruction to that of the shells.

There was more value in mastery than in destruction or in freedom of observation, for it affected the enemy's *morale*. A soldier likes to see his own planes in the air and the enemy's being driven away. The aerial influence on his psychology is enormous, for he can watch the planes as he lies in a shell-crater with his machine gun or stands guard in the trench; he has glimpses of passing wings overhead between the bursts of shells. To know that his guns are not replying adequately and that every time one of his planes appears it is driven to cover takes the edge off initiative, courage and discipline, in the resentment that he is handicapped.

German prisoners used to say on the Somme that their aviators were "funks," though the Allied aviators knew that it was not their opponents' lack of courage which was the principal fault, even if they had lost *morale* from being the under dog and lacked British and French initiative, but numbers and material. It was resource against resource again; a fight in the delicate business of the manufacture of the fragile framework, of the wonderful engines with their short lives, and of the skilled battalions of workers in factories. The Germans had to bring more planes from another front in order to restore the balance. The Allies foreseeing this brought still more themselves, till the numbers were so immense that when a battle between a score of planes on either side took place no one dared venture the opinion that the limit had been reached—not while there was so much room in the air and volunteers for the aviation corps were so plentiful.

XXIII

A PATENT CURTAIN OF FIRE

Thiepval again—Director of tactics of an army corps—Graduates of Staff Colleges—Army jargon—An army director's office—"Hope you will see a good show"—"This road is shelled; closed to vehicles"—A perfect summer afternoon—The view across No Man's Land—Nests of burrowers more cunning than any rodents—men—Tranquil preliminaries to an attack—The patent curtain of fire—Registering by practice shots—Running as men will run only from death—The tall officer who collapsed—"The shower of death."

"We had a good show day before yesterday," said Brigadier-General Philip Howell, when I went to call on him one day. "Sorry you were not here. You could have seen it excellently."

The corps of which he was general staff officer had taken a section of first-line trench at Thiepval with more prisoners than casualties, which is the kind of news they like to hear at General Headquarters. Thiepval was always in the background of the army's mind, the symbol of rankling memory which irritated British stubbornness and consoled the enemy for his defeat of July 15th and his gradual loss of the Ridge. The Germans, on the defensive, considered that the failure to take Thiepval at the beginning of the Somme battle proved its impregnability; the British, on the offensive, considered no place impregnable.

Faintly visible from the hills around Albert, distinctly from the observation post in a high tree, the remains of the village looked like a patch of coal dust smeared in a fold of the high ground. When British fifteen-inch shells made it their target some of the dust rose in a great geyser and fell back into place; but there were cellars in Thiepval which even fifteen-inch shells could not penetrate.

"However, we'll make the Germans there form the habit of staying indoors," said a gunner.

Howell who had the Thiepval task in hand I had first known at Uskub in Macedonia in the days of the Macedonian revolution, when Hilmi Pasha was juggling with the Powers of Europe and autonomy—days which seem far away. A lieutenant then, Howell had an assignment from *The Times*, while home on leave from India, in order to make a study of the Balkan situation. In our walks around Uskub as we discussed the politics and the armies of the world I found that all was grist that came to his keen mind. His ideas about soldiering were explicit and practical. It was such hard-working, observant officers as he, most of them students at one time or another at the Staff

College, who, when the crisis came, as the result of their application in peace time, became the organizers and commanders of the New Army. The lieutenant I had met at Uskub was now, at thirty-eight, the director of the tactics of an army corps which was solving the problem of reducing the most redoubtable of field works.

Whenever I think of the Staff College I am reminded that at the close of the American Civil War the commanders of all the armies and most of the corps were graduates of West Point, which serves to prove that a man of ability with a good military education has the start of one who has not, though no laws govern geniuses; and if we should ever have to fight another great war I look for our generals to have studied at Leavenworth and when the war ends for the leaders to be men whom the public did not know when it began.

"We shall have another show to-morrow and I think that will be a good one, too," said Howell.

All attacks are "shows;" big shows over two or three miles or more of front, little shows over a thousand yards or so, while five hundred yards is merely "cleaning up a trench." It may seem a flippant way of speaking, but it is simply the application of jargon to the everyday work of an organization. An attack that fails is a "washout," for not all attacks succeed. If they did, progress would be a matter of marching.

"Zero is at four; come at two," Howell said when I was going.

At two the next afternoon I found him occupied less with final details than with the routine business of one who is clearing his desk preparatory to a week-end holiday. Against the wall of what had been once a bedroom in the house of the leading citizen of the town, which was his office, he had an improvised bookkeeper's desk and on it were the mapped plans of the afternoon's operation, which he had worked over with the diligence and professional earnestness of an architect over his blue prints. He had been over the ground and studied it with the care of a landscape gardener who is going to make improvements.

"A smoke barrage screen along there," he explained, indicating the line of a German trench, "but a real attack along here"—which sounded familiar from staff officers in chateaux.

Every detail of the German positions was accurately outlined, yard by yard, their machine guns definitely located.

"We're uncertain about that one," he remarked, laying his pencil on the map symbol for an M.G.

Trench mortars had another symbol, deep dugouts another. It was the business of somebody to get all this information without being communicative about his methods. Referring to a section of a hundred yards or more he remarked that an eager company commander had thought that he could take a bit of German trench there and had taken it, which meant that the gunners had to be informed so as to rearrange the barrage or curtain of fire with the resulting necessity of fresh observations and fresh registry of practice shots. I judged that Howell did not want the men to be too eager; he wanted them just eager enough.

This game being played along the whole front has, of course, been likened to chess, with guns and men as pieces. I had in mind the dummy actors and dummy scenery with which stage managers try out their acts, only in this instance there was never any rehearsal on the actual stage with the actual scenery unless a first attack had failed, as the Germans will not permit such liberties except under machine gun fire. A call or two came over the telephone about some minor details, the principal ones being already settled.

"It's time to go," he said finally.

The corps commander was downstairs in the dining-room comfortably smoking his pipe after tea. There would be nothing for him to do until news of the attack had been received. "I hope you will see a good show," he remarked, by way of *au revoir*.

How earnestly he hoped it there is no use of mentioning here. It is taken for granted. Carefully thought out plans backed by hundreds of guns and the lives of men at stake—and against the Thiepval fortifications!

"Yes, we'll make it nicely," concluded Howell, as we went down the steps. A man used to motoring ten miles to catch the nine-thirty to town could not have been more certain of the disposal of his time than this soldier on the way to an attack. His car which was waiting had a right of way up to front such as is enjoyed only by the manager of the works on his own premises. Of course he paid no attention to the sign, "This road is shelled; closed to vehicles," at the beginning of a stretch of road which looked unused and desolate.

"A car in front of me here the other day received a direct hit from a 'krump,' and car and passengers practically disappeared before my eyes," he remarked, without further dwelling on the incident; for the Germans were, in turn, irritated with the insistence of these stubborn British that they could take Thiepval.

Three prisoners in the barbed-wire inclosure that we passed looked lonely. They must have been picked up in a little bombing affair in a sap.

"I think that they will have plenty of companions this evening," said Howell. "How they will enjoy their dinner!" He smiled in recollection as did I of that familiar sight of prisoners eating. Nothing excites hunger like a battle or gives such zest to appetite as knowledge that you are out of danger. I know that it is true and so does everybody at the front.

As his car knew no regulations except his wishes he might take it as far as it could go without trying to cross trenches. I wonder how long it would have taken me if I had had a map and asked no questions to find my way to the gallery seat which Howell had chosen for watching the show. After we had passed guns with only one out of ten firing leisurely but all with their covers off, the gunners near their pieces and ample ammunition at hand, we cut straight up the slope, Howell glancing at his wrist watch and asking if he were walking too fast for me. We dropped into a communication trench at a point which experience had proven was the right place to begin to take cover.

"This is a good place," he said at length, and we rubbed our helmets with some of the chalk lumps of the parapet, which left the black spot of our field glasses the only bit of us not in harmony with our background.

It was a perfect afternoon in late summer, without wind or excessive heat, the blue sky unflecked; such an afternoon as you would choose for lolling in a hammock and reading a book. The foreground was a slope downward to a little valley where the usual limbless tree-trunks were standing in a grove that had been thoroughly shelled. No one was in sight there, and an occasional German five-point-nine shell burst on the mixture of splinters and earth.

On the other side of the valley was a cut in the earth, a ditch, the British first-line trench, which was unoccupied, so far as I could see. Beyond lay the old No Man's Land where grass and weeds had grown wild for two seasons, hiding the numerous shell-craters and the remains of the dead from the British charge of July 1st which had been repulsed. On the other side of this was two hundred yards of desolate stretch up to the wavy, chalky excavation from the deep cutting of the German first-line trench, as distinct as a white line on dark-brown paper. There was no sign of life here, either, or to the rear where ran the network of other excavations as the result of the almost two years of German digging, the whole thrown in relief on the slope up to the bare trunks of two or three trees thrust upward from the smudge of the ruins of Thiepval.

Just a knoll in rolling farm country, that was all; but it concealed burrows upon burrows of burrowers more cunning than any rodents—men. Since July 1st the Germans had not been idle. They had had time to profit from the lesson of the attack with additions and improvements. They had deepened dugouts and joined them by galleries; they had Box and Cox hiding-places; nests defensible from all sides which became known as Mystery Works and Wonder Works. The message of that gashed and spaded hillside was one of mortal defiance.

Occasionally a British high explosive broke in the German trench and all up and down the line as far as we could see this desultory shell fire was proceeding, giving no sign of where the next attack was coming, which was part of the plan.

"It's ten to four!" said Howell. "We were here in ample time. I hope we get them at relief," which was when a battalion that had been on duty was relieved by a battalion that had been in rest.

He laid his map on the parapet and the location and plan of the attack became clear as a part of the extensive operations in the Thiepval-Mouquet Farm sector. The British were turning the flank of these Thiepval positions as they swung in from the joint of the break of July 1st up to the Pozières Ridge. A squeeze here and a squeeze there; an attack on that side and then on this; one bite after another.

"I hope you will like our patent barrage," said the artillery general, as he stopped for a moment on the way to a near-by observation post. "We are thinking rather well of it ourselves of late." He did not even have to touch a pushbutton to turn on the current. He had set four as zero.

I am not going to speak of suspense before the attack as being in the very air and so forth. I felt it personally, but the Germans did not feel it or, at least, the British did not want them to feel it. There was no more sign of an earthly storm brewing as one looked at the field than of a thunderstorm as one looked at the sky. Perfect soporific tranquillity possessed the surroundings except for shell-bursts, and their meagerness intensified the aspect, strangely enough, on that battlefield where I had never seen a quieter afternoon since the Somme offensive had begun. One could ask nothing better than that the tranquillity should put the Germans to sleep. To the staff expert, however, the dead world lived without the sight of men. Every square rod of ground had some message.

Of course, I knew what was coming at four o'clock, but I was amazed at its power and accuracy when it did come—this improved method of artillery preparation, this patent curtain of fire. An outburst of screaming shells overhead that became a continuous, roaring sweep like that of a number of endless railroad trains in the air signified that the guns which had been idle were all speaking. Every one by scattered practice shots had registered on the German first-line trench at the point where its shell-bursts would form its link in the chain of bursts. Over the wavy line of chalk for the front of the attack broke the flashes of cracking shrapnel jackets, whose bullets were whipping up spurts of chalk like spurts of dust on a road from a hailstorm.

As the gun-blasts began I saw some figures rise up back of the German trench. I judged that they were the relief coming up or a working party that had been under cover. These Germans had to make a quick decision: Would they try a leap for the dugouts or a leap to the rear? They decided on flight. A hundred-yard sprint and they would be out of that murderous swath laid so accurately on a narrow belt. They ran as men will only run from death. No goose-stepping or "after you, sir" limited their eagerness. I had to smile at their precipitancy and as some dropped it was hard to realize that they had fallen from death or wounds. They seemed only manikins in a pantomime.

Then a lone figure stepped up out of a communication trench just back of the German first line. This tall officer, who could see nothing between walls of earth where he was, stood up in full view looking around as if taking stock of the situation, deciding, perhaps, whether that smoke barrage to his right now rolling out of the British trench was on the real line of attack or was only for deception; observing and concluding what his men, I judge, were never to know, for, as a man will when struck a hard blow behind the knees, he collapsed suddenly and the earth swallowed him up before the bursts of shrapnel smoke had become so thick over the trench that it formed a curtain.

There must have been a shell a minute to the yard. Shrapnel bullets were hissing into the mouths of dugouts; death was hugging every crevice, saying to the Germans:

"Keep down! Keep out of the rain! If you try to get out with a machine gun you will be killed! Our infantry is coming!"

XXIV

WATCHING A CHARGE

The British trench comes to life—The line goes forward—A modern charge no chance for heroics—Machine-like forward movement—The most wicked sound in a battle—The first machine gun—A beautiful barrage—The dreaded "shorts"—The barrage lifts to the second line—The leap into the trenches—Figures in green with hands up—Captured from dugouts—A man who made his choice and paid the price—German answering fire—Second part of the program—Again the protecting barrage—Success—Waves of men advancing behind waves of shell fire—Prisoners in good fettle—Brigadier-General Philip Howell.

Now the British trench came to life. What seemed like a row of khaki-colored washbasins bottom side up and fast to a taut string rose out of the cut in the earth on the other side of the valley, and after them came the shoulders and bodies of British soldiers who began climbing over the parapet just as a man would come up the cellar stairs. This was the charge.

Five minutes the barrage or curtain of fire was to last and five minutes was the allotted time for these English soldiers to go from theirs to the German trench which they were to take. So many paces to the minute was the calculation of their rate of progress across that dreadful No Man's Land, where machine guns and German curtains of fire had wrought death in the preceding charge of July 1st.

Every detail of the men's equipment was visible as their full-length figures appeared on the background of the gray-green slope. They were entirely exposed to fire from the German trench. Any tyro with a rifle on the German parapet could have brought down a man with every shot. Yet none fell; all were going forward.

I would watch the line over a hundred yards of breadth immediately in front of me, determined not to have my attention diverted to other parts of the attack and to make the most of this unique opportunity of observation in the concrete.

The average layman conceives of a charge as a rush. So it is on the drill-ground, but not where its movement is timed to arrival on the second before a hissing storm of death, and the attackers must not be winded when there is hot work awaiting them in close encounters around traverses and at the mouths of dugouts. No one was sprinting ahead of his companions; no one crying, "Come on, boys!" no one swinging his steel helmet aloft, for he needed it for protection from any sudden burst of shrapnel. All were advancing at a rapid pace, keeping line and intervals except where they had to pass around shell-craters.

If this charge had none of the display of other days it had all the more thrill because of its workmanlike and regulated progress. No get-drunk-six-days-of-the-week-and-fight-like-h—l-on-Sunday business of the swashbuckling age before Thiepval. Every man must do his part as coolly as if he were walking a tight rope with no net to catch him, with death to be reckoned with in the course of a systematic evolution.

"Very good! A trifle eager there! Excellent!" Howell sweeping the field with his glasses was speaking in the expert appreciation of a football coach watching his team at practice. "No machine guns yet," he said for the second time, showing the apprehension that was in his mind.

I, too, had been listening for the staccato of the machine gun, which is the most penetrating, mechanical and wicked, to my mind, of all the instruments of the terrible battle orchestra, as sinister as the clicking of a switch which you know will derail a passenger train. The men were halfway to the German trench, now. Two and a half minutes of the allotted five had passed. In my narrow sector of vision not one man had yet fallen. They might have been in a manoeuver and their goal a deserted ditch. Looking right and left my eye ran along the line of sturdy, moving backs which seemed less concerned than the spectator. Not only because you were on their side but as the reward of their steadiness, you wanted them to conquer that stretch of first-line fortifications. Any second you expected to see the first shell-burst of the answering German barrage break in the midst of them.

Then came the first sharp, metallic note which there is no mistaking, audible in the midst of shell-screams and gun-crashes, off to the right, chilling your heart, quickening your observation with awful curiosity and drawing your attention away from the men in front as you looked for signs of a machine gun's gathering of a human harvest. Rat-tat-tat-tat in quick succession, then a pause before another series instead of continuous and slower cracks, and you knew that it was not a German but a British machine gun farther away than you had thought.

More than ever you rejoiced in every one of the bursts of stored lightning thick as fireflies in the blanket of smoke over the German trench, for every one meant a shower of bullets to keep down enemy machine guns. The French say "*Belle!*" when they see such a barrage, and beautiful is the word for it to those men who were going across the field toward this shell-made nimbus looking too soft in the bright sunlight to have darts of death. All the shell-bursts seemed to be in a breadth of twenty or thirty yards. How could guns firing at a range of from two to five thousand yards attain such accuracy!

The men were three-quarters of the distance, now. As they drew nearer to the barrage another apprehension numbed your thought. You feared to see a "short"—one of the shells from their own guns which did not carry far enough bursting among the men—and this, as one English soldier who had been knocked over by a short said, with dry humor, was "very discouraging, sir, though I suppose it is well meant." A terrible thing, that, to the public, killing your own men with your own shells. It is better to lose a few of them in this way than many from German machine guns by lifting the barrage too soon, but fear of public indignation had its influence in the early days of British gunnery. The better the gunnery the closer the infantry can go and the greater its confidence. A shell that bursts fifteen or twenty yards short means only the slightest fault in length of fuse, error of elevation, or fault in registry, back where the muzzles are pouring out their projectiles from the other side of the slope. And there were no shorts that day. Every shell that I saw burst was "on." It was perfect gunnery.

Now it seemed that the men were going straight into the blanket over the trenches still cut with flashes. Some forward ones who had become eager were at the edge of the area of dust-spatters from shrapnel bullets in the white chalk. Didn't they know that another twenty yards meant death? Was their methodical phlegm such that they acted entirely by rule? No, they knew their part. They stopped and stood waiting. Others were on the second of the five minutes' allowance as suddenly all the flashes ceased and nothing remained over the trench but the mantle of smoke. The barrage had been lifted from the first to the second-line German trench as you lift the spray of a hose from one flower bed to another.

This was the moment of action for the men of the charge, not one of whom had yet fired a shot. Each man was distinctly outlined against the white background as, bayonets glistening and hands drawn back with bombs ready to throw, they sprang forward to be at the mouths of the dugouts before the Germans came out. Some leaped directly into the trench, others ran along the parapet a few steps looking for a vantage point or throwing a bomb as they went before they descended. It was a quick, urgent, hit-and-run sort of business and in an instant all were out of sight and the fighting was man to man, with the guns of both sides keeping their hands off this conflict under ground. The entranced gaze for a moment leaving that line of chalk saw a second British wave advancing in the same way as the first from the British first-line trench.

"All in along the whole line. Bombing their way forward there!" said Howell, with matter-of-fact understanding of the progress of events.

I blinked tired eyes and once more pressed them to the twelve diameters of magnification, every diameter having full play in the clear light. I saw nothing but little bursts of smoke rising out of the black streak in the chalk which was the trench itself, each one from an egg of high explosive thrown at close quarters but not numerous enough to leave any doubt of the result and very evidently against a few recalcitrants who still held out.

Next, a British soldier appeared on the parapet and his attitude was that of one of the military police directing traffic at a busy crossroads close to the battle front. His part in the carefully worked out system was shown when a figure in green came out of the trench with hands held up in the approved signal of surrender the world over. The figure was the first of a file with hands up—and very much in earnest in this attitude, too, which is the one that the British and the French consider most becoming in a German—who were started on toward the first-line British trench. All along the front small bands of prisoners were appearing in the same way. There would have been something ridiculous about it, if it had not been so real.

For the most part, the prisoners had been breached from dugouts which had no exit through galleries after the Germans had been held fast by the barrage. It was either a case of coming out at once or being bombed to death in their holes; so they came out.

"A live prisoner would be of more use to his fatherland one day than a dead one, even though he had no more chance to fight again than a rabbit held up by the ears," as one of the German prisoners said.

"More use to yourself, too," remarked his captor.

"That had occurred to me, also," admitted the German.

During the filing out of the different bags of prisoners two incidents passed before my eye with a realism that would have been worth a small fortune to a motion picture man if equally dramatic ones had not been posed. A German sprang out of the trench, evidently either of a mind to resist or else in a panic, and dropped behind one of the piles of chalk thrown up in the process of excavation. A British soldier went after him and he held up his hands and was dispatched to join one of the groups. Another who sought cover in the same way was of different temperament, or perhaps resistance was inspired by the fact that he had a bomb. He threw it at a British soldier who seemed to dodge it and drop on all fours, the bomb bursting behind him. Bombs then came from all directions at the German. There was no time to parley; he had made his choice and must pay the price. He rolled over after the smoke had risen from the explosions and then remained a still green blot against the chalk. A British soldier bent over the figure in a hasty examination and then sprang into the trench, where evidently he was needed.

"The Germans are very slow with their shell fire," said Howell in the course of his ejaculations, as he watched the operations.

Answering barrages, including a visitation to our own position which was completely exposed, were in order. Howell himself had been knocked over by a shell here during the last attack. One explanation given later by a German officer for the tardiness of the German guns was that the staff had thought the British too stupid to attack from that direction, which pleased Howell as showing the advantage of racial reputation as an aid to strategy.

However, the German artillery was not altogether unresponsive. It was putting some "krumps" into the neighborhood of the British first line and one of the bands of prisoners ran into the burst of a five-point-nine. Ran is the word, for they were going as fast as they could to get beyond their own curtain of fire, which experience told them would soon be due. I saw this lot submerged in the spout of smoke and dust but did not see how many if any were hit, as the sound of a machine gun drew my attention across the dead grass of the old No Man's Land to the German—I should say the former German—first-line trench where an Englishman had his machine gun on the *parados* and was sweeping the field across to the German second-line trench. Perhaps some of the Germans who had run away from the barrage at the start had been hiding in shell-craters or had shown signs of moving or there were targets elsewhere.

So far so good, as Howell remarked. That supposedly impregnable German fortification that had repulsed the first British attempt had been taken as easily as if it were a boy's snow fort, thanks to the patent curtain of fire and the skill that had been developed by battle lessons. It was retribution for the men who had fallen in vain on July 1st. Howell was not thinking of that, but of the second objective in the afternoon's plan. By this time not more than a quarter of an hour had elapsed since the first charge had "gone over the lid." Out of the cut in the welt of chalk the line of helmets rose again and England started across the field toward the German second-line trench, which was really a part of the main first-line fortification on the slope, in the same manner as toward the first.

What about their protecting barrage? My eyes had been so intently occupied that my ears had been uncommunicative and in a start of glad surprise I realized that the same infernal sweep of shells was going overhead and farther up on the Ridge fireflies were flashing out of the mantle of smoke that blanketed the second line. Now the background better absorbed the khaki tint and the figures of the men became more and more hazy until they disappeared altogether as the flashes in front of them ceased. Howell had to translate from the signals results which I could not visually verify. One by one items of news appeared in rocket flashes through the gathering haze which began to obscure the slope itself.

"I think we have everything that we expected to take this afternoon," said Howell, at length. "The Germans are very slow to respond. I think we rather took them by surprise."

They had not even begun shelling their old first line, which they ought to have known was now in British possession and which they must have had registered, as a matter of course; or possibly their own intelligence was poor and they had no real information of what had been proceeding on the slope under the clouds of smoke, or their wires had been cut and their messengers killed by shell fire. This was certain, that the British in the first-line German trench had a choice lot of dugouts in good condition for shelter, as the patent barrage does not smash in the enemy's homes, only closes the doors with curtains of death.

"I hope you're improving your dugouts," British soldiers would call out across No Man's Land, "as that is all the better for us when we take them!"

We stayed on till Howell's expert eye had had its fill of details, with no burst of shells to interfere with our comfort; though by the rules we ought to have had a good "strafing," which was another reminder of my debt to the German for his consideration to the American correspondent at the British front.

"What do you think of our patent barrage, now?" said the artillery general returning from his post of observation.

"Wonderful!" was all that one could say.

"A good show!" said Howell.

The rejoicing of both was better expressed in their eyes than in words. Good news, too, for the corps commander smoking his pipe and waiting, and for every battalion engaged—oh, particularly for the battalions!

"Congratulations!" The exclamation was passed back and forth as we met other officers on our way to brigade headquarters in a dugout on the hillside, where Howell's felicitations to the happy brigadier on the way that his men had gone in were followed by suggestions and a discussion about future plans, which I left to them while I had a look through the brigadier's telescope at Thiepval Ridge under the patterns of shell fire of average days, which proved that the Germans were making no attempt at a counter-attack to recover lost ground. I imagined that the German staff was dumfounded to hear that their redoubtable old first line could possibly have been taken with so little fireworks.

It was when I came to the guns on our return that I felt an awe which I wanted to translate into appreciation. They were firing slowly now or not firing at all, and the idle gunners were lounging about. They had not seen their own curtain of fire or the infantry charge; they had been as detached from the action as the crew of a battleship turret. It was their accuracy and their coördination with the infantry and the infantry's coördination with the barrage that had expressed better than volumes of reports the possibilities of the offensive with waves of men advancing behind waves of shell fire, which was applied in the taking of Douaumont later and must be the solution of the problem of a decision on the Western front.

Above the communication trenches the steel helmets of the British and the gray fatigue caps of German prisoners were bobbing toward the rear and at the casualty clearing station the doctor said, "Very light!" in answer to the question about losses. The prisoners were in unusually good fettle even for men safe out of shell fire; many had no chalk on their clothes to indicate a struggle. They had been sitting in their dugouts and walked out when an Englishman appeared at the door. Yes, they said that they had been caught just before relief, and the relief had been carried out in an unexpected fashion. If they must be taken they, too, liked the patent barrage.

"I'll let you know when there's to be another show," said Howell, as we parted at corps headquarters; but none could ever surpass this one in its success or its opportunity of intimate observation.

This was the last time I saw him. A few days later, on one of his tours to study the ground for an attack, he was killed by a shell. Army custom permits the mention of his name because he is dead. He was a steadfast friend, an able soldier, an upright, kindly, high-minded gentleman; and when I was asked, not by the lady who had never kept up her interest so long in anything as in this war, but by another, if living at the front is a big strain, the answer is in the word that comes that a man whom you have just seen in the fulness of life and strength is gone.

XXV

CANADA IS STUBBORN

What is Canada fighting for?—The Kaiser has brought Canadians together—The land of immense distances—Canada's unfaltering spirit—Canada our nearest neighbor geographically and sentimentally—Ypres salient mud—Canadians invented the trench raid—A wrestling fight in the mud—Germans "try it on" the Canadians—"The limit" in artillery fire—Maple Leaf spirit—Baseball talk on the firing line—A good sprinkling of Americans.

One day the Canadians were to lift their feet out of the mire of the Ypres salient and take the high, dry road to the Somme front, and anyone with a whit of chivalry in his soul would have rejoiced to know that they were to have their part in the big movement of Sept. 15th. But let us consider other things and other fighting before we come to the taking of Courcelette.

When I was home in the winter of 1915-16, for the first time the border between the United States and Canada drew a line in sharp contrasts. The newspapers in Canada had their casualty lists, parents were giving their sons and wives their husbands to go three thousand miles to endure hardship and risk death for a cause which to them had no qualifications of a philosophic internationalism. Everything was distinct. Sacrifice and fortitude, life and death, and the simple meaning words were masters of the vocabulary.

Some people might ask why Canada should be pouring out her blood in Europe; what had Flanders to do with her? England was fighting to save her island, France for the sanctity of her soil, but what was Canada fighting for? As I understood it, she was fighting for Canada. A blow had been struck against her, though it was struck across the Atlantic, and across the Atlantic she was going to strike back.

She had had no great formative war. Pardeburg was a kind of expedition of brave men, like the taking of San Juan Hill. It did not sink deep into the consciousness of the average Canadian, who knew only that some neighbor of his had been in South Africa. Our own formative war was the Revolution, not the Civil War where brother fought brother. The Revolution made a mold which, perhaps, instead of being impressed upon succeeding generations of immigrants may have only given a veneer to them. A war may be necessary to make them molten for another shaping.

No country wanted war less than Canada, but when war came its flame made Canada molten with Canadian patriotism. As George III. brought the Carolinas and Massachusetts together, so the Kaiser has brought the Canadian provinces together. The men from that cultivated, rolling country of Southern Ontario, from New Brunswick and the plains and the coast and a quota from the neat farms of Quebec have met face to face, not on railroad trains, not through representatives in Parliament or in convention, but in billets and trenches. Whatever Canada is, she is not small. She is particularly the land of immense distances; her breadth is greater than that of the United States. All of the great territorial expanse of Canada in its manhood, in the thoughts of those at home, was centered in a few square miles of Flanders.

I was in Canada when only the first division had had its trial and recruiting was at full blast; and again when three hundred and fifty thousand had joined the colors and Canada, now feeling the full measure of loss of life, seemed unfaltering, which was the more remarkable in a new country where livelihood is easy to gain and Opportunity knocks at the door of youth if he has only the energy to take her by the hand and go her way. I may add that not all the youth about Toronto or any other town who gave as their reason for not enlisting that they were American citizens actually were. They were not "too *proud* to fight," whatever other reason they had, for they had no pride; and if honest Quakers they would not have given a lying excuse.

Out in France I heard talk about this Canadian brigade being better than that one, and that an Eastern Canada man wanted no leading from a Western Canada man, and that not all who were winning military crosses were hardy frontiersmen but some were lawyers and clerks in Montreal or Toronto—or should I put Toronto first, or perhaps Ottawa or Winnipeg—and more talk expressive of the rivalry which generals say is good for spirit of corps. Moose Jaw Street was across from Halifax Avenue and Vancouver Road from Hamilton Place in the same community.

As I was not connected with any part of Canada, the Canadians, with their Maple Leaf emblem, were all Canadians to me; men across the border which we pass in coming and going without change of language or steam-heated cars or iced-water tanks. Some Canadians think that the United States with its more than a hundred millions may feel patronizing toward their eight millions, when after Courcelette if a Canadian had patronized the United States I should not have felt offended. I have even heard some fools say that the two countries might yet go to war, which shows how absurd some men have to be in order to attract attention. All of this way of thinking on both sides should be placed on a raft in the middle of Lake Erie and supplied with bombs to fight it out among themselves under a curtain of fire; and their relatives ought to feel a deep relief after the excursion steamers that came from Toronto, Cleveland and Buffalo to see the show had returned home.

To listen to certain narrators you might think that it was the Allies who always got the worst of it in the Ypres salient, but the German did not like the salient any better than they. I never met anybody who did like it. German prisoners said that German soldiers regarded it as a sentence of death to be sent to the salient. There are many kinds of mud and then there is Ypres salient mud, which is all kinds together with a Belgian admixture. I sometimes thought that the hellish outbreaks by both sides in this region were due to the reason which might have made Job run amuck if all the temper he had stored up should have broken out in a storm.

This is certain, that the Canadians took their share in the buffets in the mud, not through any staff calculation but partly through German favoritism and the workings of German psychology. Consider that the first volunteer troops to be put in the battle line in France weeks before any of Kitchener's Army was the first Canadian division, in answer to its own request for action, which is sufficient soldierly tribute of a commander to Canadian valor! That proud first division, after it had been well mud-soaked and had its hand in, was caught in the gas attack. It refused to yield when it was only human to yield, and stood resolute in the fumes between the Germans and success and even counter-attacked. Moreover, it was Canadians who introduced the trench raid.

If the Canadians did not particularly love the Germans, do you see any reason why the Germans should love the Canadians? It was unpleasant to suffer repulse by troops from an unmilitary, new country. Besides, German psychology reasoned that if Canadians at the front were made to suffer heavy losses the men at home would be discouraged from enlisting. Why not? What had Canada to gain by coming to fight in France? It does not appear an illogical hypothesis until you know the Canadians.

However, it must not be understood that other battalions, brigades and divisions, English and Scotch, did not suffer as heavily as the Canadians. They did; and do not forget that in the area which has seen the hardest, bloodiest, meanest, nastiest, ghastliest fighting in the history of the world the Germans, too, have had their full share of losses. The truth is that if any normal man was stuck in the mud of the Ypres salient and another wanted his place he would say, "Take it! I'm only trying to get out! We've got equally bad morasses in the Upper Yukon;" and retire to a hill and set up a machine gun.

When a Canadian officer was asked if he had organized some trenches that his battalion had taken his reply, "How can you organize pea soup?" filled a long-felt want in expression to characterize the nature of trench-making in that kind of terrain. Yet in that sea of slimy and infected mush men have fought for the possession of cubic feet of the mixture as if it had the qualities of Balm of Gilead—which was also logical. What appears most illogical to the outsider is sometimes most logical in war. It was a fight for mastery, and mastery is the first step in a war of frontal positions.

Many lessons the Canadians had to learn about organization and staff work, about details of discipline which make for homogeneity of action, and the divisions that came to join the first one learned their lessons in the Ypres salient school, which gave hard but lasting tuition. I was away when at St. Eloi they were put to such tests as only the salient can provide. The time was winter, when chill water filled the shell-craters and the soil oozed out of sandbags and the mist was a cold, wet poultice. Men bred to a dry climate had to fight in a climate better suited to the Englishman or the German than to the Canadian. There could be no dugouts. Lift a spade of earth below the earth level and it became a puddle. It was a wrestling fight in the mud, this, holding onto shell-craters and the soft remains of trenches. The Germans had heard that the Canadians were highstrung, nervous, quick for the offensive, but badly organized and poor at sticking. The Canadians proved that they could be stubborn and that their soldiers, even if they had not had the directing system of an army staff that had prepared for forty years, with two years of experience could act on their own in resisting as well as in attacking. "Our men! our men!" the officers would say. That was it: Canada's men, learning tactics in face of German tactics and holding their own!

When all was peaceable up and down the line, with the Grand Offensive a month away, the Germans once more "tried it on" the Canadians in the Hooge and Mount Sorrell sector, where the positions were all in favor of the Germans with room to plant two guns to one around the bulging British line. For many days they had been quietly registering as they massed their artillery for their last serious effort during the season of 1916 in the north.

Anything done to the Canadians always came close home to me; and news of this attack and of its ferocity to anyone knowing the positions was bound to carry apprehension, lasting only until we learned that the Canadians were already counter-attacking, which set your pulse tingling and little joy-bells ringing in your head. It meant, too, that the Germans could not have developed any offensive that would be serious to the situation as a whole at that moment, in the midst of preparations for the Somme. Nothing could be seen of the fight, even had one known that it was coming, in that flat region where everyone has to follow a communication trench with only the sky directly overhead visible.

There was an epic quality in the story of what happened as you heard it from the survivors. It was an average quiet morning in the first-line trenches when the German hurricane broke from all sides; but first-line trenches is not the right phrase, for all the protection that could be made was layers of sandbags laboriously filled and piled to a thickness sufficient to stop a bullet at short range.

What luxury in security were the dugouts of the Somme hills compared to the protection that could be provided here! When the first series of bursts announced the storm you could not descend a flight of steps to a cavern whose roof was impenetrable even by five-hundred-pound shells. Little houses of sandbags with corrugated tin roofs, in some instances level with the earth, which any direct hit could "do in" were the best that generous army resources could permit. High explosive shells must turn such breastworks into rags and heaps of earth. There was nothing to shoot at if a man tried to stick to the parapet, for fresh troops fully equipped for their task back in the German trenches waited on demolition of the Canadian breastworks before advancing under their own barrage. Shrapnel sent down its showers, while the trench walls were opened in great gaps and tossed heavenward. Officers clambered about in the midst of the spouts of dust and smoke over the piles and around the craters, trying to keep in touch with their men, when it was a case of every man taking what cover he could.

"The limit!" as the men said. "The absolute limit in an artillery concentration!"

But they did not go—not until they had orders. This was their kind of discipline under fire; they "stayed on the job." One group charged out beyond the swath of fire to meet the Germans in the open and there fought to the death in expression of characteristic initiative. When word was passed to retire, some grudgingly held on to fight the outnumbering Germans in the midst of the débris and escaped only by passing through the German barrage placed between the first and second line to cover the German advance on the second. The supports themselves under the carefully arranged pattern of shell fire held as the rallying-points of the survivors, who found the communication trenches so badly broken that it was as well to keep in the open. Little knots of men with their defenses crushed held from the instinctive sense of individual stubbornness.

To tell the whole story of that day as of many other days where a few battalions were engaged, giving its fair due to each group in the struggle, is not for a correspondent who had to cover the length of the battle line and sees the whole as an example of Maple Leaf spirit. The rest is for battalion historians, who will find themselves puzzled about an action where there was little range of vision and this obscured by shell-smoke and the preoccupation of each man trying to keep cover and do his own part to the death.

In the farmhouses afterward, as groups of officers tried to assemble their experiences, I had the feeling of being in touch with the proof of all that I had seen in Canada months previously. Losses had been heavy for the battalions engaged though not for the Canadian corps as a whole, no heavier than British battalions or the Germans had suffered in the salient. Canada happened to get the blow this time.

The men, after a night's sleep and writing home that they were safe and how comrades had died, might wander about the roads or make holiday as they chose. They were not casual about the fight, but outspoken and frank, Canadian fashion. They realized what they had been through and spoke of their luck in having survived. From the fields came the cry of, "Leave that to me!" as a fly rose from the bat, or, "Out on first!" as men took a rest from shell-curves and high explosives with baseball curves and hot liners between the bases, which was very homelike there in Flanders. Which of the players was American one could not tell by voice or looks, for the climate along the border makes a type of complexion and even of features with the second generation which is readily distinguished from the English type.

"What part of Canada do you come from?" asked an officer of a private.

"Out west, sir!"

"What part of the west?"

"'Way out west, sir!"

"An officer is asking you. Be definite."

"Well, the State of Washington, sir."

There was a good sprinkling of Americans in the battle, including officers; but on the baseball field and the battlefield they were a part of the whole, performing their task in a way that left no doubt of their quality. Whether the spirit of adventure or the principle at stake had brought her battalions to Flanders, Canada had proved that she could be stubborn. She was to have her chance to prove that she could be quick.

XXVI

THE TANKS ARRIVE

The New Army Irish—Irish wit—And Irish courage—Pompous Prussian Guard officer—The British Guards and their characteristics—Who invented the tank?—The great secret—Combination of an armadillo, a caterpillar, a diplodocus, a motor car and a traveling circus—Something really new on the front—Gas attacks—A tank in the road—A moving "strong point"—Making an army laugh—Suspense for the inmates of the untried tanks.

The situation on the Ridge was where we left it in a previous chapter with all except a few parts of it held, enough for a jumping-off place at all points for the sweep down into the valley toward Bapaume. In the grim preliminary business of piecemeal gains which should make possible an operation over a six-mile front on Sept. 15th, which was the first general attack since July 14th, the part that the Irish battalions played deserves notice, where possibly the action of the tried and sturdy English regiments on their flanks need not be mentioned, as being characteristic of the work they had been doing for months.

They were the New Army Irish, all volunteers, men who had enlisted to fight against Germany when their countrymen were largely disaffected, which requires more initiative than to join the colors when it is the universal passion of the community. Many stories were told of this Irish division. If there are ten Irishmen among a hundred soldiers the stories have a way of being about the ten Irishmen.

I like that one of the Connaught man who, on his first day in the trenches, was set to digging out the dirt that had been filled into a trench by a shell-burst. Along came another shell before he was half through his task; the burst of a second knocked him over and doubled the quantity of earth before him. When he picked himself up he went to the captain and threw down his spade, saying:

"Captain, I can't finish that job without help. They're gaining on me!"

Some people thought that the Sinn Fein movement which had lately broken out in the Dublin riots would make the new Irish battalions lukewarm in any action. They would go in but without putting spirit into their attack. Other skeptics questioned if the Irish temperament which was well suited to dashing charges would adapt itself to the matter-of-fact necessities of the Somme fighting. Their commander, however, had no doubts; and the army had none when the test was made.

Through Guillemont, that wicked resort of machine guns, which had been as severely hammered by shell fire after it had repulsed British attacks as any village on the Somme, the Irish swept in good order, cleaning up dugouts and taking prisoners on the way with all the skill of veterans and a full relish of the exploit, and then forward, as a well-linked part of a successful battle line, to the sunken road which was the second objective.

"I thought we were to take a village, Captain," said one of the men, after they were established in the sunken road. "What are we stopping here for?"

"We have taken it. You passed through it—that grimy patch yonder"—which was Guillemont's streets and houses mixed in ruins five hundred yards to the rear.

"You're sure, Captain?"

"Quite!"

"Well, then, I'd not like to be the drunken man that tried to find his keyhole in that town!"

It was a pity, perhaps, that the Irish who assisted in the taking of Ginchy, which completed the needful mastery of the Ridge for British purposes, could not have taken part in the drive that was to follow. We had looked forward to this drive as the reward of a down hill run after the patient labor of wrenching our way up hill. Even the Germans, who had suffered appalling losses in trying to hold the Ridge, must have been relieved that they no longer had to fight against the inevitable.

Again the clans were gathering and again there ran through the army the anticipation which came from the preparation for a great blow. The Canadians were appearing in billets back of the front. If in no other way, I should have known of their presence by their habit of moving about roads and fields getting acquainted with their surroundings and finding out if apples were ripe. For other portions of the country it was a little unfair that these generous and well-paid spenders should take the place of the opulent Australians in villages where small boys already had hordes of pennies and shopkeepers were hastening to replenish their stocks to be equal to their opportunities.

At last the Guards, too, were to have their turn, but not to go in against the Prussian Guard, which those with a sense of histrionic fitness desired. When a Prussian Guard officer had been taken at Contalmaison he had said, "The Prussian Guard feels that it is surrendering to a foe worthy of its steel when it yields to superior numbers of the English Guard!" or words to that effect according to reports, only to receive the answer that his captors were English factory hands and the like of the New Army, whose officers excused themselves, in the circumstances, for their identity as politely as they could.

Grenadiers, Coldstreams, Scottish, or Irish, the Guards were the Guards, England's crack regiments, the officers of each wearing their buttons in a distinctive way and the tall privates saluting with the distinctive Guards' salute. In the Guards the old spirit of gaiety in face of danger survived. Their officers out in shell-craters under curtains of fire joked one another with an aristocratic, genial sangfroid, the slender man who had a nine-inch crater boasting of his luck over the thickset man who tried to accommodate himself to a five-inch, while a colonel blew his hunting-horn in the charge, which the Guards made in a manner worthy of tradition.

Though the English would have been glad to go against the Prussian Guard with bayonet or bomb or a free-for-all, army commanders in these days are not signaling to the enemy, "Let us have a go between your Guards and our Guards!" but are putting crack regiments and line regiments in a battle line to a common task, where the only criterion is success.

The presence of the Guards, however, yielded interest to another new arrival on the Somme front. When the plan for a style of armored motor car which would cross shell-craters and trenches was laid before an eminent general at the War Office, what he wrote in dismissing it from further consideration might have been more blasphemous if he could have spared the time to be anything but satirically brief. Such conservatives probably have prevented many improvements from materializing, and probably they have also saved the world from many futile creations which would only have wasted time and material.

Happily both for geniuses and fools, who all, in the long run, let us hope, receive their just deserts, there is no downing an idea in a free country where continued knocking at doors and waiting in hallways eventually secure it a trial. Then, if it succeeds, the fellow who thought that the conception was original with him finds his claims disputed from all points of the compass. If it fails, the poor thing goes to a fatherless grave.

I should like to say that I was the originator of the tank—one of the originators. In generous mood, I am willing to share honors with rivals too numerous to mention. Haven't I also looked across No Man's Land toward the enemy's parapet? Whoever has must have conjectured about a machine that would take frontal positions with less loss of life than is usual and would solve the problem of breaking the solid line of the Western front. The possibility has haunted every general, every soldier.

Some sort of armadillo or caterpillar which would resist bullet fire was the most obvious suggestion, but when practical construction was considered, the dreamer was brought down from the empyrean, where the aeroplane is at home, to the forge and the lathe, where grimy machinists are the pilots of a matter-of-fact world. Application was the thing. I found myself so poor at it that I did not even pass on my plan to the staff, which had already considered a few thousand plans. Ericsson conceiving a gun in a revolving turret was not so great a man as Ericsson making the monitor a practicable engine of war.

To Lieutenant-Colonel Swinton, of the Engineers, was given the task of transforming blue-print plans into reality. There was no certainty that he would succeed, but the War Office, when it had need for every foundry and every skilled finger in the land, was enterprising enough to give him a chance. He and thousands of workmen spent months at this most secret business. If one German spy had access to one workman, then the Germans might know what was coming. Nobody since Ericsson had a busier time than Swinton without telling anybody what he was doing. The whisperers knew that some diabolical surprise was under way and they would whisper about it. No censor regulations can reach them. Sometimes the tribe was given false information in great confidence in order to keep it too occupied to pass on the true.

The new monster was called a tank because it was not like a tank; yet it seemed to me as much like a tank as like anything else. As a tank is a receptacle for a liquid, it was a name that ought to mask a new type of armored motor car as successfully as any name could. Flower pot would have been too wide of the mark. A tank might carry a new kind of gas or a burning liquid to cook or frizzle the adversary.

Considering the size of the beast, concealment seemed about as difficult as for a suburban cottager to keep the fact that he had an elephant on the premises from his next-door neighbor; but the British Army has become so used to slipping ships across the channel in face of submarine danger that nobody is surprised at anything that appears at the front unheralded.

One day the curtain rose, and the finished product of all the experiments and testing appeared at the British front. Hundreds of thousands of soldiers were now in the secret. "Have you seen the tanks?" was the question up and down the line. All editors were inventing their own type of tank. Though I have patted one on the shoulder in a familiar way, as I might stroke the family cat, it neither kicked nor bit me. Though I have been inside of one, I am not supposed to know at this writing anything about its construction. Unquestionably the tank resembles an armadillo, a caterpillar, a diplodocus, a motor car, and a traveling circus. It has more feet than a caterpillar, and they have steel toenails which take it over the ground; its hide is more resistant than an armadillo's, and its beauty of form would make the diplodocus jealous. No pianist was ever more temperamental; no tortoise ever more phlegmatic.

In summer heat, when dust clouds hung thick on the roads behind the shell clouds of the fields, when the ceaseless battle had been going on for two months and a half, the soldiers had their interest stimulated by a mechanical novelty just before a general attack. Two years of war had cumulatively desensitized them to thrills. New batteries moving into position were only so many more guns. Fresh battalions marching to the front were only more infantry, all of the same pattern, equipped in the same way, moving with the same fixed step. Machine gun rattles had become as commonplace as the sound of creaking caisson wheels. Gas shells, lachrymatory shells and *Flammenwerfer* were as old-fashioned as high explosives and shrapnel. Bombing encounters in saps had no variation. The ruins of the village taken to-day could not be told from the one taken yesterday except by its location on the map. Even the aeroplanes had not lately developed any sensational departures from habit. One paid little more attention to them than a gondolier pays to the pigeons of St. Mark's. Curtains of fire all looked alike. There was no new way of being killed—nothing to break the ghastly monotony of charges and counter-charges.

All the brains of Europe had been busy for two years inventing new forms of destruction, yet no genius had found any sinuous creature that would creep into dugouts with a sting for which there was no antidote. Everybody was engaged in killing, yet nobody was able to "kill to his satisfaction," as the Kentucky colonel said. The reliable methods were the same as of old and as I have mentioned elsewhere: projectiles propelled by powder, whether from long-necked naval guns at twenty thousand yards, or short-necked howitzers at five thousand yards, or rifles and machine guns at twenty-five hundred yards, or trench mortars coughing balls of explosives for one thousand yards.

True, the gas attack at Ypres had been an innovation. It was not a discovery; merely an application of ghastliness which had been considered too horrible for use. As a surprise it had been successful—once. The defense answered with gas masks, which made it still more important that soldiers should not be absent-minded and leave any of their kit out of reach. The same amount of energy put into projectiles would have caused more casualties. Meanwhile, no staff of any army, making its elaborate plans in the use of proved weapons, could be certain that the enemy had not under way, in this age of invention which has given us the wireless, some new weapon which would be irresistible.

Was the tank this revolutionary wonder? Its sponsors had no such hope. England went on building guns and pouring out shells, cartridges and bombs. At best, the tanks were another application of an old, established form of killing in vogue with both Daniel Boone and Napoleon's army—bullets.

The first time that I saw a tank, the way that the monster was blocking a road gorged with transport had something of the ludicrousness of, say, a pliocene monster weighing fifty tons which had nonchalantly lain down at Piccadilly Circus when the traffic was densest. Only the motor-truck drivers and battalions which were halted some distance away minded the delay. Those near by were sufficiently entertained by the spectacle which stopped them. They gathered around the tank and gaped and grinned.

The tank's driver was a brown-skinned, dark-haired Englishman, with a face of oriental stolidity. Questions were shot at him, but he would not even say whether his beast would stand without hitching or not; whether it lived on hay, talcum powder, or the stuff that bombs are made of; or what was the nature of its inwards, or which was the head and which the tail, or if when it seemed to be backing it was really going forward.

By the confession of some white lettering on its body, it was officially one of His Majesty's land ships. It no more occurred to anyone to suggest that it move on and clear the road than to argue with a bulldog which confronts you on a path. I imagined that the feelings of the young officer who was its skipper must have been much the same as those of a man acting as his own chauffeur and having a breakdown on a holiday in a section of town where the population was as dense as it was curious in the early days of motoring. For months he had been living a cloistered life to keep his friends from knowing what he was doing, as he worked to master the eccentricities of his untried steed, his life and the lives of his crew depending upon this mastery. Now he had stepped from behind the curtain of military secrecy into the full blaze of staring, inquiring publicity.

The tank's inclination was entirely reptilian. Its body hugged the earth in order to expose as little surface as possible to the enemy's fire; it was mottled like a toad in patches of coloring to add to its low visibility, and there was no more hop in it than in the Gila monster.

The reason of its being was obvious. Its hide being proof against the bullets of machine guns and rifles, it was a moving "strong point" which could go against the enemy's fixed strong points, where machine guns were emplaced to mow down infantry charges, with its own machine guns. Only now it gave no sign of moving. As a mechanical product it was no more remarkable than a steam shovel. The wonder was in the part that it was about to play. A steam shovel is a labor-saving, and this a soldier-saving, device.

For the moment it seemed a leviathan dead weight in the path of traffic. If it could not move of itself, the only way for traffic to pass was to build a road around it. Then there was a rumbling noise within its body which sounded like some unnatural gasoline engine, and it hitched itself around with the ponderosity of a canal boat being warped into a dock and proceeded on its journey to take its appointed place in the battle line.

Did the Germans know that the tanks were building? I think that they had some inkling a few weeks before the tanks' appearance that something of the sort was under construction. There was a report, too, of a German tank which was not ready in time to meet the British. Some German prisoners said that their first intimation of this new affliction was when the tanks appeared out of the morning mist, bearing down on the trenches; others said that German sausage observation balloons had seen something resembling giant turtles moving across the fields up to the British lines and had given warning to the infantry to be on the lookout.

Thus, something new had come into the war, deepening the thrill of curiosity and intensifying the suspense before an attack. The world, its appetite for novelty fed by the press, wanted to know all about the tanks; but instead of the expected mechanical details, censorship would permit only vague references to the tanks' habits and psychology, and the tanks were really strong on psychology—subjectively and objectively. It was the objective result in psychology that counted: the effect on the fighting men. Human imagination immediately characterized them as living things; monstrous comrades of infantry in attack.

Blessed is the man, machine, or incident that will make any army laugh after over two months of battle. Individuals were always laughing over incidents; but here hundreds of thousands of men were to see a new style of animal perform elephantine tricks. The price of admission to the theater was the risk of a charge in their company, and the prospect gave increased zest to battalions taking their place for next day's action. What would happen to the tanks? What would they do to the Germans?

The staff, which had carefully calculated their uses and limitations, had no thought that the tanks would go to Berlin. They were simply a new auxiliary. Probably the average soldier was skeptical of their efficiency; but his skepticism did not interfere with his curiosity. He wanted to see the beast in action.

Christopher Columbus crossing uncharted seas did not undertake a more daring journey than the skippers of the tanks. The cavalryman who charges the enemy's guns in an impulse knows only a few minutes of suspense. A torpedo destroyer bent on coming within torpedo range in face of blasts from a cruiser's guns, the aviator closing in on an enemy's plane, have the delirium of purpose excited by speed. But the tanks are not rapid. They are ponderous and relatively slow. Columbus had already been to sea in ships. The aviator and the commander of a destroyer know their steeds and have precedent to go by, while the skippers of the tanks had none. They went forth with a new kind of ship on a new kind of sea, whose waves were shell-craters, whose tempests sudden concentrations of shell fire.

The Germans might have full knowledge of the ships' character and await their appearance with forms of destruction adapted to the purpose. All was speculation and uncertainty. Officers and crew were sealed up in a steel box, the sport of destiny. For months they had been preparing for this day, the crowning experiment and test, and all seemed of a type carefully chosen for their part, soldiers who had turned land sailors, cool and phlegmatic like the monsters which they directed. Each one having given himself up to fate, the rest was easy in these days of war's superexaltation, which makes men appear perfectly normal when death hovers near. Not one would have changed places with any infantryman. Already they had *esprit de corps*. They belonged to an exclusive set of warriors.

Lumberingly dipping in and out of shell-craters, which sometimes half concealed the tanks like ships in a choppy sea, rumbling and wrenching, they appeared out of the morning mist in face of the Germans who put up their heads and began working their machine guns after the usual artillery curtain of fire had lifted.

XXVII

THE TANKS IN ACTION

How the tanks attacked—A tank walking up the main Street of a village—Effect on the Germans—Prussian colonel surrenders to a tank—Tanks against trees—The tank in High Wood—The famous Crème de Menthe—Demolishing a sugar factory—Germans take the tanks seriously—Differences of opinion regarding tanks—Wandering tanks—German attack on a stranded tank—Prehistoric turtles—Saving twenty-five thousand casualties.

With the reverse slope of the Ridge to conceal their approach to the battle line, the tanks squatting among the men at regular intervals over a six-mile front awaiting the cue of zero for the attack at dawn and the mist still holding to cover both tanks and men, the great Somme stage was set in a manner worthy of the début of the new monsters.

A tactical system of coördinated action had been worked out for the infantry and the untried auxiliary, which only experienced soldiers could have applied with success. According to the nature of the positions in front, the tanks were set definite objectives or left to find their own objectives. They might move on located machine gun positions or answer a hurry call for help from the infantry. Ahead of them was a belt of open field between them and the villages whose capture was to be the consummation of the day's work. While observers were straining their eyes to follow the progress of the tanks and seeing but little, corps headquarters eagerly awaited news of the most picturesque experiment of the war, which might prove ridiculous, or be a wonderful success, or simply come up to expectations.

No more thrilling message was ever brought by an aeroplane than that which said that a tank was "walking" up the main street of Flers surrounded by cheering British soldiers, who were in possession of the village. "Walking" was the word officially given; and very much walking, indeed, the tank must have seemed to the aviator in his swift flight. An eagle looked down on a tortoise which had a serpent's sting. This tank, having attended to its work on the way, passed on through Flers bearing a sign: "Extra Special! Great Hun Victory!" Beyond Flers it found itself alongside a battery of German field guns and blazed bullets into the amazed and helpless gunners.

The enemy may have heard of the tanks, but meeting them was a different matter. After he had fought shells, bullets, bombs, grenades, mortars, bayonets and gas, the tank was the straw that broke the camel's back of many a German. A steel armadillo laying its bulk across a trench and sweeping it on both sides with machine guns brought the familiar complaint that this was not fighting according to rules in a war which ceased to have rules after the bombing of civilian populations, the sinking of the *Lusitania*, and the gas attack at Ypres. It depends on whose ox is gored. There is a lot of difference between seeing the enemy slaughtered by some new device and being slaughtered by one yourself. No wonder that German prisoners who had escaped alive from a trench filled with dead, when they saw a tank on the road as they passed to the rear threw up their hands with a guttural: "Mein Gott! There is another! There is no fighting that! This is not war; it is butchery!" Yes, it was butchery—and butchery is war these days. Wasn't it so always? And as a British officer remarked to the protestants:

"The tank is entirely in keeping with Hague rules, being only armor, machinery and machine guns."

Germans surrendered to a tank in bodies after they saw the hopelessness of turning their own machine gun and rifle fire upon that steel hide. Why not? Nothing takes the fight out of anyone like finding that his blows go into the air and the other fellow's go home. There seemed a strange loss of dignity when a Prussian colonel delivered himself to a tank, which took him on board and eventually handed him over to an infantry guard; but the skipper of the tank enjoyed it if the colonel did not.

The surprising thing was how few casualties there were among the crews of the tanks, who went out prepared to die and found themselves safe in their armored shells after the day's fight was over, whether their ships had gone across a line of German trenches, developed engine trouble, or temporarily foundered in shell-holes. Bullets had merely made steel-bright flecks on the tanks' paint and shrapnel had equally failed to penetrate the armor.

Among the imaginary tributes paid to the tank's powers is that it "eats" trees—that is to say, it can cut its way through a wood—and that it can knock down a stone wall. As it has no teeth it cannot masticate timber. All that it accomplishes must be done by ramming or by lifting up its weight to crush an obstacle. A small tree or a weak wall yields before its mass.

As foresters, the tanks had a stiff task in High Wood, where the Germans had held to the upper corner with their nests of machine guns which the preliminary bombardment of British artillery had not silenced and they began their murderous song immediately the British charge started. They commanded the front and the flanks if the men continued to advance and therefore might make a break in the whole movement, which was precisely the object of the desperate resistance that had preserved this strong point at any cost against the rushes of British bombers, trench mortars and artillery shells for two months.

Soldiers are not expected to undertake the impossible. Nobody who is sane will leap into a furnace with a cup of water to put out the fire. Only a battalion commander who is a fool will refuse, in face of concentrated machine gun fire, to stop the charge.

"Leave it to me!" was the unspoken message communicated to the infantry by the sight of that careening, dipping, clambering, steel body as it rumbled toward the miniature fortress. And the infantry, as it saw the tank's machine guns blazing, left it to the tank, and, working its way to the right, kept in touch with the general line of attack, confident that no enemy would be left behind to fire into their backs. Thus, a handful of men capable, with their bullet sprays, of holding up a thousand men found the tables turned on them by another handful manning a tank. They were simply "done in," as the tank officer put it. Safe behind his armor, he had them no less at his mercy than a submarine has a merchant ship. Even if unarmed, a tank could take care of an isolated machine gun position by sitting on it.

One of the most famous tanks was Crème de Menthe. She had a good press agent and also made good. She seemed to like sugar. At least, her glorious exploit was in a sugar factory, a huge building of brick with a tall brick chimney which had been brought down by shell fire. Underneath the whole were immense dugouts still intact where German machine gunners lay low, like Br'er Rabbit, as usual, while the shells of the artillery preparation were falling, and came out to turn on the bullet spray as the British infantry approached. British do the same against German attacks; only in the battle of the Somme the British had been always attacking, always taking machine gun positions.

Crème de Menthe, chosen comrade of the Canadians on their way to the taking of Courcelette, was also at home among débris. The Canadians saw that she was as she moved toward it with the glee of a sea lion toward a school of fish. She did not go dodging warily, peering around corners with a view to seeing the enemy before she was seen. Whatever else a tank is, it is not a crafty boy scout. It is brazenly and nonchalantly public in its methods, like a steam roller coming down the street into a parade without regard to the rules of the road. Externally it is not temperamental. It does not bother to follow the driveway or mind the "Keep Off the Grass" sign when it goes up to the entrance of a dugout.

And Crème de Menthe took the sugar factory and a lot of prisoners. "Why not?" as one of the Canadians said. "Who wouldn't surrender when a beast of that kind came up to the door? It was enough to make a man who had drunk only light Munich beer wonder if he had 'got 'em!'"

Prisoners were a good deal of bother to the tanks. Perhaps future tanks will be provided with pockets for carrying prisoners. But the future of tanks is wrapped in mystery at the present.

This is not taking them seriously, you may say. In that case, I am only reflecting the feelings of the army. Even if the tanks had taken Bapaume or gone to the Kaiser's headquarters, the army would have laughed at them. It was the Germans who took the tanks seriously; and the more seriously the Germans took the tanks the more the British laughed.

"Of all the double-dyed, ridiculous things, was the way that Crème de Menthe person took the sugar factory!" said a Canadian, who broke into a roar at the recollection of the monster's antics. "Good old girl, Crème de Menthe! Ought to retire her for life and let her sit up on her haunches in a café and sip her favorite tipple out of barrel with a garden hose for a straw—which would be about her size."

However, there was a variation of opinions among soldiers about tanks drawn from personal experience, when life and death form opinions, of the way it had acted as an auxiliary to their part of the line. A tank that conquered machine-gun positions and enfiladed trenches was an heroic comrade surrounded by a saga of glorious anecdotes. One which became stalled and failed in its enterprise called for satirical comment which was applied to all.

We did not personify machine guns, or those monstrous, gloomy, big howitzers with their gaping maws, or other weapons; but every man in the army personified the tanks. Two or three tanks, I should have remarked, did start for Berlin, without waiting for the infantry. The temptation was strong. All they had to do was to keep on moving. When Germans scuttling for cover were the only thing that the skippers could see, they realized that they were in the wrong pew, or, in strictly military language, that they had got beyond their "tactical objective."

Having left most of their ammunition where they thought that it would do the most good in the German lines, these wanderers hitched themselves around and waddled back to their own people. For a tank is an auxiliary, not an army, or an army staff, or a curtain of fire, and must coöperate with the infantry or it may be in the enemy's lines to stay. There was one tank which found itself out of gasoline and surrounded by Germans. It could move neither way, but could still work its guns. Marooned on a hostile shore, it would have to yield when the crew ran out of food.

The Germans charged the beast, and got under its guns, pounded at the door, tried to bomb and pry it open with bayonets and crawled over the top looking for dents in the armor with the rage of hornets, but in vain. They could not harm the crew inside and the crew could not harm them.

"A noisy lot!" said the tank's skipper.

Tactical objective be—British soldiers went to the rescue of their tank. Secure inside their shell, the commander and crew awaited the result of the fight. After the Germans were driven away, someone went for a can of gasoline, which gave the beast the breath of life to retreat to its "correct tactical position."

Even if it had not been recovered at the time, the British would have regained possession with their next advance; for the Germans had no way of taking a tank to the rear. There are no tractors powerful enough to draw one across the shell-craters. It can be moved only by its own power, and with its engine out of order it becomes a fixture on the landscape. Stranded tanks have an appearance of Brobdingnagian helplessness. They are fair targets for revenge by a concentration of German artillery fire; yet when half hidden in a gigantic shell-hole which they could not navigate they are a small target and, their tint melting into the earth, are hard to locate.

Seen through the glasses, disregarding ordinary roads and traveled routes, the tanks' slatey backs seemed like prehistoric turtles whose natural habitat is shell-mauled earth. They were the last word in the business of modern war, symbolic of its satire and the old strife between projectile and armor, offensive and defensive. If two tanks were to meet in a duel, would they try to ram each other after ineffectually rapping each other with their machine guns?

"I hope that it knows where it is going!" exclaimed a brigadier-general, as he watched one approach his dugout across an abandoned trench, leaning over a little as it dipped into the edge of a shell-crater some fifteen feet in diameter with its sureness of footing on a rainy day when a pedestrian slipped at every step.

There was no indication of any guiding human intelligence, let alone human hand, directing it; and, so far as one could tell, it might have mistaken the general's underground quarters for a storage station where it could assuage its thirst for gasoline or a blacksmith's shop where it could have a bent steel claw straightened. When, finally, it stopped at his threshold, the general expressed his relief that it had not tried to come down the steps. A door like that of a battleship turret opened, and out of the cramped interior where space for crew and machinery is so nicely calculated came the skipper, who saluted and reported that his ship awaited orders for the next cruise.

Soon the sight of tanks became part of the routine of existence, and interest in watching an advance centered on the infantry which they supported in a charge; for only by its action could you judge whether or not machine gun fire had developed and, later, whether or not the tanks were silencing it. The human element was still supreme, its movement and its losses in life the criterion of success and failure, with an eternal thrill that no machine can arouse. If the tanks had accomplished nothing more than they did in the two great September attacks they would have been well worth while. I think that they saved twenty-five thousand casualties, which would have been the additional cost of gaining the ground won by unassisted infantry action. When machines manned by a few men can take the place of many battalions in this fashion they exemplify the essential principle of doing the enemy a maximum of damage with a minimum to your own forces.

XXVIII

CANADA IS QUICK

Canada's first offensive—The "surprise party"—Over nasty ground—Canada's hour—Germans amazed—Business of the Canadians to "get there"—Two difficult villages—Canadians make new rules—Canada's green soldiers accomplish an unheard of feat—Attacking on their nerve—The last burst—Fewer Canadians than Germans, but—"Mopping up"—Rounding up the captives—An aristocratic German and a democratic Canadian—French-Canadians—Thirteen counter-attacks beaten—Quickness and adaptability—Canada's soldiers make good.

The tanks having received their theatric due, we come to other results of Sept. 14th when the resistance of the right was stiff and Canada had her turn of fortune in sharing in the brilliant success on the left.

It was the Canadians' first offensive. They knew that the eyes of the army were upon them. Not only for themselves, after parrying blows throughout their experience at the front, but in the name of other battalions that had endured the remorseless grind of the Ypres salient they were to strike the blows of retribution. The answer as to how they would charge was written in faces clear-cut by the same climate that gave them their nervous alertness.

On that ugly part of the Ridge where no stable trench could be made under the vengeful German artillery fire and small numbers were shrewdly distributed in shell-craters and such small ditches as could be maintained, they crept out in the darkness a few days before the attack to "take over" from the Australians and familiarize themselves with this tempest-torn farming land which still heaved under tornadoes of shells. The men from the faraway island continent had provided the jumping-off place and the men from this side of the Pacific and the equator were to do the jumping, which meant a kind of overseas monopoly of Pozières Ridge.

The Germans still hated the idea of yielding all the crest that stared down on them and hid the slope beyond which had once been theirs. They would try again to recover some of it, but chose a time for their effort which was proof enough that they did not know that a general attack was coming. Just before dawn, with zero at dawn, when the Canadians were forming on the reverse slope for their charge, the Germans laden with bombs made theirs and secured a footing in the thin front line among the shell-craters and, grim shadows in the night lighted by bursts of bombs and shells, struggled as they have on many similar occasions.

Then came the "surprise party." Not far away the Canadian charge waited on the tick of the second which was to release the six-mile line of infantry and the tanks.

"We were certainly keyed up," as one of the men said. "It was up to us all right, now."

Breasting the tape in their readiness for the word, the dry air of North America with its champagne exhilaration was in their lungs whipping their red corpuscles. They had but one thought and that was to "get there." No smooth drill-ground for that charge, but earth broken with shell-craters as thick as holes in a pepper-box cover! A man might stumble into one, but he must get up and go on. One fellow who twisted his ankle found it swollen out of all shape when the charge was over. If he had given it such a turn at home he would not have attempted to move but would have called for a cab or assistance. Under the spell of action he did not even know that he was hurt.

It was Canada's hour; all the months of drill at home, all the dreams on board the transport of charges to come, all the dull monotony of billets, all the slimy vigil of trenches, all the labor of preparation come to a head for every individual. Such was the impulse of the tidal wave which broke over the crest upon the astounded Germans who had gained a footing in the trench, engulfing them in as dramatic an episode as ever occurred on the Somme front.

"Give yourselves up and be quick about it! We've business elsewhere!" said the officers.

Yes, they had business with the German first-line trench when the artillery curtain lifted, where few Germans were found, most of them having been in the charge. The survivors here put up their hands before they put up their heads from shelter and soon were on their way back to the rear in the company of the others.

"I guess we had the first batch of prisoners to reach an inclosure on the morning of the 14th," said one Canadian. "We had a start with some coming into our own front line to be captured."

On the left Mouquet Farm, which, with its unsurpassed dugouts and warrens surrounded by isolated machine gun posts, had repulsed previous attacks, could not resist the determined onslaught which will share glory, when history is written, with the storming of Courcelette. Down hill beside the Bapaume Road swept the right and center, with shell-craters still thick but growing fewer as the wave came out into open fields in face of the ruins of the sugar factory, with the tank Crème de Menthe ready to do her part. She did not take care of all the machine guns; the infantry attended to at least one, I know. The German artillery turned on curtains of fire, but in one case the Canadians were not there when the curtain was laid to bar their path. They had been too rapid for the Germans. No matter what obstacle the Germans put in the way the business of the Canadians was to "get there"— and they "got there." The line marked on their map from the Bapaume Road to the east of the sugar factory as their objective was theirs. In front of them was the village of Courcelette and in front of the British line linked up on their right was Martinpuich.

Spades now! Dig as hard as you have charged in order to hold the freshly won position, with "there" become "here" and the Ridge at your backs! The London song of "The Byng Boys are Here," which gave the name of the Byng Boys to the Canadians after General Byng took command of their corps, had a most realistic application.

With the news from the right of the six-mile front that of a continuing fierce struggle, word from the left had the definite note of success. Was General Byng pleased with his Byng Boys? Was his superior, the army commander, pleased with the Canadians? They had done the trick and this is the thing that counts on such occasions; but when you take trenches and fields, however great the gain of ground, they lack the concrete symbol of victory which a village possesses.

And ahead were Courcelette and Martinpuich, both only partially demolished by shell fire and in nowise properly softened according to the usual requirements for capitulation, with their cellars doubtless heavily reinforced as dugouts. Officers studying the villages through their glasses believed that they could be taken. Why not try? To try required nerve, when it was against all tactical experience to rush on to a new objective over such a broad front without taking time for elaborate artillery preparation. General Byng, who believed in his men and understood their initiative, their "get there" quality, was ready to advance and so was the corps commander of the British in front of Martinpuich. Sir Douglas Haig gave consent.

"Up and at them!" then, with fresh battalions hurried up so rapidly that they had hardly time to deploy, but answering the order for action with the spirit of men who have been stalled in trenches and liked the new experience of stretching their legs. With a taste of victory, nothing could stop these highstrung reserves, except the things that kill and wound. The first charge had succeeded and the second must succeed.

German guns had done the customary thing by laying barrages back of the new line across the field and shelling the crest of the Ridge to prevent supports from coming up. It was quite correct form for the German commander to consider the ceremony of the day over. The enemy had taken his objective. Of course, he would not try for another immediately.

Meanwhile, his tenure of new line must be made as costly as possible. But this time the enemy did not act according to rules. He made some new ones.

The reserve battalions which were to undertake the storming of the village had gone over the ground under the barrages and were up to the first objective, and when through the new line occupied by the men who made the first charge they could begin their own charge. As barrages are intermittent, one commander had his men lie down behind one until it had ceased. Again, after waiting on another for a while he decided that he might be late in keeping his engagement in Courcelette and gave the order to go through, which, as one soldier said, "we did in a hundred-yard dash sprinting a double quick—good reason why!" When the fresh wave passed the fellows in the new line the winners of the first objective called, "Go to it!" "You'll do it!" "Hurrah for Canada!" and added touches of characteristic dry humor which shell fire makes a little drier, such as a request to engage seats for the theatre at Courcelette that evening.

Consider that these battalions which were to take Courcelette had to march about two miles under shell fire, part of the way over ground that was spongy earth cut by shell-craters, before they could begin their charge and that they were undertaking an innovation in tactics, and you have only half an understanding of their task. Their officers were men out of civil life in every kind of occupation, learning their war in the Ypres salient stalemate, and now they were to have the severest possible test in directing their units in an advance.

There had been no time to lay out pattern plans for each company's course in this second rush according to map details, which is so important against modern defenses. The officers did not know where machine guns were hidden; they were uncertain of the strength of the enemy who had had all day to prepare for the onslaught on his bastions in the village. It was pitched battle conditions against set defenses. Under curtains of fire, with the concentration heavy at one point and weak at another, with machine gun or sniping fire developing in some areas, with the smoke and the noise, with trenches to cross, the business of keeping a wave of men in line of attack for a long distance—difficult enough in a manoeuver—was possible only when the initiative and an understanding of the necessities of the situation exist in the soldiers themselves. If one part of the line was not up, if a section was being buffeted by salvos of shells, the officers had to meet the emergency; and officers as well as men were falling, companies being left with a single officer or with only a "non-com" in charge. Unless a man was down he knew that his business was to "get there" and his direction was straight ahead in line with the men on his right and left.

With dead and wounded scattered over the field behind them, all who could stand on their feet, including officers and men knocked over and buried by shells and with wounds of arms and heads and even legs which made them hobble, reached the edge of the village on time and lay down to await the lifting of the fire of their own guns before the final rush.

After charging such a distance and paying the toll of casualties exacted they enjoyed a breathing space, a few minutes in which to steady their thoughts for the big thing before, "lean for the hunt," they sprang up to be in for the fray with the burst of the last shells from their guns. They knew what to do. It had been drilled into them; they had talked it and dreamed it in billets when routine became humdrum, these men with practical minds who understood the essentials of their task.

There were fewer Canadians charging through the streets than there were Germans in the village at that moment. The Canadians did not know it, but if they had it would have made no difference, such was their spirit. Secure in their dugouts from bombardment, the first that the Germans, in their systematized confidence that the enemy would not try for a second objective that day, knew of the presence of the Canadians was when the attackers were at the door and a St. Lawrence River incisiveness was calling on the occupants to come out as they were prisoners—which proves the advantage of being quick. The second wave was left to "mop up" while the first wave passed on through the village to nail down the prize by digging new trenches. Thus, they had their second objective, though on the left of the line where the action had been against a part of the old first-line system of trenches progress had been slow and fighting bitter.

The Canadians who had to "mop up" had the "time of their lives" and some ticklish moments. What a scene! Germans in clean uniforms coming out of their dugouts blinking in surprise at their undoing and in disgust, resentment and suppressed rage! Canadians, dust-covered from shell-bursts, eyes flashing, laughing, rushing about on the job in the midst of shouts of congratulation and directions to prisoners among the ruins, and the German commander so angered by the loss of the village that he began pouring in shells on Germans and Canadians at the same time! Two colonels were among the captured, a regimental and a battalion commander. The senior was a baron—one cannot leave him out of any narrative—and inclined to bear himself with patrician contempt toward the Canadian democracy, which is a mistake for barons in his situation with every Canadian more or less of a king that day. When he tried to start his men into a revolt his hosts acted promptly, with the result that the uprising was nipped in the bud and the baron was shot through the leg, leaving him still "fractious and patronizing." Then the little colonel of the French-Canadians said, "I think I might as well shoot you in a more vital part and have done with it!" or something equally to the point and suddenly the baron became quite democratic himself.

One of the battalions that took Courcelette was French-Canadian. No other Canadian battalion will deny them the glory that they won that day, and it must have been irritating to the German baron to surrender superior numbers to the stocky type that we see in New England factory towns and on their farms in Quebec, for they now formed the battalion, the frontiersmen, the *courrier de bois*, having been mostly killed in the salient. Shall I forget that little private, forty years old if he were a day, with a hole from shrapnel in his steel helmet and the bit of purple and white ribbon worn proudly on his breast, who, when I asked him how he felt after he received the clout from a shell-fragment, remarked blandly that it had knocked him down and made his head ache!

"You have the military cross!" I said.

"Yais, sir. I'm going to win the Victoria Cross!" he replied, saluting. Talk about "the spirit that quickeneth!"

Or, shall I forget the French-Canadian colonel telling his story of how he and the battalion on his left in equal difficulties held the line beyond Courcelette with his scattered men against thirteen counter-attacks that night; how he had to go from point to point establishing his posts in the dark, and his repeated "'I golly!" of wonder at how he had managed to hold on, with its ring of naïve unrealization of the humor of being knocked over by a shell and finding, "'I golly!" that he had not been hurt! They had not enlisted freely, the French-Canadians, but those who had proved that if the war emotion had taken hold of them as it had of the rest of Canada they would not have been found wanting.

"'I golly!" they had to fight from the very fact that there were only a few to strike for old France and for the martial honor of Quebec. And they held all they took as sturdily as the other Canadian battalion in front of the village when the Germans awakened to revenge for the loss of Courcelette.

From start to finish of that great day it had been quickness that counted; quickness to realize opportunities; alertness of individual action in "mopping up" after the village was taken; prompt adaptability to situations which is the gift of the men of a new country; and that individual confidence of the Canadian once he was not tied to a trench and might let his initiative have full play, man to man, which is not a thing of drill or training but of inheritance and environment. On the right, Martinpuich was taken by the British and also held.

It was in rain and mist after the battle, while the dead still lay on the field, that I went over the Ridge and along the path of the Canadian charges, wondering how they had passed through the curtains of fire when I saw shrapnel cases so thick that you could step from one to another; wondering how men could survive in the shell-craters and the poor, tumbled trenches in the soft, shell-mashed earth; wondering at the whole business of their being here in France, a veteran army two years after the war had begun. I saw them dripping from the rains, mud-spattered, but in the joy of having made good when their turn came, and in a way that was an exemplification of Canadian character in every detail. "Heap good!" I suppose that big Sioux Indian, looking as natural seated in a trench in his imperturbability as if he were seated in front of his tepee, would have put it. He was seeing a strange business, but high explosives shaking the earth, aeroplanes overhead, machine guns rattling in the war of the Pale Faces he accepted without emotion.

With the second battle of Ypres, with St. Eloi, Hooge, Mount Sorrell, and Observatory Ridge, Courcelette had completed the cycle of soldierly experiences for those who bore the Maple Leaf in France of the *Fleur-de-lis*. Officers and men of every walk of life called to a new occupation, a democracy out of the west submitting to discipline had been inured and trained to a new life of risk and comradeship and sacrifice for a cause. It will seem strange to be out of khaki and to go to the office, or the store, or to get up to milk the cows at dawn; "but," as one man said, "we'll manage to adapt ourselves to it without spending nights in a mud hole or asking the neighbors to throw any bombs over the fence in order to make the change gradual."

XXIX

THE HARVEST OF VILLAGES

High and low visibilities—Low Visibility a pro-German—High Visibility and his harvest smile—Thirty villages taken by the British—The 25th of September—The Road of the Entente—Twelve miles of artillery fire—Two villages taken—Combles—British and French meet in a captured village—English stubbornness—Dugouts holding a thousand men—Capture of Thiepval.

Always we were talking of the two visibilities, high and low. I thought of them as brothers with the same meteorological parent, one a good and the other an evil genius. Every morning we looked out of doors to see which had the stage. Thus, we might know whether or not the "zero" of an attack set for to-day would be postponed, as it was usually if the sun gave no sign of appearing, though not always; sometimes the staff gave those who tried to guess what was in its mind a surprise.

Low Visibility, a pro-German who was in his element in the Ypres salient in midwinter, delighted in rain, mist, fog and thick summer haze—anything that prevented observers from seeing the burst of shells, transformed shell-craters into miniature lakes and fields into mire to founder charges, and stalled guns.

High Visibility was as merry as his wicked brother was dour. He sent the sunlight streaming into your room in the morning, washed the air of particles enabling observers to see shell-bursts at long range, and favored successful charges under accurate curtains of fire—the patron saint of all modern artillery work, who would be most at home in Arizona where you could carry on an offensive the year around.

During September his was a glad harvest smile which revealed figures on the chalk welts a mile away as clearly as if within a stone's throw under the glasses and limned the tree-trunks of ruined villages in sharp outlines. He was your companion now when you might walk up the Ridge and, standing among shell-craters still as a frozen sea where but lately an inferno had raged, look out across the fields toward new lines of shell fire and newly won villages on lower levels. He helped to make the month of September when he was most needed the most successful month of the offensive, with its second great attack on the 25th turning the table of losses entirely against the Germans and bringing many guests to the prisoners' inclosures.

These were days that were rich with results, days of harvest, indeed, when the ceaseless fighting on the Ridge and the iron resolution of a commander had its reward; when advances gathered in villages till the British had taken thirty and the French, with fresh efforts after their own chipping away at strong points, also had jumping-off places for longer drives as they swung in with their right on the Somme in combination with British attacks.

The two armies advanced as one on the 25th. The scene recalled the splendor of the storming of Contalmaison which, if not for its waste and horror, might lead men to go to war for the glory of the panorama—glorious to the observer in this instance when he thought only of the spectacle, in a moment of oblivion to the hard work of preparation and the savage work of execution. Our route to a point of observation for the attack which was at midday took us along the Road of the Entente, as I called it, where French battalions marched with British battalions, stately British motor trucks mixed with the lighter French vehicles, and Gaul sat resting on one side of the road and Briton on the other as German prisoners went by, and there was a mingling of blue and khaki which are both of low visibility against the landscape yet as distinct as the characters of the two races, each with its own way of fighting true to racial bent yet accomplishing its purpose.

Just under the slope where we sat the British guns linked up with the French. To the northward the British were visible right away past Ginchy and Guillemont to Flers and the French clear to the Somme. We were almost midway of a twelve-mile stretch of row upon row of flashes of many calibers, the French more distinct at the foot of a slope fearlessly in the open like the British, a long machine-loom of gunnery with some monsters far back sending up great clouds of black smoke from Mt. St. Quentin which hid our view of Péronne.

Now it was all together for the guns in the preliminary whirlwind, with *soixante-quinzes* ahead sparkling up and down like the flashes of an automatic electric sign, making a great, thrumming beat of sound in the valley, and the 120's near by doing their best, too, with their wicked crashes, while the ridges beyond were a bobbing canopy of looming, curling smoke. The units of the two armies might have been wired to a single switchboard with heartbeats under blue and khaki jackets timed together in the final expression of *entente cordiale* become *entente furieuse*.

The sunlight had the golden kindness of September and good Brother High Visibility seemed to make it a personal matter to-day against the Kaiser. Distinct were the moving figures of the gunners and bright was the gleam of the empty shells dropping out of the breach of the *soixante-quinze* as the barrel swung back in place and of the loaded shells going home; distinct were paths and trenches and all the detail of the tired, worn landscape, with the old trenches where we were sitting tumbling in and their sides fringed with wild grass and weeds, which was Nature's own little say in the affair and a warning that in a few years after the war she and the peasant will have erased war's landmarks.

The lifting of the barrage as the infantry went in was signaled to the eye when the canopy of shell-smoke began to grow thin and gossamery for want of fresh bursts and another was forming beyond, as if the master hand at such things had lifted a long trail of cloud from one set of crests to another; only, nature never does things with such mathematical precision. All in due order to keep its turn in the program the German artillery began to reply according to its system of distribution, with guns and ammunition plentiful but inferior in quantity to the French. They did not like that stretch of five hundred yards behind a slope where they thought that the most troublesome batteries were, and the puffs of shrapnel smoke thickened dimming the flashes from the bursting jackets until a wall of mist hung there. A torrent of five-point-nines was tearing up fresh craters with high explosives back of other gun positions, and between the columns of smoke we saw the French gunners going on unconcerned by this plowing of the landscape which was not disturbing them.

Far off on the plain where a British ammunition train was visible the German loosed more anger, whipping the fields into geysers; but the caissons moved on as if this were a signal of all aboard for the next station without the Germans being aware that their target was gone. A British battery advancing at another point evidently was not in view of the Germans two thousand yards away, though good Brother High Visibility gave our glasses the outline of the horses at five thousand yards.

Thus, you watched to see what the Germans were shooting at, with suspense at one point and at another the joy of the observer who sees the one who is "it" in blind man's buff missing his quarry. Some shrapnel searching a road in front and a scream overhead indicated a parcel of high explosives for a village at the rear. In Morval where houses were still standing, their white walls visible through the glasses, there was a kind of flash which was not that of a shell but prolonged, like a windowpane flaming under the sun, which we knew meant that the village was taken, as was also Gueudecourt we learned afterward.

Reserves were filing along a road between the tiers of guns, helmets on the backs of heads French fashion when there is no fire, with the easy marching stride of the French and figures disappeared and reappeared on the slope as they advanced. Wounded were coming along the winding gray streak of highway near where we sat and a convoy of prisoners passed led by a French guard whose attitude seemed to have an eye-twinkling of "See who's here and see what I've got!" Not far away was a French private at a telephone.

"It goes well!" he said. "Rancourt is taken and we are advancing on Frégicourt. Combles is a ripe plum."

All the while Combles had been an oasis in the shell fire, the one place that had immunity, although it had almost as much significance in the imagination of the French people as Thiepval in that of the English. They looked forward to its storming as a set dramatic event and to its fall as one of the turning-points in the campaign. Often a position which was tactically of little importance, to our conception, would become the center of great expectations to the outside world, while the conquest of a strong point with its nests of machine guns produced no responsive thrill.

Combles was a village and a large village, its size perhaps accounting for the importance associated with it when it had almost none in a military sense. Yet correspondents knew that readers at the breakfast table would be hungry for details about Combles, where the taking of the Schwaben Redoubt or Regina Trench, which were defended savagely, had no meaning. Its houses were very distinct, some being but little damaged and some of the shade trees still retaining their branches. This town nestling in a bowl was not worth the expenditure of much ammunition when what the Germans wanted to hold and the Anglo-French troops to gain was the hills around it. Rancourt was the other side of Combles, which explains the plum simile.

The picturesque thing was that the British troops were working up on one side of Combles and the French on the other side; and the next morning after the British had gathered in some escaping Germans who seemed to have lost their way, the blue and the khaki met in the main street without indulging in formal ceremonies and exchanged a "Good morning!" and "*Bon jour!*" and "Here we are! Voyla! Quee pawnsays-vous!" and "Ça va bien! Oh, yais, I tink so!" and found big piles of shells and other munitions which the Germans could not take away and cellars with many wounded who had been brought in from the hills—and that was all there was to it: a march in and look around, when for glory's sake, at least, the victors ought to have delivered congratulatory addresses. But tired soldiers will not do that sort of thing. I shall not say that they are spoiling pictures for the Salon, for there are incidents enough to keep painters going for a thousand years; which ought to be one reason for not having a war for another thousand!

As for Thiepval, the British staff, inconsiderate of the correspondents this time—they really were not conducting the war for us—did not inform us of the attack, being busy those days reaping villages and trenches after they were over the Ridge while High Visibility had Low Visibility shut up in the guardhouse. Besides, the British were so near Thiepval as the result of their persistent advances that its taking was only another step forward, one of savage fighting, however, in the same kind of operations that I have described in the chapter on "Watching a Charge." The débris beaten into dust had been so scattered that one could not tell where the village began or ended, but the smudge was a symbol to the army no less than to the British public—a symbol of the boasted impregnability of the first-line German fortifications which had resisted the attack of July 1st—and its capture a reward of English stubbornness appealing to the race which is not unconscious of the characteristic that has carried its tongue and dominion over the world.

Point was given, too, by the enormous dugouts, surpassing previous exhibits, capable of holding a garrison of a thousand men and a hospital which, under the bursts of huge shells of the months of British bombardment, had been safe under ground. The hospital was equipped with excellent medical apparatus as well as anæsthetics manufactured in Germany, of which the British were somewhat short. The German battalion that held the place had been associated with the work of preparing its defenses and were practically either all taken prisoner or killed, so far as could be learned. They had sworn that they would never lose Thiepval; but the deeper the dugouts the farther upstairs men inside have to climb in order to get to the door before the enemy, who arrives at the threshold as the whirlwind barrage lifts.

As I have said, Thiepval was not on the very crest of the Ridge and on the summit the same elaborate works had been built to hold this high ground. We watched other attacks under curtains of fire as the British pressed on. Sometimes we could see the Germans moving out in the open from their dugouts at the base of the hill in St. Pierre Divion and driven to cover as the British guns sniped at them with shrapnel. Resistlessly the British infantry under its covering barrages kept on till the crest and all its dugouts and galleries were gained, thus breaking back the old first-line fortifications stage by stage and forcing the German into the open, where he must dig anew on equal terms.

The capture of Thiepval did not mean that its ruins were to have any rest from shells, for the German guns had their turn. They seemed fond of sending up spouts from a little pond in the foreground, which had no effect except to shower passing soldiers with dirty water. However much the pond was beaten it was still there; and I was struck by the fact that this was a costly and unsuccessful system of drainage for such an efficient people as the Germans to apply.

XXX

FIVE GENERALS AND VERDUN

Sixty miles an hour to meet General Joffre—Joffre somewhat like Grant—Two figures which France will remember for all time—Joffre and Castelnau—Two very old friends—At Verdun—What Napoleon and Wellington might have thought—A staff whose feet and mind never dragged—The hero of Douaumont, General Nivelle—Simplicity—Men who believe in giving blows—A true soldier—A prized photograph of Joffre—The drama of Douaumont—General Mangin, corps commander at Verdun—An eye that said "Attack!"—A five-o'clock-in-the-morning corps—The old fortress town, Verdun—The effort of Colossus—Germany's high water mark—Thrifty fighters, the French—Germany good enough to win against Rumania, but not at Verdun.

That spirited friend Lieutenant T., at home in an English or a French mess or walking arm-in-arm with the *poilus* of his old battalion, required quick stepping to keep up with him when we were not in his devil of a motor car that carried me on a flying visit to the French lines before I started for home and did not fail even when sixty miles an hour were required to keep the appointment with General Joffre—which we did, to the minute.

Many people have told of sitting across the table in his private office from the victor of the Marne; and it was when he was seated and began to talk that you appreciated the power of the man, with his great head and its mass of white hair and the calm, largely-molded features, who could give his orders when the fate of France was at stake and then retire to rest for the night knowing that his part was done for the day and the rest was with the army. In common with all men when experience and responsibility have ripened their talents, though lacking in the gift of formal speech-making, as Grant was, he could talk well, in clear sentences, whose mold was set by precise thought, which brought with it the eloquence that gains its point. It was more than personality, in this instance, that had appeal. He was the personification of a great national era.

In view of changes which were to come, another glimpse that I had of him in the French headquarters town which was not by appointment is peculiarly memorable. When I was out strolling I saw on the other side of the street two figures which all France knew and will know for all time. Whatever vicissitudes of politics, whatever campaigns ensue, whatever changes come in the world after the war, Joffre's victory at the Marne and Castelnau's victory in Lorraine, which was its complement in masterly tactics, make their niches in the national Pantheon secure.

The two old friends, comrades of army life long before fame came to them one summer month, Commander-in-Chief and Chief of Staff, were taking their regular afternoon promenade—Joffre in his familiar short, black coat which made his figure the burlier, his walk affected by the rheumatism in his legs, though he certainly had no rheumatism in his head, and Castelnau erect and slight of figure, his slimness heightened by his long, blue overcoat— chatting as they walked slowly, and behind them followed a sturdy guard in plain clothes at a distance of a few paces, carrying two cushions. Joffre stopped and turned with a "you-don't-say-so" gesture and a toss of his head at something that Castelnau had told him.

Very likely they were not talking of the war; indeed, most likely it was about friends in their army world, for both have a good wit, a keen and amiable understanding of human nature. At all events, they were enjoying themselves. So they passed on into the woods, followed by the guard who would place their cushions on their favorite seat, and the two who had been lieutenants and captains and colonels together would continue their airing and their chat until they returned to the business of directing their millions of men.

It was raining in this darkened French village near Verdun and a passing battalion went dripping by, automobiles sent out sprays of muddy water from their tires, and over in the crowded inclosures the German prisoners taken at Douaumont stood in the mud waiting to be entrained. Occasionally a soldier or an officer came out of a doorway that sent forth a stream of light, and upstairs in the municipal building where we went to pay our respects to the general commanding the army that had won the victory which had thrilled France as none had since the Marne, we found that it was the regular hour for his staff to report. They reported standing in the midst of tables and maps and standing received their orders. In future, when I see the big room with its mahogany table and fat armchairs reserved for directors' meetings I shall recall equally important conferences in the affairs of a nation that were held under simpler auspices.

This conference seemed in keeping with the atmosphere of the place: nobody in any flurry of haste and nobody wasting time. One after another the officers reported; and whatever their ages, for some would have seemed young for great responsibilities two years before, they were men going about their business alert, self-possessed, reflective of the character of their leader as staffs always are, men whose feet and whose minds never dragged. When they spoke to anybody politeness was the lubricant of prompt exchange of thought, a noiseless, eight-cylinder, hundred-horse-power sort of staff. If the little Corsican could have looked on, if he could have seen the taking of Douaumont, or if Wellington could have seen the taking of the Ridge, I think that they would have been well satisfied—and somewhat jealous to find that military talent was so widespread.

The man who came out of the staff-room would have won his marshal's baton in Napoleon's day, I suppose, though he was out of keeping with those showy times. I did not then know that he was to be Commander-in-Chief; only that all France thrilled with his name, which time will forever associate with Douaumont. At once you felt the dynamic quality under his agreeable manner and knew that General Nivelle did things swiftly and quietly, without wasteful expenditure of reserve force, which he could call upon when needed by turning on the current.

There was a stranger come to call; it was a rainy night; we had better not drive back to the hotel at Bar-le-Duc, he suggested, but find a billet in town, which was hospitality not to be imposed upon when one could see how limited quarters were in this small village. Some day I suppose a plaque will be put up on the door of that small house, with its narrow hall and plain hat-rack and the sitting-room turned into a dining-room, saying that General (perhaps it will be Marshal) Nivelle lived here during the battle of Verdun. It is a fine gift, simplicity. Some great men, or those who are called great, lack it; but nothing is so attractive in any man. No sentry at the door, no servant to open it. You simply went in, hung up your cap and took off your raincoat.

Hundreds of staffs were sitting down to the same kind of dinner with a choice of red or white wine and the menu was that of an average French household. I recall this and other staff dinners, in contrast to costly plate and rich food in a house where a gold Croesus with diamond eyes and necklace should have been on the mantelpiece as the household god, with the thought that even war is a good thing if it centers ambition on objects other than individual gain. Without knowing it, Joffre, Castelnau, Foch, Pétain, Nivelle and others were the richest men in France.

A colonel when the war began, in the sifting by Father Joffre to find real leaders by the criterion of success General Nivelle had risen to command an army. Wherever he was in charge he got the upper hand of the enemy. All that he and his officers said reflected one spirit—that of the offensive. They were men who believed in giving blows. A nation looking for a man who could win victories said, "Here he is!" when its people read the *communiqué* about Douaumont one morning. He had been going his way, doing the tasks in hand according to his own method, and at one of the stations fame found him. Soldiers have their philosophy and these days when it includes fame, probably fame never comes. This time it came to a soldier without any of the showy qualities that fame used to prefer, one who, I should say, was quite unaffected by it owing to a greater interest in his work; a man without powerful influence to urge his promotion. If you had met him before the war he would have impressed you with his kindly features, well-shaped head and vitality, and if you know soldiers you would have known that he was highly trained in his profession. His staff was a family, but the kind of family where every member has telepathic connection with its head; I could not imagine that any officer who had not would be at home in the little dining-room. Readiness of perception and quickness of action in intelligent obedience were inherent.

Over in his office in the municipal building where we went after dinner the general took something wrapped in tissue paper out of a drawer and from his manner, had he been a collector, I should have known that it was some rare treasure. When he undid the paper I saw a photograph of General Joffre autographed with a sentiment for the occasion.

"He gave it to me for Douaumont!" said General Nivelle, a touch of pride in his voice—the only sign of pride that I noticed.

There spoke the soldier to whom praise from his chief was the best praise and more valued than any other encomium.

When I spoke of Douaumont he drew out the map and showed me his order of the day, which had a soldierly brevity that made words keen-edged tools. The attacking force rushed up overnight and appeared as a regulated tidal wave of men, their pace timed under cover of curtains of fire which they hugged close, then over the German trenches and on into the fort. Six thousand prisoners and forty-five hundred French casualties! It was this dramatic, this complete and unequivocal success that had captured the imagination of France, but he was not dramatic in telling it. He made it a military evolution on a piece of paper; though when he put his pencil down on Douaumont and held it fast there for a moment, saying, "And that is all for the present!" the pencil seemed to turn into steel.

All for the present! And the future? That of the army of France was to be in his hands. He had the supreme task. He would approach it as he had approached all other tasks.

You had only to look at General Mangin commanding the corps before Verdun to know that attack was not alone a system but a gospel with him. Five stripes on his arm for wounds, all won in colonial work, sun-browned, swart, with a strong, abutting chin which might have been a fit point for Nivelle's pencil, an eye that said "Attack!" and could twinkle with the wisdom of many campaigns!

"General Joffre sat in that chair two hours before the advance," he said, with the same respectful awe that other generals had exhibited toward the Commander-in-Chief.

The time had come for the old leader, grown weary, to go; for the younger men of the school which the war has produced, with its curtains of fire and wave attacks, to take his place. But the younger ones in the confidence of their system could look on the old leader while he lived as the great, indomitable figure of the critical stages of the war.

A man of iron, Mangin, with a breadth of chest in keeping with his chin, who could bear the strain of command which had brought down many generals from sheer physical incapacity. Month after month this chin had stood out against German drives, all the while wanting to be in its natural element of the offensive. His resolute, outright solution of problems by human ratios would fit him into any age or any climate. He was at home leading a punitive expedition or in the complicated business of Verdun. Whether he was using a broadsword or a curtain of fire he proposed to strike his enemy early and hard and keep on striking. In the course of talking with him I spoke of the contention that in some cases in modern war men could be too brave.

"Rarely!" he replied, a single word which had the emphasis of both that jaw and that shrewd, piercing eye.

"What is the best time to go out to the front?" I asked the general.

"Five o'clock in the morning!"

The officer who escorted me did not think anything of getting up at that hour. Mangin's is a five-o'clock-in-the-morning corps.

Shall I describe that town on the banks of the Meuse which has been described many times? Or that citadel built by Vauban, with dynamos and electric light in its underground chambers and passages, its hospitals, shops, stores and barrack room, so safe under its walls and roof of masonry that the Germans presciently did not waste their shells on it but turned them with particular vengeance on the picturesque old houses along the river bank, neglecting the barracks purposely in view of their usefulness to the conquerors when Mecca was theirs. There must be something sacred to a Frenchman in the citadel which held life secure and in the ruins which bore their share of the blows upon this old fortress town in the lap of the hills, looking out toward hills which had been the real defense.

Interest quickened on the way to the Verdun front as you came to the slopes covered with torn and fallen trees, where the Germans laid their far-reaching curtains of fire to catch the French reserves struggling through mud and shell-craters on those February and March days to the relief of the front line.

Only when you have known the life of an army in action in winter in such a climate can you appreciate the will that drove men forward to the attack and the will of the defenders against outnumbering guns, having to yield, point by point, with shrewd thrift, small bands of men in exposed places making desperate resistance against torrents of shells.

Verdun was German valor at its best and German gunnery at its mightiest, the effort of Colossus shut in a ring of steel to force a decision; and the high-water mark of German persistence was where you stood on the edge of the area of mounds that shells had heaped and craters that shells had scooped by the concentration of fire on Fort Souville. A few Germans in the charge reached here, but none returned. The survivors entered Verdun, the French will tell you with a shrug, as prisoners. Down the bare slope with its dead grass blotched by craters the eye travels and then up another slope to a crest which you see as a cumulus of shell-tossed earth under an occasional shell-burst. That is Douaumont, whose taking cost the Germans such prolonged and bloody effort and aroused the Kaiser to a florid outburst of laudation of his Brandenburgers who, by its capture, had, as Germany then thought, brought France to her death-gasp.

On that hill German prestige and system reached their zenith; and the answer eight months later was French *élan* which, in two hours, with the swiftness and instinctive cohesion of democracy drilled and embattled and asking no spur from an autocrat, swept the Germans off the summit. From other charges I could visualize the precise and spirited movement of those blue figures under waves of shell fire in an attack which was the triumphant example of the latest style of offensive against frontal positions. There was no Kaiser to burst into rhetoric to thank General Nivelle, who had his reward in an autographed photograph from Father Joffre; and the men of that charge had theirs in the gratitude of a people.

Fort Vaux, on another crest at the right, was still in German hands, but that, too, was to be regained with the next rush. Yes, it was good to be at Verdun after Douaumont had been retaken, standing where you would have been in range of a German sniper a week before. Turning as on a pivot, you could identify through the glasses all the positions whose names are engraved on the French mind. Not high these circling hills, the keystone of a military arch, but taken together it was clear how, in this as in other wars, they were nature's bastion at the edge of the plain that lay a misty line in the distance.

Either in front or to the rear of Souville toward Verdun the surprising thing was how few soldiers you saw and how little transport within range of German guns; which impressed you with the elastic system of the French, who are there and are not there. Let an attack by the Germans develop and soldiers would spring out of the earth and the valleys echo with the thunder of guns. A thrifty people, the French.

When studying those hills that had seen the greatest German offensive after I had seen the offensive on the Somme, I thought of all that the summer had meant on the Western front, beginning with Douaumont lost and ending with Douaumont regained and the sweep over the conquered Ridge; and I thought of another general, Sir Douglas Haig, who had had to train his legions, begin with bricks and mortar to make a house under shell fire and, day by day, with his confidence in "the spirit that quickeneth" as the great asset, had wrought with patient, far-seeing skill a force in being which had never ceased attacking and drawing in German divisions to hold the line that those German divisions were meant to break.

Von Falkenhayn was gone from power; the Crown Prince who thirsted for war had had his fill and said that war was an "idiocy." It was the sentiment of the German trenches which put von Falkenhayn out; the silent ballots of that most sensitive of all public opinion, casting its votes with the degree of its disposition to stand fire, which no officer can control by mere orders.

With the Verdun offensive over, the German soldiers struggling on the Ridge had a revelation which was translated into a feeling that censorship could not stifle of the failure of the campaign to crush France. They called for the man who had won victories and the Kaiser gave them von Hindenburg, whom fortune favored when he sent armies inspirited by his leadership against amateur soldiers in veteran confidence, while the weather had stopped the Allied offensive in the West.

Imagine Lee's men returning from Gettysburg to be confronted by inexperienced home militia and their cry, "The Yanks have given us a rough time of it, but you fellows get out of the way!" Such was the feeling of that German Army as it went southward; not the army that it was, but quite good enough an army to win against Rumania with the system that had failed at Verdun.

XXXI

AU REVOIR, SOMME!

Sir Douglas Haig—Atmosphere at headquarters something of Oxford and of Scotland—Sir Henry Rawlinson—"Degumming" the inefficient—Back on the Ridge again—The last shell-burst—Good-bye to the mess—The fellow war-correspondents—*Bon voyage*.

The fifth of the great attacks, which was to break in more of the old first-line fortifications, taking Beaumont-Hamel and other villages, was being delayed by Brother Low Visibility, who had been having his innings in rainy October and early November, when the time came for me to say good-byes and start homeward.

Sir Douglas Haig had been as some invisible commander who was omnipresent in his forceful control of vast forces. His disinclination for reviews or display was in keeping with his nature and his conception of his task. The army had glimpses of him going and coming in his car and observers saw him entering or leaving an army or a corps headquarters, his strong, calm features expressive of confidence and resolution.

There were many instances of his fine sensitiveness, his quick decisions, his Scotch phrases which could strip a situation bare of non-essentials. It was good that a man with his culture and charm could have the qualities of a great commander. In the chateau which was his Somme headquarters where final plans were made, the final word given which put each issue to the test, the atmosphere had something of Oxford and of Scotland and of the British regular army, and everything seemed done by a routine that ran so smoothly that the appearance of routine was concealed.

Here he had said to me early in the offensive that he wanted me to have freedom of observation and to criticise as I chose, and he trusted me not to give military information to the enemy. When I went to take my leave and thank him for his courtesies the army that he had drilled had received the schooling of battle and tasted victory. How great his task had been only a soldier could appreciate, and only history can do justice to the courage that took the Ridge or the part that it had played in the war.

Upstairs in a small room of another chateau the Commander-in-Chief and the Commander of the Fourth of the group of armies under Sir Douglas— who had played polo together in India as subalterns, Sir Henry Rawlinson being still as much of a Guardsman as Sir Douglas was a Scot—had held many conferences. Sir Henry could talk sound soldierly sense about the results gained and look forward, as did the whole army, to next summer when the maximum of skill and power should be attained. In common with

Nivelle, both were leaders who had earned their way in battle, which was promoting the efficient and shelving or "degumming," in the army phrase, the inefficient. Every week, every day, I might say, the new army organization had tightened.

With steel helmet on and gas mask over the shoulder for the last time, I had a final promenade up to the Ridge, past the guns and Mouquet Farm, picking my way among the shell-craters and other grisly reminders of the torment that the fighters had endured to a point where I could look out over the fields toward Bapaume. For eight and ten miles the way had been blazed free of the enemy by successive attacks. Five hundred yards ahead "krumps" splashing the soft earth told where the front line was and around me was the desert which such pounding had created, with no one in the immediate neighborhood except some artillery officers hugging a depression and spotting the fall of shells from their guns just short of Bapaume and calling out the results by telephone, over one of the strands of the spider's web of intelligence which they had unrolled from a reel when they came. I joined them for a few minutes in their retreat below the skyline and listened to their remarks about Brother Low Visibility, who soon was to have the world for his own in winter mists, rain and snow, limiting the army's operations by his perversity until spring came.

And so back, as the diarists say, by the grassless and blasted route over which I had come. After I was in the car I heard one of the wicked screams with its unpleasant premonition, which came to an end by whipping out a ball of angry black smoke short of a near-by howitzer, which was the last shell-burst that I saw.

Good-bye, too, to my English comrades in a group at the doorway: to Robinson with his poise, his mellowness, his wisdom, his well-balanced sentences, who had seen the world around from mining camps of the west to Serbian refugee camps; to "our Gibbs," ever sweet-tempered, writing his heart out every night in the human wonder of all he saw in burning sentences that came crowding to his pencil-point which raced on till he was exhausted, though he always revived at dinner to undertake any controversy on behalf of a better future for the whole human race; to blithesome Thomas who will never grow up, making words dance a tune, quoting Horace in order to forget the shells, all himself with his coat off and swinging a peasant's scythe; to Philips the urbane, not saying much but coming to the essential point, our scout and cartographer, who knew all the places on the map between the Somme and the Rhine and heard the call of Pittsburgh; to Russell, that pragmatic, upstanding expert in squadrons and barrages, who saved all our faces as reporters by knowing news when he saw it, arbiter of mess conversations, whose pungent wit had a movable zero—luck to them all! May Robinson have a stately mansion on the Thames where he can study nature at leisure; Gibbs never want for something to write about; Thomas have six crops of hay a year to mow and a garden with a different kind of bird nesting in every tree; Philips a new pipe every day and a private yacht sailing on an ocean of maps; Russell a home by the sea where he can watch the ships come in—when the war is over.

It happened that High Visibility had slightly the upper hand over his gloomy brother the day they bade me *bon voyage*. My last glimpse of the cathedral showed it clear against the sky; and ahead many miles of rich, familiar landscape of Picardy and Artois were to unfold before I took the cross-channel steamer. I knew that I had felt the epic touch of great events.

THE END

Milton Keynes UK
Ingram Content Group UK Ltd.
UKHW012312040624
443649UK00007B/567